Signal Coms.   £18.6.

To a friend of school
day[...] , Ishmay,
with [...] es.
2.

Of Ploughs, Planes and Palliasses

PERCY WILSON CARRUTHERS
(D.F.M., M.i.D.)

Woodfield
ARUNDEL · SUSSEX · ENGLAND

First published in 1992 by

WOODFIELD PUBLISHING
Woodfield House, Arundel Road, Fontwell,
West Sussex BN18 0SD, England.

© Percy Wilson Carruthers, 1992

All rights reserved.
No part of this publication may be reproduced
or transmitted in any form or by any means,
electronic or mechanical, nor may it be stored
in any information storage and retrieval system,
without prior permission from the publisher.

British Library Cataloguing in Publication Data

Carruthers, Percy W.
  Of planes, ploughs and palliasses
  I. Title.

ISBN 1-873203-21-7

Printed in Great Britain

I STARTED TO READ AN ADVENTURE STORY. IT SOON BECAME A WAR BOOK WITH PLENTY OF ACTION, ALL ACTION, UNTIL THE FIGHTING, FLYING MACHINE OF PERCY W. CARRUTHERS, DFM, MiD, COULD NOT TAKE ANY MORE. THEN I GOT A CHRONICLE OF EVENTS THAT WERE MORE OF AN EYE-OPENER THAN ANYTHING THAT WENT BEFORE.

IT IS NOT FICTION. IT ALL HAPPENED. I KNOW. I WAS THERE.

F. ALAN HAMER
WOP/AG, 'RAINGILLS'
COCKERHAM ROAD, FORTON PR3 0A

To Olivia, Debra and Paul

PREFACE

I remember reading somewhere that a book, like any other piece of writing, is conceived, it gestates and the delivery is frequently overdue being accompanied by severe labour pains.

This writing was conceived, I suppose, in the early 1940's when I kept notes, sometimes in the form of a diary, of wartime activities and wrote rhyming verse about certain events.

Then passed some thirty-five years without any development whatsoever when one chose to push the memory of those wartime experiences out of mind and get on with living.

Gestation then commenced, about the year 1980, when Olivia, my eldest daughter said "Daddy you never speak of the past or of the war, why not write something down before you snuff it, then at least we shall all be able to read something about it?"

That remark was somewhat alarming, reminding me that I had already passed the sixtieth milestone, and it was perhaps a little later than I realised.

My thanks to the Imperial War Museum for allowing me to use photographs of most of the types of aircraft which I flew.

No attempt has been made to write of wartime activities in any official manner, I simply record what I saw, heard and experienced at that time. The words of conversation may not be exact, but they do depict the mood at the time, and are in essence what was then said.

During my note-compiling exercise, I decided I would be better equipped to give a more detailed account of some of the Wartime events if I were able to recruit the assistance of some of the boys who were 'there at the time'.

From my wartime documents I extracted over a hundred addresses, over thirty-five years old, wrote to them, putting suitable remarks on the envelopes to encourage the postmen to assist in bringing the letters to the new homes of the addressees, and waited.

What an amazing degree of success. The enthusiastic replies were electrifying and delightful to read. The anticipation of meeting up again was so keen that I was encouraged to arrange a re-union for all concerned.

The volume of correspondence grew dramatically as new leads came in. Following these up, replying, circulating addresses, arranging a venue, accommodation, talking terms, sending invitations and hosts of other matters became an all absorbing occupation.

The hopes of now having time to 'write something down' had receded somewhat. I was too busy attending the demands of what had now become an organisation which threatened to take up, and swallow a great deal of my time as the volume of correspondence snowballed.

I named our group 'KRIEGIE CALL', the word Kriegie being an abbreviation of the German word KRIEGSGEFANGENER, (prisoner of war). We meet annually at the Sywell Motel, which is the old RAF mess, modernised, and situated on the Sywell aerodrome near Northampton. The last count of attenders was 123 with a total on the mailing list, covering the British Isles, Canada, Eire, USA, Tahiti, New Zealand, Australia, South Africa, Zimbabwe and Czechoslovakia, of 218. I have scores of names of others who cannot yet be traced and news of very many who unfortunately have died.

Sywell is a most suitable venue having been a wartime E.F.T.S. where some of our members actually carried out their initial flight. The aerodrome is still active as a commercial and private landing ground, being the base of a private flying club. I have landed there on many occasions during my private flying, becoming acquainted with Mike Newton, airport manager, and Keith and Diana West, proprietors of the Motel.

Twelve years have now passed since writing those letters and I now find time to 'write something down' for Olivia, Debra and Paul to read at their leisure. Thanks also to Jean for her help in those many hours of typewriter clatter whilst I concentrated on the job in hand, through long periods of nil communicado.

I am indebted to my revered flying friends and prisoner of war comrades for refreshing my memory on many incidents during the war years. I also appreciate many of them allowing me reference to their writings, sketches and memos.

I therefore write with confidence, that it may not be said, as Coriolanus,

>"The dust of antique time would lie unswept, mountainous error be too highly heaped, for truth to o'er peer."

·CHAPTER 1·
AT HOME

Grecian House nestled snugly at the foot of the hill on entering the tiny village of Sunderland where in 1919 I was born, two years before the tragic death of my father in a road accident. My only brother was born six months after the death of my father in 1921 and my mother died shortly afterwards. Twenty-three years later, after having served in the RAF during World War Two, my brother Jerry was also fatally injured in a road accident.

It was at Ivy Hall, a small farm, in the village of Bothel, Cumberland, some three miles from Sunderland, that Jerry and I were to spend our early years with our maternal grandparents and Uncle Joe and Auntie Bly (who was their youngest of nine, and only eleven years my senior).

Uncle Joe was the special of the family, having lost the use of both legs at the age of twelve after a serious attack of measles. He was the most determined character I have ever met in my life. It was to be no wheelchair life for him, as no such things as invalidity or mobility allowances existed at that time.

Such determination and ingenuity combined to make him entirely self mobile, enabling him to milk the cows, mow the crops, house the hay, dress the

Uncle Joe at the farm, 'Ivy Hall', Bothel, Cumbria, c.1940.

hedges and generally attend to farm repairs and maintenance. He was also the village barber and refuse disposal man, and was to be reported on in the press as far distant as Australia.

The implement of his mobility was his 'Box'. This was of his own design and manufacture. It was, in essence, an inverted box of wood with the two side pieces extending down and being rounded to form a rocker type contact with the ground, the edges being clad with either narrow metal or rubber strips. The top of the box was padded to make seating more comfortable.

With his emaciated limbs tucked up to the right he would strap himself firmly onto the contraption and with two eighteen inch long T-shaped crutches firmly gripped in his hands, with powerful arms and shoulders he would swing the whole box forward, clear of the ground, a distance of about two feet and rock forward into another lift. This display of strength and co-ordination, acquired through persistent practice, was quite outstanding and would propel him a good mile to the village rugger pitch on a Saturday afternoon to every home game.

His creations in carved wood furniture from solid oak were the hallmark of perfection.

It was not until some years later that I realised the tremendous influence which Uncle Joe had exerted on me, when the local Headmaster dubbed me 'Percy-verence'.

Farming life in the thirties was hard and demanding and although I enjoyed it, along with the rugger, tennis and fell-running, it was the attraction to aircraft which I found paramount. By chance, early one morning at about 6am, when collecting the cows for milking, I saw the *Graf Zeppelin* pass by, parallel to the Cumbrian coast about three miles distant. I would also occasionally see a couple of old biplanes pass overhead and would stand enthralled until they totally disappeared from sight.

Dad "did not hold with such thundering things" and to contemplate entering the RAF was, in his opinion, complete insanity. Perhaps it was my Percy-verence which at last, in 1937, brought about a softening of his attitude to my wishes and he agreed – reluctantly – to give his parental consent to me going into the RAF.

This of course would mean leaving the land that I loved. The lakes of Bassenthwaite, Ullswater, Derwentwater, Crummock, Buttermere, Ennerdale and all the surrounding beauty. This was Wordsworth country. It was also John Peel country, Caldbeck, Bewaldeth, Brayton and Skiddaw, Binsey, Isel, White Fields and galloping steeds, and many other place names featuring in many of the John Peel songs.

Aunt Frances was landlady at the Oddfellows Arms in Caldbeck, where the John Peel annual meet was held. Everybody went: men women and children by the hundred, horses and hounds by the score. Beer was always flowing freely, topping up the swill casks for Auntie's pigs (and if you have never tasted bacon from a beer swilling pig I can claim with total confidence that you have a treat

The Author, born 16th February 1919, entered the RAF 15th November 1937.

in store). The supply of Cumberland Tatie Hot Pot seemed endless. It was studded with the most delicious home made black puddings and was hot from morning till night.

The story goes that the lyrics of the song 'John Peel' were composed in the bar parlour of Auntie's pub, and whenever I pass through Caldbeck, where John Peel lies buried, I recall with some nostalgia the sound of the voices at 'The Meet'.

I also remember the Reverend Charles Wilfred Howard and his weekly bible classes with tea and cakes in the Vicarage, and how he corresponded with me during the whole of World War Two, and how the 'Song of Home' would come to mind.

> Away down yonder how I do long to wander,
> In the Cumberland mountains, in the land that I love.
> I'm always dreaming of the silver moon beaming
> In the Cumberland mountains in the land that I love.
> Oh the Mocking Bird is singing in the twilight
> And the evening sun is sinking o'er the hills,
> And I'm still yearning, and my poor heart's burning
> For those Cumberland mountains, in the land that I love.

Rugger tore a cartilage in my right knee and I spent the time in hospital over the period when King George the Fifth died. Ploughing an arrow-like furrow with the two old Clydesdales soon toughened up the knee in preparation for attending the RAF medical.

> In Wordsworth land as schoolboy dour,
> I'd work and toil for many an hour
> In farm fields steeped in meadowsweet
> And new mown hay. I'd contemplate
> How in the future I would rate
> The calls of life to size and meet.
>
> The west coast bounding Cumbrian Lakes
> Found living standards, beyond the gates
> Of farmsteads, meagre beyond doubt.
> Horizons clear and far were seen,
> To offer tracks anew and green,
> Ambitions to achieve and scout.
>
> To dream of winged machines so free
> Was I so wont to do with glee.
> Fetters to this by Dad were tied
> So tightly, that I dared not say
> Before all else, an aircraft gay
> With sovereign colours I would ride.
>
> Year thirty-seven proved to see
> A weakness creep o'er Dad's decree,
> A severance of his fetters fast
> Was my release, and to my joy,

OF PLOUGHS, PLANES & PALLIASSES

Reluctantly he said, "My boy
You go your airplane to at last".

Worthwhile my eighteen years then seemed
To have been spent with plough and field,
But duties were first well removed
From what intentions I had schemed.
No aircraft was to me bequeathed,
I may as well been quite four hoofed.

But close to those machines of flight
At least was I, and in the night
Of navigation, theory, maths,
Mercators, four stroke, met and plot
I'd read, and find what was my lot
If I were bent along those paths.

At last, as were Dad's fetters cut,
Surmounted I the earthly rut
As pupil pilot three years on
I gained my wings, so proudly worn,
An aircraft in the sky at dawn
I'd fly alone, in cloud and sun.

The enemy now was threatening strong,
To fly for pleasure, gone ere long,
Into the battle one must go,
The Hun to keep from off our land,
And what was more from Egypt's sand,
To brave the guns and deal a blow.

Comrades fell and aircraft hit,
But bombs found targets, and they lit
The desert sand around, and smoked
A thousand feet towards the sky.
The enemy tanks and Huns must die,
The world to save from being choked.

Enemy flak and fighters brash
Our planes attacked, would often smash
Whole pieces off and claim my friends,
But guardian wings for thirty three
Attacks on enemy shielded me,
Whilst some much earlier met their ends.

But came one burst of deadly shell,
When bombs we dropped into Hun's Hell.
The aircraft lurched as mortal slain,
One total engine came adrift
And earthward plunged, no more to lift.
To stay therein was nought to gain.

Falling to earth benumbed and gashed,
The Hun below triumphant gnashed,
His teeth with glee, and stuck a steel
Blade in my ribs, as parachute
I pressed release and minus boot

I hopped and stumbled without feel.

In Lazarette three months I lay,
Crete, Athens, and Bari, till one day
The 'Wounded' train to Munich took
Me. From then on to Dulag Luft,
And on. Were glad to eat a tuft
Of grass or any food to cook.

The 'Insterburg' that ship of hell,
the hunger and that awful smell,
The dogs upon us loosed with leer,
Whilst chains and handcuffs clanged and cut,
I'd change it for that 'English Rut',
Which then was bad but now most dear.

Escape came, from a cattle truck,
Tunnels and wire-cuts came unstuck,
Many had paid the price supreme
By being shot, cold blooded, down
A meadow green, without a frown,
Freedom now was like a dream.

But seven days was all we had.
Three hungry airmen, badly clad
Were found one morn in farmer's straw.
"'Tis sabotage". was all we heard,
"For this it's death," the hun concurred
The solit'ry cell now to withdraw.

Six hundred miles we walked in pain,
Three months slept we in snow and rain
In woods and fields and barns and ricks,
And ate what ere we found in the fields,
And friends too ill to bear would yield
And die. The Hun had deadly tricks.

"Sixth Airborne," shouted we with glee,
At last thank God we're really free,
Through this we've come, our lives are spared,
And now Great Britain shall we build.
To what we'd hoped, our hopes fulfilled.
To doubt all this we'd never dared.

For bursting tanks and killing Huns,
For sinking ships and bombing runs,
I got a note to make my way
To Palace Buckingham, noting
That day that I would meet the King
My chest a medal to array.

A mention too for what I'd done
Whilst keeping Jerry on the run,
'Despatches' showed I'd done my bit.
But then for thousands who had died
No recognition could be plied,
Except the letters R.I.P.

OF PLOUGHS, PLANES & PALLIASSES

Since this is now all in the past,
And other forces formed the cast,
The Britain we had hoped to glean
Then far receded from the show,
A workforce new, all ebb and flow,
Let union Commies rule the scene.

It's oft forgot there was a spot
In recent years, when not a lot
Lay in between our total loss
And our survival as a land,
Hinged upon Egypt's golden sand.
Alas our stones have gathered moss.

Britons today should start to pay
True tribute practical in a way
To those brave boys who fought and died.
No personal risk is now involved.
Just effort and guts means problems solved,
Then those brave boys could rest with pride.

· CHAPTER 2 ·

PROP – AGANDA

It was 15th November 1937 when I set out for Recruits Reception Centre, West Drayton, Middlesex, and after interview, medial and kitting out, I and other new entrants set out for Recruits Training Centre, Cardington, Bedfordshire. Here stood an old Hawker Hind, quite unserviceable, but still an item of adoration used in the instruction of aircraft handling, propeller swinging and general familiarisation.

PROP-AGANDA

When you give a prop a swing
Don't do gymnastics on the thing.
Even if the switch is 'OFF',
The engine may still give a cough.
'Dead' motors have been known to kick
And slice an arm off mighty quick.
Your head entangled in the works
Will make the engine go in jerks
And aeroplanes do not fly better
With 'swinger' in the carburettor".

Here too at Cardington stood the massive hangers which housed the ill-fated airship R101. The mooring mast dominated the far end of the airfield, a solemn reminder of the absent ship.

I enjoyed the parade ground drill, and the antics of poor of old Varley with two left feet. My greatest enjoyment came from the long hours spent voluntarily in the well equipped gymnasium. Wall bars, vaulting horse, mat work, leading to handsprings and upstarts. My thin wispy flaxen haired Geordie friend, (Curly Topper), was equally enthusiastic and we encouraged each other. I still have my 'cross country' and 'athletic standard' medallion. I was grateful to the RAF for the wonderful opportunities for sport and enjoyed representing 'The Station' at many places at rugger. Physical fitness to me was a wonderful investment and was, I believe, the major factor in saving my life some five years later.

Interest in the initial entry trade of Flight Mechanic had seriously wilted in the aura of Physical Training and within a few months I entered the RAF School of Physical Training at Uxbridge as a pupil and came out some eighteen weeks later with the top mark of 91%.

The advance party to open the new RAF Station at St Athan, South Wales, was due to move off, and I, as a very junior Corporal, was to escort the party

OF PLOUGHS, PLANES & PALLIASSES 9

by rail. The final stage of the journey was a march from the railway station to the camp. The locals had not yet experienced the pleasure of the company of a large squad of very smart young airmen but intended to find out through dozens of invitations out to tea.

Rugby and boxing teams were found in profusion up the Welsh valleys where I was to learn a new dimension in dedication and fanaticism.

We were now into 1939 with the political scene on the continent not at all pretty. Recruitment to the RAF was decidedly gaining momentum and soon I was posted to open up a new Recruits Training Depot at Driffield home of 77 and 102 Squadrons, flying Whitleys, and who were later (in June 1940) to be the first squadrons, along with 10 and 51 to carry out a bombing attack on the mainland, namely Turin. It was here that I conducted the mass Physical Training Demonstration from atop a rickety trestle table with the other instructors standing around my platform. One of the recruits from that first entry greeted me some two years later at an overseas station I was visiting.

Driffield was only half as far from home as St Athan and the journey in wintry conditions via Thirsk, Scotch Corner and Bowes Moor mostly in the dark, was a barrel of fun. I would stop en-route at RAF Leeming for a hot mug of tea before tackling the Moors on my old 250cc BSA. The Bowes Moor road was winding, undulating and unfenced. The road would radiate off the heat collected during the day and attract the sheep to lay down for the night. The radiation would allow the cold air to flow down into the hollows where low thick fog would form hiding the reposing sheep. Imagine some of the incidents which took place. A fast moving motor cycle with black-out fittings on the headlamp ploughing through a clear night approaching the foggy hollows. These days there was so little traffic the sheep had an almost uninterrupted night's rest. In virgin snow the roadway was not to be recognised from the surrounding moorland, and presented me with an additional hazard.

Station Sports Day was a new responsibility, Field layout, tracks, lanes, staggered starts, hurdles, shot, discus and the one thousand other duties, got me "...a ratherish perennial ritual" as the sports officer put it. I ventured, with respect, that that was not the object of the exercise and I came out of that quite well with a posting to N°·6 F.T.S., Tern Hill, Shropshire.

It was now June 1939 the sinister rumblings emanating from Germany became even more disturbing. The goose-stepping Wehrmacht featured more in the news with the ranting disturbing speeches of the leaders of the Reich even more vitriolic.

I loved being at Tern Hill. I exchanged the old 250 Beezer for a 350 Empire Star, sneaked a bit of bowser juice to augment the meagre petrol ration and did frequent home runs. At least at Tern Hill I was at a Flying Training School, although not a pupil but I worked hard at my ground duties and got my third stripe, just turned twenty. My duties kept me in close and constant touch with the office of the S/Ldr Admin, which gave additional support to my pilot application. I also forged a lasting link with the local squadron the of Air Training Corps in nearby Market Drayton, giving them regular instruction.

Then there was the Dodd family who took me in their home as one of their own. Sixteen years later I was privileged once more to visit their home, when on opening the door Mrs Dodd cried, "Oh, it's my son. My son." She already had two of her own much older than me.

Old friends from Tern Hill cropped up at times in the most unexpected places, sometimes very conveniently. Some three years later I led a flight of three aircraft into an M.U. at Kasfareet, South of Cairo for a modification job and quite by chance the Flt/Sgt in charge was an old Tern Hill acquaintance. We arranged a mutually agreeable time for the completion of the job, if you follow.

· CHAPTER 3 ·

A SCRAP OF PAPER

It was now September 1939. Chamberlain's 'scrap of paper' which he brandished on his return from Germany some months earlier then proved to be the 'scrap', interpreted literally.

I was in one of the barracks calling up the boys for Church Parade that Sunday morning, 3rd September, when from a nearby radio I heard the news we all dreaded...

"...and we are therefore in a state of war with Germany."

There was a new and vigorous dimension to efficiency. In addition to routine PT and drill training for the trainee pilots there was concentrated fire drill and something entirely new, aerodrome defence. General Duties airmen were busy with armament lectures, gun stripping and target practice. Tents and gun posts were situated at strategic points, manned on rota by the airman and I was NCO in charge of perimeter posts. I paid a visit to the Isle of Man in a twenty-foot fishing boat in order to take a course on the 20mm Hispano Suiza cannon, at Jurby. Such a journey I would not seek to repeat. Here, in Douglas, was my first glimpse of captivity. The seafront hotels were wired off, housing hundreds of internees, arrogant and belligerent.

It was the intention to equip all gun posts with a telephone link and arm them with the 20mm cannon. Winter conditions made life in the tents most uncomfortable and I would visit the perimeter posts each morning, from 0600 hrs on, clad in PT kit, at the double. The airmen were frozen. Following my inspection one morning I was entering the Mess for breakfast about 0700 hrs when the sound of unfamiliar aero engines broke the stillness, approaching from the north at a height of about 20 feet. Coming in fast, the aircraft could be seen beyond the parade ground and all eyes turned to the north-facing windows. Someone said it was a Blenheim from the MU sited on the far edge of the aerodrome, when suddenly proof came that it was not. It zoomed over at about a hundred feet, all guns blazing, bullets spurting soil in the flower borders and heading straight for No. 1 hangar. The bomb aimer placed his bombs neatly, close in by the side of the hanger. One airman coming out of a small side door had the door thrown at him with the blast and a fire started. Airmen showed great resourcefulness, quickly wheeling aircraft out of the hanger, one after the other.

The party soon put an end to the fire, and aircraft damage was minimal. Damage to the hanger was soon put right. I clearly remember the JU88 banking

11

slightly to the left as it sped away across the landing ground to the left of the MU. He obviously had no bombs left. I immediately made my way to the nearest gun post which was less than 100 yards from the mess only to find they were not able to get the gun covers off before the fun was over. Not a single shot had been fired by our guns. The crews were in for a right rollicking because very shortly I would have to be down to the S/Ldr's office with some answers – and no doubt they would not be suitable. I would go down early. The P/O always arrived early and often asked my opinion rather than give me his. I could prime him and disappear round the perimeter posts. I had some rockets to deliver.

It was about 0900 hrs when I returned. I usually looked in the Orderly Room before knocking on the door of the S/Ldr, just to test the atmosphere.

"Christ there's some hub-hub this morning Sergeant," said the Orderly Room Corporal. "Where have you been? The P/O said you had gone round the gun posts but the runner couldn't find you".

"He wouldn't be running fast enough to catch me, I can assure you Corporal. Why, what's the flap?"

"Squadron Leader Admin wants to see you quicker than possible." said he, "Wing have been on the phone and his in-tray is a foot high."

I jerked the tails of my tunic, checked my tie, Glengarry at correct angle, and did my usual three taps on the door just as you would tap out 'R' on the morse key. He recognised it immediately.

"Enter!"

I did, and stood to attention. He didn't hold with saluting in the office.

"It seems to me Carruthers," he said pinning me straight in the eyes, (he never addressed me by rank) that you are the only one on this station this morning with any good news. You're on the next Pilot's Selection Board". I felt like shouting, but it was not quite the time.

"Congratulations," said he, "I'm pleased for you. I shall be sorry to lose you".

"Thank you Sir..." I commenced, but he cut me short.

"Now what about this shambles this morning?"

I knew it had to come, but it was not as disastrous as I had imagined.

"I want a written report, signed and dated by 1200 hours. Why was that aircraft not fired on this morning? Wing want a full report."

"Every gun post was manned Sir, half the men were at breakfast, but gun covers were still on as per instructions. Until we get authority to instruct that the actual weapon be manned at all hours we are not going to get these quick lone raiders."

"Put that in your report. Remember 1200 hrs."

I got out of that easier than I had dared to hope. On the way out I ran into F/Sgt Black who was really my immediate superior, but it was well known that we all side-stepped him, including the officers, because we got things done much better without him. I always hoped he would be posted, as he was in my way.

"What are you looking so bloody pleased about? I thought you'd be up to the ears in the fertilizer this morning," was his greeting.

"I was, but Wing sent me down a shovel to get me out," I replied.

"Yes, and I'll bet it was in the shape of a rocket!" claimed Flight.

"Truth is, I'm posted next week Flight," I told him.

"No bloody wonder after this morning's debacle," he returned.

"Pilot's course at last Flight, so the baby's yours, soggy nappy and all that."

He shuffled into the Orderly Room and became their problem.

* * *

In May 1940 the enemy had begun the invasions of Holland, Belgium and Luxembourg preceded by massive air attacks in which thousands of civilians had perished. We had been conditioned to think that bombs should not be dropped if there was a risk of civilians being hit. How naive could we be? We did not realise that the Nazi rulers would conduct themselves in such dishonourable ways – that they were totally without conscience, or that they would stoop to force such inhuman circumstances and utter degradation on their captives as they eventually did.

British forces on the continent were now in deep trouble and the infamous name of Dunkirk was on the lips of everyone.

"Victory at all costs," roared Churchill, "victory in spite of all terror, victory however long and hard the road may be, for without victory there is no survival." Within a few weeks he was back on the air again urging the nation forward and giving the facts. "The Battle of Britain is about to begin".

July found the Luftwaffe attacking our Channel convoys whilst the RAF were attending to barges being concentrated presumably for the invasion of Britain; German bomber hordes were crossing our coastlines preparing the way for the invasion. So was the first stage of the Battle of Britain. The second stage was to come in August when activity against our shipping convoys began to assume quite serious proportions. Attacks against coastal towns and airfields were stepped up to destroy resistance and keep the RAF on the ground. But it was the gross underestimation by Adolf Hitler of the capabilities of the RAF Hurricanes and Spitfires, which proved to be one of the many incidents of his erroneous judgments. By the end of August one might claim that the third stage was about to develop. Heavy bombing of the City of London in addition to the daylight raids on the Midlands. Then the dramatic increase of night operations on these same targets. The daylight raids however were to fizzle out by the end of October, a great victory for the RAF, which prompted the immortal Churchill claim that, "Never in the field of human conflict has so much been owed by so many to so few."

I attended Aircrew Selection Board, and having shown the necessary aptitude on spatial judgement and other strange tests I was off to the Initial Training

Wing, billeted in the boarding houses of Aberystwyth. Lectures were even held in the lovely old university. I supervised the Entry for PT and Drill. It worked like a charm. We moved on to the RAF Melksham in Wiltshire where night after night we listened to the de-synchronised engines of the Luftwaffe as they flew over en-route to Coventry and Liverpool – the fires from which could be clearly seen on the horizon. They consistently flew a precise course which to my reckoning could only have been projected on a beam – and so it later proved to be.

An overseas posting was indicated, so I set off for home to deposit the old Beezer and brass cornet I kept by me. A good neighbour stripped down the old Beezer and stored it for me until I returned some years later.

North Africa was now newsworthy. General Irwin Rommel, ex Panzer Commander in France, landed to support the ailing forces of Mussolini. General Sir Archibald Wavell's forces, under Gen O'Connor, met the Germans for the first time at Ageila (Cyrenaica). Air Commodore Collishaw was in charge of the RAF operating in North Africa (both Bombers and Fighters), whilst keeping an eye on Greece – where great danger loomed. He fell ill and was relieved by AVM Teddar who acted as deputy to Air Marshall Longmore.

· CHAPTER 4 ·
DESTINATION UNKNOWN

West Kirby, Liverpool was seething with airmen when I arrived – but how wonderful was the organisation of ferrying groups down the Mersey to the troopships anchored in the bay. What a lovely target for enemy aircraft, but Hurricanes dodged about keeping a watchful eye in the air and the sea approaches.

I took up residence on ship G.17. (Dutch Dempo on 'A' Deck, Cabin 202. I took charge of the deck's airmen, arranging PT for them without delay, but allowing Corporal and above to join in on a voluntary basis. Such differentiation was quite unnecessary, they joined me to a man. I strove to make the classes amusing, racy and thought-provoking which proved a great success throughout the entire trip to Cape Town. Dutch food aboard was excellent. You could also get 4oz of Bruno for 2/- and 50 Goldflake for 1/8d. From the Bridge it was interesting to read the Aldis Signals morse, ship to ship, passing amongst the twenty ships forming the convoy. Reading this morse, I know, was the basis of my success in getting a 100% pass, some months later, in Wings examinations.

I calculated we were aiming for a call on the Gold Coast. Ships frequently changed station and when near at hand I listed their names: *Duke of York; Andes; Viceroy of India; Strathalan; Johan van Oldenbarne Velt; Georgic; Marnes; Majestic; Stirling Castle; Orion* (which I know was at one time *The Yarrow* which plied between Silloth and Dublin); *Oranto; Orcades; Glenorchy; Strathmore; Pasteur; Strathnaver.* Including our *Dempo* this totalled only seventeen, – I would watch for the other three. Suddenly, where did all this lovely fresh fruit come from? The reason for such an appearance was explained by a notice the following day that we would shortly be arriving in port and in no circumstances should fruit be brought from the natives. The sea was becoming more green rather than black and a strong sea-side smell pervaded. Flying fish rocketed out of the water in shoals, lovely dolphins performed their acrobatics and the sun went down as though it had fallen out of the sky. A Walrus flying-boat circled the convoy and soon we sighted the mountain range behind Sierra Leone. The scenery was truly lovely. Golden sands, lined with dark green palm trees and a background of golden hills.

Natives in their dug-out canoes were scudding around from 0700 hrs attempting to sell their wares. Fruit, fowls, monkeys and silk handiwork. Their diving was superb for Liverpool sixpences and Glasgow shillings.

After dark the hillsides around were ablaze with fires, some so large that it appeared the whole vegetation was alight. We needn't have had any fears, the solution came about 0400 hrs. Blinding lightning clearly illuminated the surrounding hills as though it were daylight and the rain came down with a fury I had not before witnessed. Come daylight however the clear blue vaults of the heavens awaited us with the merciless sun from which there was little escape.

The *Nelson* headed off very impressively to investigate a sighting on the horizon and did not rejoin us for many hours. We learned from two ship engineers that recently German U boats had claimed a victory in this very area.

The constellation of the Southern Cross was now visible at reasonable declination and yet the Great Bear was still quite easily discernible although not Polaris itself.

A few old Ansons appeared patrolling the outskirts of the convoy and soon we saw the top of the unmistakable Table Mountain. Our journey had taken a glorious twenty-seven days and as we drew into port the crowds on the quayside jostled and scrambled vigorously for a front line position calling loudly for coins. The police appeared and the crowds just melted away. We only spent four hours in Capetown and were entrained for Bulawayo on a train more suitably equipped for a thirty mile journey than for one of 1300 miles which for the next three days was to be what we thought, at that time, to be the journey of a lifetime. But better was yet to come.

The train was fitted with seats of slatted wood with not a trace of upholstery: no kitchen, no diner, no bar and no comforts. The primitive engine was small indeed and for such a steam power unit to haul a thousand airmen 1300 miles through the arid Kalahari Desert, appeared to be far too optimistic. The scenery en-route was so varied and so very lovely that one could, with pleasure, write at length.

We had miles of thickly wooded areas, then miles of flat denuded country with a very occasional tree. Then scores of peculiar rounded heaps of stones, rather like cairns, perhaps some type of burial demarcation. Cactus plants of all sizes, isolated houses or settlements all with their own windmill for drawing water or generating electricity. Numerous groups of mud huts occupied by natives who grew large scrawny crops of perhaps yams, very much resembling vegetable marrows. Hundreds of native children were gathered in groups to watch the train go by. They gazed in total wonderment. They were so very beautiful yet so dirty and ill clad, or totally unclad. We had passed Kimberley aerodrome, we had passed gold mines and thousands of ant heaps three to five feet high.

We stopped at Kimberley station where it seemed the whole population, both black and white, had assembled to see the 'War Train'. The white population was extremely well represented by the ladies, and most surprisingly by many lovely young ladies who were there with their tea, sandwiches and cake stalls. There was an absolutely endless supply of gallons of lovely hot tea, all free, and beautiful fruit, most certainly the best I had ever tasted. The ladies were so kind to us. Had we any buttons which needed sewing on? Was there any stitching to be done?

"Hold my tea Perc whilst I rip a sleeve out of my tunic," said Syd as a gorgeous twenty-year-old headed in our direction with a beautiful smile and a sewing box. Oh, and what about writing paper and envelopes with which to write home? What about razor blades? Oh, and drinks for the next 200 miles?

"Shame there's no beds on this cursed train" said Sandy, "I could just do with a good cabin maid." It was no wonder the train was without refreshments.

Within an hour and a half we were gone. What a pity to leave such hospitality behind. It was so obvious how all those ladies enjoyed the wonderful voluntary work they were doing, and how they enjoyed seeing us from England.

We had quite forgotten what it was like to be fussed over with such enthusiasm. I wondered if I had got all my bods back on this expedition. We passed over a river complex and through the area known as The Fourteen Streams, a panorama I shall always remember. Through Werewton, Penwani, Pudimo, Dry Hart, Quarry and Vryburg was no less than astounding. The number of English and Dutch ladies was overpowering. Again, gallons of lovely hot tea and mountains of good things to eat, all quite free. Hundreds of free books, cigarettes and other items were being offered. What wonderful generous people who strove to make our lot an enjoyable journey.

We had now been on a steady incline for some time, and some gradients were indicated as much as 1:35. The rails were much more slender and a maximum speed of 35 mph was indicated by the side of the track. Looking along the track, the undulating switchbacks could be clearly seen, the rails disappearing entirely from line of sight in the dips reminding me of a fairground fun ride. We saw

Some of the tribesmen we met on our safari.

natives gathering their crops on carts drawn by between twenty and thirty donkeys to one cart. Perhaps it was some kind of status symbol. We passed through Paradise, an amusing paradox, and then to Devondale 4129 feet above sea level, 790 miles from Cape.

That night was to be punctuated by some of the most spectacular lightening one could ever hope to see. It was quite captivating and spell-binding. Some of the flashes did not appear to have either source or direction. No origin or location. They were just spread all around you. They appeared to illuminate the whole landscape from one horizon to the opposite one and would occur in such quick succession there would be a continuous shimmering white/blue light, vivid yet soft and pleasing to the eyes. The horizon would be silhouetted in lovely sharp relief. But where was the thunder? Not a sound. I recall how I enjoyed rumbling along in the dark, mile upon mile, with lights visible in profusion either side of the track. Fires burning freely around which sat perhaps twenty to thirty natives, or in family groups eating their final meal of the day or drinking their local beer and I would contrast the blackout at home with this wonderful scene of total freedom.

The receptions at previous halts had indeed been beyond belief, but the welcome which awaited us at Mafeking was to out-do them all. The crowds were very much larger and the fare much more generous and lavish. The buffet, for one thousand hungry airmen, was superb and must have taken this army of ladies hours to prepare. It was satisfying and perhaps just a little touching to see all those dedicated ladies taking such pride in seeing all their lovely fare disappearing down the cavernous throats of "all the boys from home on the War Train". The magnificent efforts of all these lovely ladies were deserving of a much longer stay. One of the ladies pressed a New Testament souvenir into my hand and introduced me to a kindly gentleman who was the area postmaster. To mark the occasion of our meeting he offered to send a cablegram to my folks at home, immediately and quite free of charge. They later confirmed receipt.

We had recently experienced much wheel slip on the rails, where much steam and water had to be directed onto the wheels where they made contact with the rails. The excessive slip would cause the overloaded train to slow down to a mere walking pace, whereupon one thousand airmen would leap from the train and commence to push. When 65 tons of bodies disgorged themselves from the train and supplied a forward pressure of one thousand man power, to assist that poor old overworked engine, it was amazing how it responded. The problem then was how to get back on board as the pace quickened. There was much hilarity as access to the passing coaches was denied by hundreds of other bodies. By the time the last coach hove into view there were so many hangers on that any San Francisco tram would have been a picnic.

The hard working train crew was to be greatly admired for dedication and persistence and found much entertainment from our antics especially when some of our boys were slightly under the influence of some of that lovely white South African wine we would pick up at some of the halts.

Tomatoes were growing wild in profusion at Raneguane. Natives were busy digging in the many dry river beds to locate water in this northern area of the Kalahari Desert. We passed through Vagaganga at an altitude of 4520 feet and signed 1291 miles from the Cape. Syringa, Marula and Khami followed Plumtree, then on to Bulawayo where that wonderful train crew waved us a rather affectionate farewell. I thought of them doing the return trip and wondered how many such trips they would complete before we again returned south.

Rhodesia was lovely, well elevated with superb weather and lovely people. At RAF Kumalo I soon rustled up a rugger team to compete against the tough and determined local teams. I loved flying the Tiger Moth especially the rolls and loops following my first exciting solo after six and a half hours dual.

During free time we visited the Wankie Game Reserve and the Victoria Falls on the Zambesi. The thunderous roar of the water could be heard miles away, deep-throated and ominous in all its power. Monkeys played their noisy games in the trees and Baboons spanked their young when they misbehaved. Without waterproofs you got uncomfortably wet even a mile distant from the fine misty rain billowing up from the Falls. Beautiful miniature rainbows crowned the glory of this wonderful natural phenomenon which I have ever since recalled with pleasure. We went to Gwelo and Umtali where the locals almost pulled us into their sumptuous houses and where a dear old lady loaned me her Austin Ruby for

Syd (centre) and friends in Rhodesia.

my stay. The roads between towns were not specifically good, being two tarmac strips on which you attempted to navigate. On meeting an oncoming car each would take one strip with the other wheel on the hard baked earth. Regaining your two strips at times could be fun – especially when the dust clouds were reluctant to clear.

Doug would hire an old crate one weekend, for which there were much too many occupants. But piled high we set forth with a slightly inebriated Doug at the wheel. Doug reasoned that the quicker you motored the easier it was to retain your strips. He could with equal justification have reasoned that once you lost the strips it would be easier to maintain one's course off them, which proved to be the case. At one point on this vertiginous escapade, the hard core surface bordering the strips had become somewhat sunken, the strips standing up well proud of the base. Doug now driving and singing like some cycloid frenetic, suddenly lost his strips and no amount of frantic persuasion would force or coax the old crate back on to them. The vehicle would ricochet from the edges of the strips as though bouncing off a crash barrier. With one vigorous heave Doug locked over, bodies piling on top of each other. The old crate accepted the challenge, leapt clean across both strips and plunged down an embankment catapulting all occupants into the 'Bush'. I collided with a Needle bush which grew needle-like spines about two inches long, quite unbreakable, but which detached themselves fairly easily from the branch. I was literally porcupined, and one needle had completely augured through both my nostrils. I still carry the evidence.

"We're not so bad..." said Doug, "relatively speaking," in his doctrinaire manner.

We hired some natives to canoe us up the Zambesi. A more hair-raising journey by water I have never made nor witnessed. How those boys navigated and sweated on those rapids, and daring at times to skim the noses of the lazy looking crocodiles with their deep cavernous pink throats. They scared the hell out of me, but these boys were devastatingly expert. They landed us on a small mid-river island, the thick vegetation growing right to the water edge. Tall trees reached skywards in their battle for light, barring the sun from the dense green luscious undergrowth. Beautiful birds flapped and flitted, screeching and squawking their protests. I collected some vegetable ivory nuts and still have them.

I journeyed to Chilimanzi and Fort Victoria. To the seventy acre site of the ruins of Zimbabwe some seventeen miles south of Fort Victoria. Here stands the elliptical Temple of the Valley of the Ruins and the Acropolis on the Hill. Building is attributed to the Bantu tribe from the 8th century A.D. We visited native Kraals where the men had many wives who all lived in the same thatched Kraal and who lavishly decorated their section of the internal wall to seek the favours of their husband. The children fled in terror. The Chiefs were clad in skins and feathers and one had terribly mutilated features. Many of the mothers were mere girls of 14 or 15. I later flew over the Matopas Hills and located the monument to commemorate the great Cecil Rhodes.

I well remember flying a twin-engined Oxford on a night exercise and came across a Kaffir Drink. This was an occasion on which hundreds of the natives would congregate to consume huge quantities of their home-made brew, Kaffir Beer. Such Drinks were feasts which lasted for days and the huge fires were visible for many miles. There were two tribes, the Mashonas and the Matabele. The singing from the Drinks could be heard floating on the breeze from very great distances and we were told of deaths occurring on these occasions, which was not really surprising.

We visited a monument in the memory of the dead Chief Zulu Umsilikaza. It was erected under a tree, where he used to sit, and as per custom the whole tribe had moved their settlement when the great Chief died. The going was rough at times through huge towering boulders, balanced it would seem on mere pinpoints. Small wildlife was in profusion, snakes, baboons, lizards, gazelle and many other forms including scorpion and tarantulas.

How I would love to write more fully on my visit to a very lovely country to which some day I hope to return. Wings parade topped it out with myself as top pupil on Airmanship.

On a beautiful Wednesday morning aboard the old slat-seated train, where we were to be dispatched to our various theatres of conflict, against the scourge of Nazism, we gave not a serious thought to the possible consequences of the future. It did not occur to us that within a few short months many of us would be force-landing our aircraft in blinding foul weather in which even the birds refused to fly; that we would be attempting to reach base with dead or injured crew aboard, our aircraft so badly damaged by enemy fire that it could not possibly remain airborne; that some of us would be wounded; that some would only save their lives by taking to the parachute, whilst others would not save their lives whatever action they attempted. I was not to know that apart from the latter predicament of fatality, I was to be involved in all the other situations from time to time and be favoured with the award of the Distinguished Flying Medal and later, in different circumstances, be recognised by a Mention in Despatches.

Syd was to be our first casualty. It was exactly six months to the day from commencing that train journey that he went straight down into the Mediterranean without further trace. There was no apparent explanation for his loss. No enemy aircraft had been seen, but something must have rendered him unconscious or badly injured. Syd was a good pilot and enjoyed flying at all times.

I spent five wonderful days in Durban with a family who invited me into their beautiful and lavish home. Then on to Suez on HMT.B.16 Stratheden escorted by Revenge to Mombassa where the Ceres took over and the HMT Orando joined us laden fully with coloured soldiers.

On arrival at Suez, there to our regret we saw the burned out shell of the *Georgic*, one of our Liverpool to Cape convoy.

Both Cairo and Ismalia, to us, were something entirely new both in custom and architecture. There was the contrast between the wealthy and those who lived in squalor and abject poverty of which, in Egypt, there was surely a great deal too much. Both cities had an over population of troops, just as surely they had abundant evidence of the cultural past of such an ancient land as Egypt. From the wonderful Cairo Museum, Mosque and Citadel to the chicken and goat infested dwellings of Old Cairo, it was all there. Lovely hotels, Sheppards and Groppis. Sleazy bars and clubs, crippled beggars crying 'Backsheesh', peering from filthy rags. Excellent coffee and tea bars. Beer bars overcrowded by noisy troops of various nationalities, 'better-class' bars where dark-skinned, lovely Armenian girls would snuggle up to you, stroking the wings on your well-laundered tunic, whispering in your ear "My 'ero. I giff yoo de flying fook". The shoe shine boys polishing like fury whilst their heads swivelled vigorously, left to right, looking for the next customer. The sordid exhibition side shows, touted by slimy looking doubtfuls who would surreptitiously flash a photographic example in the hope of encouraging you. The wailing doleful music which I could never appreciate; the fat Egyptians sitting at tables on the pavements sipping tea and smoking their hubbly-bubblies whilst you consciously kept your hand on your wallet and side-stepped the touts and the dirty-postcard vendors. Rickshaws sped along, some carrying fat cigar-smoking locals whilst others were full of inebriated squaddies laughing and shouting oaths at the operator who appeared to have acquired the secret of perpetual motion.

Out to Giza to the inspiring Pyramids: Cheops standing there since 2700-2500 B.C. The great Sphinx of the fourth dynasty guarding the way but under threat, at that time of being covered by the slowly creeping sands of Egypt where the great Step Pyramid of Zozer has been standing since 2600 B.C., first with its four stepped sides being later extended to six stepped.

In the northern part of the Sudan lay RAF Wadi Gazousa, 1250 miles to the south near Gebeit. At El Shellal we boarded a very old, ill equipped, flat-bottomed paddle-barge. It was extremely noisy, had no cooking facilities and like the Cape train had hard wooden slatted seats which were to serve as our beds for the next two nights. This surely was a form of punishment. Our only food was purchased form the natives en-route. The first 800 miles up the Nile were spent hungry, thirsty and most uncomfortable, but it was one of the most wonderful of my experiences.

The fascinating Nile unfolded before us, revealing its age-old treasures at every turn. On one bank one could see the harnessed cow, lazily but steadily treading its circular path as it dragged the huge wooden arm of the irrigation machinery, the Sakiya, a device of remote antiquity. Crudely connected wheel-to-wheel by large wooden cogs, which creaked and groaned with friction in the blazing sun, the huge vertical wheel, laden with leaking buckets hauled up the water from the Nile to a height of about twenty feet, and as each bucket tipped on its decent beyond the vertical the water cascaded into the wooden chute which led to the irrigation channels. Somebody sang "There's a hole in your buckets dear Liza".

We came to Asyut and Thebes of Grecian name, the ancient capital of Upper Egypt from the times of the twelfth dynasty where the Necropolis, the Valley of the Kings, and that of the Queens, and the temple of Hatshepsut and many other wonderful creations are to be found. The discovery of the tomb of Tutankhamen in 1922, revealing all the priceless treasures buried with the eighteen-year-old King in the 14th century B.C., surely established this region round Luxor as the greatest attraction of the whole very wonderful country of ancient treasures and monuments.

But I must not dwell unduly on this area, to which one could not pay true tribute in a library of books, but simply mention the temples of Abydos, chief centre of the cult of the God Osiris, the temple of Seti from the 19th Dynasty, containing a list of the Pharoes on which is based the whole chronological dating of the Dynasties, are there to be seen. Then from the Colossi of Memnon to the temple of Horus at Edfu and on to Komombo where we had to hurry to include the temple of Sobek and Haroersis, or be left behind. Wonderful carvings on the elevations, hundreds of feet high awaited us at the Temple of Philae at Aswan. Since my visit to Aswan and Wadi Halfa the Nile between these points has been considerably altered by the creation of the dam which formed the present Lake Nasser. The Temple of Abu Simbel then stood in this original position hard up to the edge of the waters of the Nile. In fact to gain entrance to the temple we had to row right into the entrance. Abu Simbel really was something different indeed, captivatingly wonderful in all its regal majesty. Cut into the living rock about 1200 B.C. the entrance to the 180 feet high vault, was certainly a great sight. From the facing rock, the four statues of Ramases the Second, each over sixty-five feet high, are carved. The Temple of Queen Nefertari, his wife, stood alongside.

We left the dutiful old paddler at Wadi Halfa. For a further two days we were to traverse the wastes of the Nubian Desert for 500 miles on hard slatted benches, by train. The heat was searing. The ominous signs above, of vultures riding the convection currents, followed us for the whole journey. I attempted to scare them off by shooting the whole of my revolver ammunition at them.

The Blenheims stood around the one strip landing ground awaiting our pleasures. Paddy looked to be three or four years older than the average, and I at 23 seemed to have the edge on most, but it seemed to go without saying that he would crew up with me as my navigator. Paddy was totally unflappable; flaxen haired with a flowing moustache, a beaming smile which exhibited a wonderfully well formed arrangement of teeth and eyes forever on the move. He was an experienced navigator having entered the RAF in 1936.

I would encourage him from time to time if we came out on the right side of a sticky patch by saying something to the effect of:

"Good effort Paddy my boy, you certainly got your sums right again!"

He would never accept a compliment without returning one and was known to reply, "You make it bloody easy Perc!" – though there was always a friendly rivalry between us. The way Paddy died some seven months later from a stray enemy bullet was indeed *mal-àpropos*, and to say the least, distressing.

Les, our gunner, was the comedian of the crew. Lean to the point of being bony, as though when skins were issued he had obtained a size too small. Curly sandy hair, bounding with energy, quick to take issue on an injustice and very much having his own views on matters. He disliked intensely being segregated from the female gender for three months at a stretch, but loved flying and was keen on his job, for which he had worked hard since entering the RAF about eighteen months prior to the war, to 'do his bit' as he explained 'before flying became dangerous'. Quiet, inoffensive Rick was Wop/AG.

The Blenheim Mark I was a delight to fly. It was so obedient. From an operational viewpoint however it was a disaster; under-powered, under-armed and much over-used. The Mark IV, the Longnose, was even more so. We did some exciting low level work nevertheless, hoping to perfect the angle of approach and for correct bomb placement get the speed and height right. Initial approach, at somewhere between ten feet and a hundred feet, depending on the terrain, was an exciting venture, but navigation at that height was not always as easy as one would have wished. Low level expertise for ground attack and shipping strikes was to be our speciality and was a contribution towards our general indifference to the rule which prohibited unauthorised low flying. From the C.O. down we would beat up the landing ground on our return, unmercifully and the habit stuck so long as I was with the squadron. From such low flying we had a completely nil accident record, but an odd complaint was known to be registered now and again.

We had been ground strafing and had some fun. On the way back we happened upon a very great acreage of lovely green waving corn and I could not resist the temptation to really get down to it and set it a-ripple. I had not been down many minutes, and was still in the Flight tent when the C.O. entered looking not a little glum. An irate farmer had been on the phone explaining how a Blenheim had cut the ears of his corn off in a swathe the length of his crop. I could not deny it was me, we were the only crew airborne, so my pleas to the C.O. could only be,

"Well you know how these types exaggerate, Sir!"

"Not in this case he doesn't," said the C.O. "You have overcooked it this time. What are those two vertical deposits of sticky green gunge on the fuselage thrown up by the props? That stuff doesn't grow in the air."

He had taken a look before the ground crew could get it washed off.

The Bostons had arrived and somehow the Blenheims were no more. What a dramatic and welcome change. One hundred miles an hour faster and a tricycle undercart. We loved the extra speed and showed it off one evening on a serious beat up. That was the first time we had succeeded in getting some of the ground staff horizontal. I really think they enjoyed it in an odd sort of way. Perhaps they felt an affectionate sort of involvement because it was their aircraft doing this to them. I was forever sorry for them not having the escape or the outlet which we as aircrew had. They were stuck with the heat, the sand and the flies of the day, the cold and the mosquitoes at night. They were hundreds of miles from anywhere, no cinema, no pubs, no lounge, no snooker table, no dining room, no bedroom, no girls, no visiting concert parties, just sand and tents and aircraft, their friends and warm beer. Whereas the aircrew could be over the Jebels and darting along the Wadis like swallows and swifts.

Boredom, frustration, dissatisfaction and anger were allowed to be expressed by civilian workers back home in Britain. Miners were even on strike. Women in factories openly complained of the monotony of their job and their lives but none of them really understood that their species of boredom was really quite comfortable and true monotony was unknown to them. It was different sleeping under the stars, being washed out of your tents by a terrific deluge or being suffocated by blinding sandstorms. Flies, thirst, desert sores and Gippo guts were only for starters. Ground staff slaved long hours to keep the aircraft in the air and such primitive conditions were mother and father to all manner of ingenious arrangements, inventions and improvisations.

Little wonder that when a few energetic and boisterous young airmen found themselves 'out in the blue' for months on end that the evenings in the bar-tent became riotously funny. There were the drinking competitions, the rugger-scrums, the de-bagging, balancing the pint, headstand drinking, tug of war along with the service songs.

> Now on yon street corner two girls you'll find standing
> One to the other in a whisper did say
> Here comes that young airman whose money we squandered
> Here comes that young airman cut down in his pride.
>
> Beat the drums loudly and play the pipes merrily,
> Play the dead march as they carry him along
> And let all his comrades fire three volleys o'er him,
> He was a young airman cut down in his prime.

Then there was Salomi, with Little Jim who was permanently 'sliding and gliding in the moonlight'. The Shiba Blues, Eskimo Nell, Sweet Violets, The airman's Lament, Bombay Troopship, One Eyed Riley, Harlots of Jerusalem, The Great Big Wheel, Sylvest and many others to which many ex-RAF readers could no doubt add, and sing. A ditty round would last for ages and usually ended up riotously funny. Someone would sing a four-lined ditty and for want of a better indication to the tune may I say it went "Too-ral-eye-ooh-ral-eye-ooh-ral-eye-aye. Some were reasonable others were just unprintable. The whole mess would then chorus, "That was a cute little rhyme sing us another one do-oo". Well you had better get thinking of one because everyone had to make his contribution otherwise pay some dreadful and sometimes undignified forfeit. I usually got mine in early or staggered off before the rough stuff commenced.

> Now I was out walking with my Uncle Jim,
> When somebody threw some tomatoes at him,
> "Now tomatoes don't hurt me he said with a grin
> But by Christ it's diff'rent when they're in a tin"
>
> "That was a cute – ".
> I said to the maiden from Mulberrry Farm,
> "Just take hold of this it'll do you no harm,
> Just slide it quite gently right into your knicks,
> Then just hold your hat on whilst I do the tricks".

We were never favoured with a piano on any desert 'drome that I can remember, which usually placed my chromatic harmonica in great demand. Apart from the mess radio all we had was an old 78 hand-wind-up type gramophone which creaked, groaned and croaked from the effects of dust, sand and old age.

Single engine performance on the Boston was alarming. One could adjust speed down to 175 mph and climb happily away on one, without any fear of critical speed taking the nose out of your hands. Such performance on one engine was better than the Blenheim could offer on two good motors. For the aeronautical minded, the stall was interesting. With airframe clean, buffeting commenced at 145 mph, the nose dropping at 126 mph with good recovery. With undercart and flaps down the story was vastly different, you needed a lot of height to survive. Aileron flutter came in at 123 mph and at 110 mph the thing just fell out of the sky with a violent starboard wing drop which definitely was not to be picked up by rudder however hard you tried.

At the far end of the take-off run there was a cross furrow, before reaching which, it was recognised you had to be airborne otherwise you were getting terribly short of runway. It was in fact quite easy to lift off before the furrow even in nil wind conditions. One day I chose to see what speed could be obtained on reaching the furrow with three wheels on the ground. The nose wheel smartly smacked the furrow at 175 mph indicated and without any interference from me the nose lifted and the crate flew itself off, hands off. Great, thought I, and told the boys in the mess that evening. Next day saw some smiling pilots hammering up the runway with throttles' friction nut nice and tight and with both hands raised, proving no holds, waiting for the furrow smack. The C.O. stopped it and gave me the job of taking up 'pupil' pilots on conversion to demonstrate how a perfectly executed take off and landing was to be done officially. Such was my punishment. It did in fact not do me any harm because I was then approached to do a few months as instructor.

· CHAPTER 5 ·

TO MEET THE ENEMY

For five whole days we 'roughed it' again on train and paddle steamer to El Maza near Heliopolis (City of the Sun), where we once again had comfortable beds and good food, neither of which we had known these last three months. Cairo (El Kahira - 'The Victorious'), awaited us with all the enchantment of that great city. We were back to the infinite variety of Minarets and the wailing calls to prayer.

Shandur aerodrome lay hard by the shore on the south west side of the Great Bitter Lake, just beyond Kasfareet. All the Suez Canal traffic therefore passed within a few hundred yards of the end of our runway. Here we met many crews already known to us and even some ground staff I had known in Britain.

The Glen Martin Maryland was our mount here, the forerunner of the Baltimore. It was not so suitable as the Boston. It was a tail dragger with twin Pratt and Whitney Wasps. The fuselage was pencil thin, directional stability was poor coupled with a violent torque swing and an undersized rudder. It took some of the boys a while to get them in the air, as the swing got out of hand unless you staggered the throttles early.

Blenheims (Imperial War Museum).

Reconnaissance duty was just about right for the Maryland so we were glad to see them go to a PR Unit. Paddy, however loved flying in the thin tubular sharp end, just below my rudder-bars. It was fully glazed and he named it his 'flying greenhouse'. It was to be about our farewell flight in the Maryland and Paddy suggested that before getting rid... "we put the bloody thing on its back Perc before we get back in the circuit."

Such manoeuvres were, of course, not standard practice, especially for a Maryland, but with bags of height there ought not to be any great problems.

"I'll put her on her back and half loop out," say I, when everyone chorused agreement.

"O.K. Check on precautions. Height, airframe clean, location free, traffic free, items loose secure, make harness tight, dinghy stowed, turret guns locked and all other odds and ends – everybody confirm."

So, over we'd go. Forward pressure and top rudder as we winged over, to the right. I crushed up against the side of the cockpit and my left leg suddenly became too short. Now into the shoulder straps for a second when masses of sand fell off the floor, down into my eyes and mouth, pencils, maps and navigational rubbish whirled and gyrated round my head (and they were all supposed to be 'secured'). A shout from the gunner suggested he was standing on his head in his department, so I could not drop the nose quick enough to ease his torture. Stick and throttles back, and on passing the vertical on the pull out it was alarming the rate at which the knots were building. The way the height was peeling off was beyond belief and objects on the ground appeared to be swelling.

'Christ I'll never make it!' thought I as I heaved back and my eyeballs became very heavy and my chin tightened the helmet strap. I ought not to have done it without my old Tiger Moth. The deck was so close. I certainly had a severe attack of the proverbial ring twitters, my ears popped like champagne corks, the aircraft protested because of the speed and the vibration suggested that something was about to fall off. My ticker was flogging like a jack-hammer and as we levelled out at about 200 feet I felt drained and relieved. Paddy was delighted with the performance and thought it had been a 'wizard show'. Little did that boy know how my skin pricked and my fingers tingled, and how dry my tongue had become, and how firmly I had already decided not to 'do it again'. What amazed me later that evening when Paddy was excitedly recounting the incident to a small group in the mess, was that he finished up by nodding in my direction saying, "...and Perc didn't even comment!"

He little knew I had been almost speechless.

* * *

We were the first squadron to be equipped with the A20, the Baltimore. It was now January 1942. It was a Glen Martin production, originally a French contract now amended to RAF specification. It was a tail dragger with two 14 cylinder double bank radial engines of 1600hp each by Wright Cyclone. The pilot had four fixed forward firing machine guns housed in the wings and four rear firing guns fixed in the fuselage aft of the trailing edge. The mid-upper gunner had two .3 guns on a scarf ring, later to be .303's in an electric hydraulic turret and the W/op, when prone, could operate the two swivel guns from the lower dorsal hatch.

It was at L.G.116, near Sidi Haneish, about 350 miles west of Cairo where we spent many months of intense activity bending the Bosche. I well remember our first introduction to L.G.116 We packed up at dead of night as though to sneak away to 116 quite unnoticed and in case the Jerry shufti-kite which came over at 40,000 feet every day should record any activity. I have never known such an uncomfortable trip, (except for flak) caused by the violent desert convection. We pitched our tents upwind of the prevailing wind and learned how to eke out our daily water ration of four pints per man to see us through shaving, washing, drinking and a contribution to help with the cooking. Our usual bath was from a tin hat denuded of its internal upholstery, upturned and wedged in the sand.

It was on an early bombing run from here, when over the sea at 18,000 feet with no enemy fighters or flak, moderate convection and accurate flying that Syd, flying only a few feet to my right, turned over and went straight into the sea.

Some of the aircraft required an adjustment to the rudder static balance, so I took a formation of six back to 107.MU in the Delta Area. For the ground staff this was a twenty hour truck drive if they were due for a few days leave, so I crammed the fuselage full of airmen much to their delight and we were there in an hour and a half. A few nods and winks on our arrival, with one of the NCO's whom I knew gave us the few days on the town to which we had been looking forward.

Hugh and I pushed off to Port Tewfik and stayed at the BelAir. The place swarmed with Nazi sympathisers, so we were extremely vigilant. They were not difficult to recognise when conversing. I allowed one of them to buy me three whiskys whilst we talked, it helped my toothache, but I think he realised that I had him weighed up and he broke off the engagement.

Oddly we all gravitated to the M.U. within a few hours of each other, (what wonderful discipline) but desert rats seemed to be that way, and in a short while we were skimming over base with just enough daylight in hand to demonstrate to the boys on the ground just how we would come in at about 300mph if we were on the attack. Many of them were prostrate, but they loved it.

It ought to be mentioned the continuous trouble we had with unsatisfactory gun operation. Breech jamming and belt feeds gave cause for concern. We dispensed with the belts and fitted pans, but with the guns being manually operated no accuracy of handling was possible owing to the violent effect of the slipstream on the pan surface. The forces were much too strong for the gunner to overcome, so we reverted once again to the belts. All aircrew were naturally anxious to have this problem solved, so whilst the armourers changed the guns, we aircrew belted 38,000 rounds of ammunition, 2 AP; 2 Ball; 1 Tracer; and so on. Where else would you find that other than in the desert?

Tight or loose breeching did not help. The fault was badly finished breeches causing uneven expansion and split cases. Enemy fighter pilots realised we had troubles when our return fire would cease, when we obviously had ammunition left, and they would close in. The situation gave us concern. Les, my gunner, was the first man to object in any positive physical way, to this situation, some weeks later.

LAC McCann was not happy about two figures who seemed to be having difficulty starting up the engine of a truck at a dispersal point. He picked up a rifle and paid them a visit and returned with two escaped German Prisoners of War.

Enemy bombers were passing our way nightly en-route to such targets as Fuka, Alexandria and other Delta Area depots. Benghazi harbour was extremely busy, where Axis ships were unloading masses of equipment and stores for the Afrika Korps. Although Wellingtons from Shalufa did their nightly 'milk-run', not without losses, the supplies were still getting through. Air Headquarters therefore decided that perhaps daylight attacks would be more effective. Our Baltimores were very much faster than the lumbering Wimpeys and so it was up to us to open up the daylight dicing. Six of us set out in crystal clear visibility to do a precision job on ships and harbour. The round trip was just over 900 miles. We took an outbound devious route and arrived over the target without seeing one enemy fighter. This was to be strictly a high level visit, so on the last leg we climbed to 18,000 feet for the bombing run.

There was very little cloud and would you believe, in the lovely African sunshine, we were flying above freezing level. With our tropical shorts and shirts no cockpit heating, it was unbelievably cold. The flak opened up as we approached. They had us ranged. The black ominous puffs of the exploding shells suddenly appeared just in front of our noses and we flew straight into them. Nostrils were filled with the acrid smell of cordite and the adrenalin flowed a bit quicker. Somehow I had forgotten the intense cold, in fact it had become quite warm – but the OAT thermometer on the screen didn't seem to know. My hands were sticky and flak kept at us only a little closer because there were some sickening thuds and the aircraft rocked. My mouth was dry and my shirt was wet and my scalp prickled under my helmet.

"R-I-G-H-T," said Paddy slowly as he gave me a correction for the bombing run. I tried to do a flat turn. I was supposed to be chatting casually to the boys on the intercom.

"Steady", said Paddy, "Right up the bloody wires."

"How about bomb doors open Paddy?" I ask.

"Yes, OK now Perc" said he.

"Scope's been hit Perc, peeled off and going down," said Rick.

"Bombs gone." called Paddy, "We must be bang on." said he in a satisfied tone.

No wonder Scope had been hit, the flak was so persistently accurate.

"Rick, get down to the bottom hatch and watch for the bomb bursts."

"Bomb bursts now Rick," squeaked Paddy excitedly. "Oh Wizzo. Right across that mole. Look at those fires starting. We've got something that burns quickly. Bang on!"

"That bloody flak was rough Perc." continued Paddy as though not terribly concerned.

We had now wheeled away to flak-free skies and I started to descend hoping for warmer air and said something about there could not be any fighters around otherwise they would have picked Scope off before now.

Not a word from Les until that moment, but he broke his silence to tell us he was ready to drop 'his bombs' when a suitable target came up. Les would have his own private 'bombing' show by arrangements with Paddy up front. If Les could leave his turret, in the absence of fighters, Rick would keep a look out, Paddy would give Les the count-down to release and Les would yank the toggles. He had previously reasoned with us, that on daylight trips, as the flare chutes would not be in use he may as well fill them up with his own missiles. To compete with the true bombs, which were fitted with 'screamers' to emit blood curdling sounds as they fell, Les would use empty bottles for this purpose which made an awful woo-woo-wooing noise as they tumbled over and over. His other missiles were rocks, stones and beer bottles filled with urine, which he collected with great anticipation. With great glee and a continuous flow of humorous remarks he would pack these weapons of destruction into the flare chutes. His armoury of secret weapons would "scare these bloody Huns clean out of Africa."

"Got to get this right," I remember him once saying. "How do you calculate the terminal velocity of a bottle of piss, Perc?"

He had us roaring with laughter. "Depends on whether you were on Nut Brown or Gippo Gut Rot Les," I parry.

We were now quite low, and quite defrosted. Paddy called that he could see a bunch of Hun vehicles ahead. Les was out of his turret like a panther to get down to the flare chutes and get his intercom plugged in. Les was flat on his stomach looking out of the bottom hatch for Paddy's sighting, chatting excitedly about the inevitable fate of the enemy below.

"Count down coming up Les", called Paddy.

"Five – four – three – two – one – GO" and with squeals of delight Les yanked the chute levers to release his powers of destruction. He made some weird and wonderful claims and we all joined in the hilarity. For anyone capable of infusing such levity into a serious function such as bombing the enemy was worth his place in any crew. His story telling in the mess when he had a few beers aboard was not to be missed. The whole squadron was aware of his contribution to the victory.

"I can see that stupid face of one of those Krauts now," he would say. "He had a twitch, and I have the tense right, 'cos this bottle of piss caught him right between the eyes, and just stopped the next twitch coming on. Corked tight for a week it was!"

We had the first 150 miles of the return trip now behind us, when ahead we saw what was unmistakably a dirty yellow veil of deteriorating visibility. It was a sandstorm borne on the deadly Khamsin wind which came up from the Sahara, hot, burning, dry, choking, feverish and merciless. This persistent wind picked up hundreds of tons of the finest sand and dust swirling it thousands of feet up into the air for hundreds of miles across the desert. To attempt to fly through it was fatal. The fine dust would choke your cockpit, the engine air filters would not cope with the volume of dust and the abrasive effect on the aircraft was serious enough to strip the paint from the leading edges of the wings and cowlings. The perspex of the windscreen could be so abrased and opaque that forward visibility beyond the nose was totally cut off. I would risk the extra fuel consumption and attempt to climb over it rather than seek the leading edge and go around it. Then climb as quickly as possible. We were to land at forward base at Baheira for refuelling but we'd never find it in this airborne sand.

I altered the course to bring us over the coast as quickly as possible, where over the sea we could let down in good visibility and nip into Baheira which was not far inland.

At 15,000 feet we were still very much enveloped in this awful trap and Paddy said that we must be now well out to sea. It was not good

Boston Mark IV (Imperial War Museum).

airmanship to continue any further out to sea in case of fuel shortage so I turned towards land and began to descend. We had no means of obtaining a barometric pressure reading to set on the altimeter, but taking our southerly bombing wind as a basis and applying Buy's Ballot Law (back to the wind, low pressure on your left), meant that we were heading towards an area of high pressure. We could therefore trade a few millibars and trust the altimeter down to some suicidal minimum. If we were where we ought to be we knew the ground to be fairly elevated but reasonably flat. We would trust down to 250 feet above ground level, thick though the airborne sand continued to be and no one voted for jumping out unless I too promised to do the same – but I didn't want to bend such a good looking aircraft. Airborne sand was much worse than fog. For one thing it was much darker and it was also the same colour as the ground. Rick was to stand by with a couple of Very lights. There was a bit of ripple in the air which is quite typical when crossing the coastline at low level and it was near enough to our ETA to convince us that we were now over land. Maximum concentration was vital – absolute. Paddy now decided we were on the Baheira Latitude, so we could only be either east or west of the 'field'.

"I'm turning now Paddy on to east/west runs. I'll do four minutes out and eight minutes back for good lateral coverage. Now everybody eyes peeled like hell and shout if you see anything", said I, and almost as an after thought, added "And I may sneak a further fifty feet off. Remember my eyes are in this bloody office."

"Four and eight are a bit much Perc. Why not two and four?", asked Paddy.

"OK by me Paddy if you feel happier", I replied, "I've got speed down to one-eighty so we have a twelve miles sweep."

First sweep over and nothing sighted and thankfully, nothing hit. I turned through 180 degrees as slowly and gingerly as treading thin ice. I straightened up and with confidence said, "Right fellows down another fifty feet. Going. Check your harness and swivel the eyeballs".

We had thirty minutes fuel left. I had traded one hundred feet which meant that we were skimming along about 150 feet above ground, but then, if pressure had increased even more than assumed, we could be 250 feet up.

"Time to turn again Perc," said Paddy, "How much are you prepared to trade now?" "When I straighten up Paddy I'm going to do the next run with the altimeter reading nil, but beyond that we're in the 'twitter' region, especially if there's any boulders scattered about", I said, feeling we were now quickly approaching some kind of solution.

"TENTS!" screamed Paddy, "Fifty feet. Just a small bunch of them. We've got the bloody height spot-on Perc!"

I was delighted. "Very lights Rick. Quick!" I shouted. "Paddy you do the second hand. Take me two minutes beyond where you think those tents are, and we'll come back on the approach. Now are you happy about the surface beyond those tents?" I question.

"Yes, great Perc. Just a bit of camel thorn", assured Paddy "Two minutes almost up Perc. Ten seconds to go." he advised.

I had pulled up a bit for the turns and ought now to be heading straight for those tents. Two minutes to go. I would now set it up. Pitch fully fine, with undercart down, full flap and bags of power. Everything stable, speed down to one-thirty. I shuffled my bottom into my seat with eyes glued on the instruments. I went down to nil feet on the altimeter once again. The engines were lovely. "Another twenty seconds Perc." said Paddy and my eyes were flashing from instruments to screen to instruments to screen.

"TENTS!" screamed Paddy just as I snatched a glance through the windscreen and spotted them. Then they were gone. I eased back on the throttles and the stick. I saw the ground and clumps of camel thorn. I chopped the throttles fully and hauled hard back standing on the brakes. We thumped and jolted over the clumps, first one wheel then the other. What a bumpy ride but at least there were no boulders. We stopped, up with the flaps and cut the motors. Magic. We were out in seconds and met under the port wing. Funny how we always did that. Paddy was on his knees, raising his head and hands, facing east. We were all smiling and shaking hands when two RASC sergeants and a few soldiers came running up, followed by the Major. They appeared to be awe-struck and overcome by wonderment. Major V. Austin introduced himself.

"We heard you around for ages it seemed, but never thought for moment you had a hope in hell of getting down. We thought at one time that you were a Jerry and had us pinpointed, as you came so low spot on the same run everytime."

They showered us with questions and were fascinated with our story as they led us over to their tentage. Major immediately mounted a guard on our aircraft.

"Lucky you stopped where you did," said Major, "another fifty yards and you would have been in deep trouble. We have laid a neat little minefield there... I shall take the officers to the mess whilst you take good care of the NCO's." he said to his Sergeant

Major was quite beyond understanding that the highest rank in our aircraft was Warrant Officer.

"What! And in charge of a machine such as that?" I rather think that he expected his crowns to drop off.

These gentlemen of the 15th Coy. RASC really treated us as royalty, or as though we were on some tettrastyle mission. Beer flowed in very generous quantities, all free, because one carries no money on bombing missions. The occasion was very well suited for Les to take over the conversation. He excelled himself. He expertly punctuated his tall stories with ample physical demonstrations of how the Huns were hit by his missiles of evil content and how the rocks cascaded from the skies as in the 'days of fire and brimstone'.

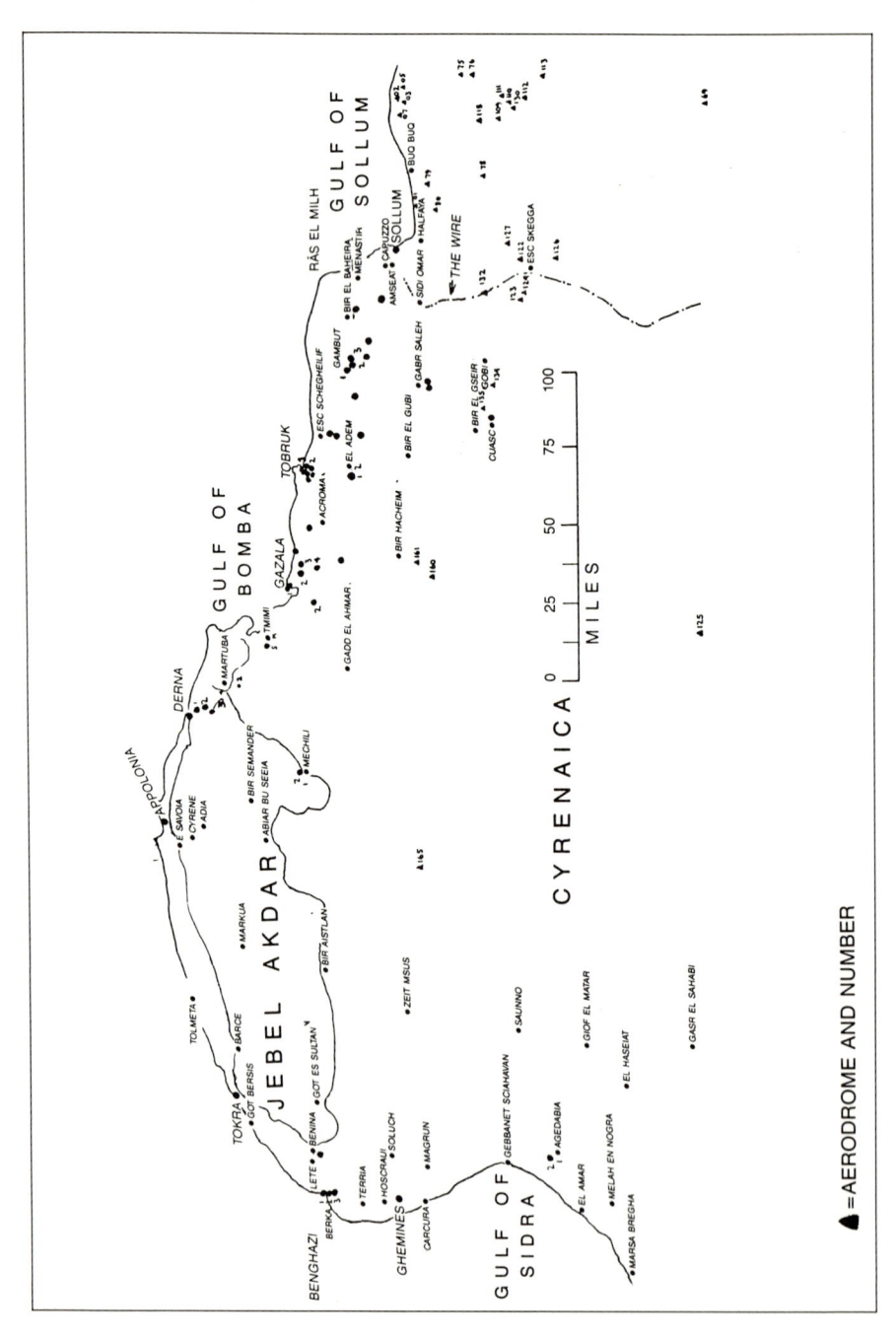

Aerodromes in Libya and Egypt.

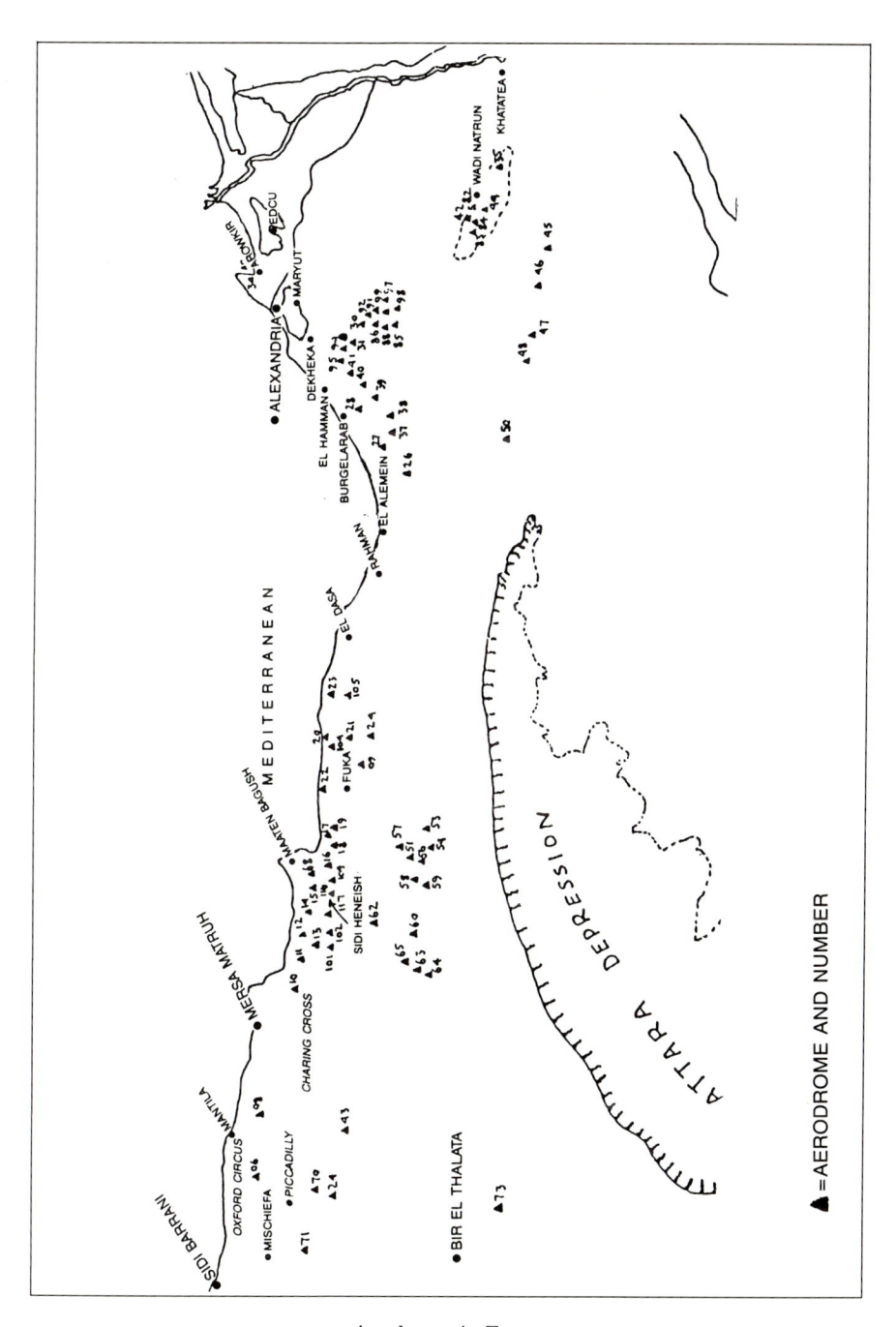

OF PLOUGHS, PLANES & PALLIASSES 37

Aerodromes in Egypt.

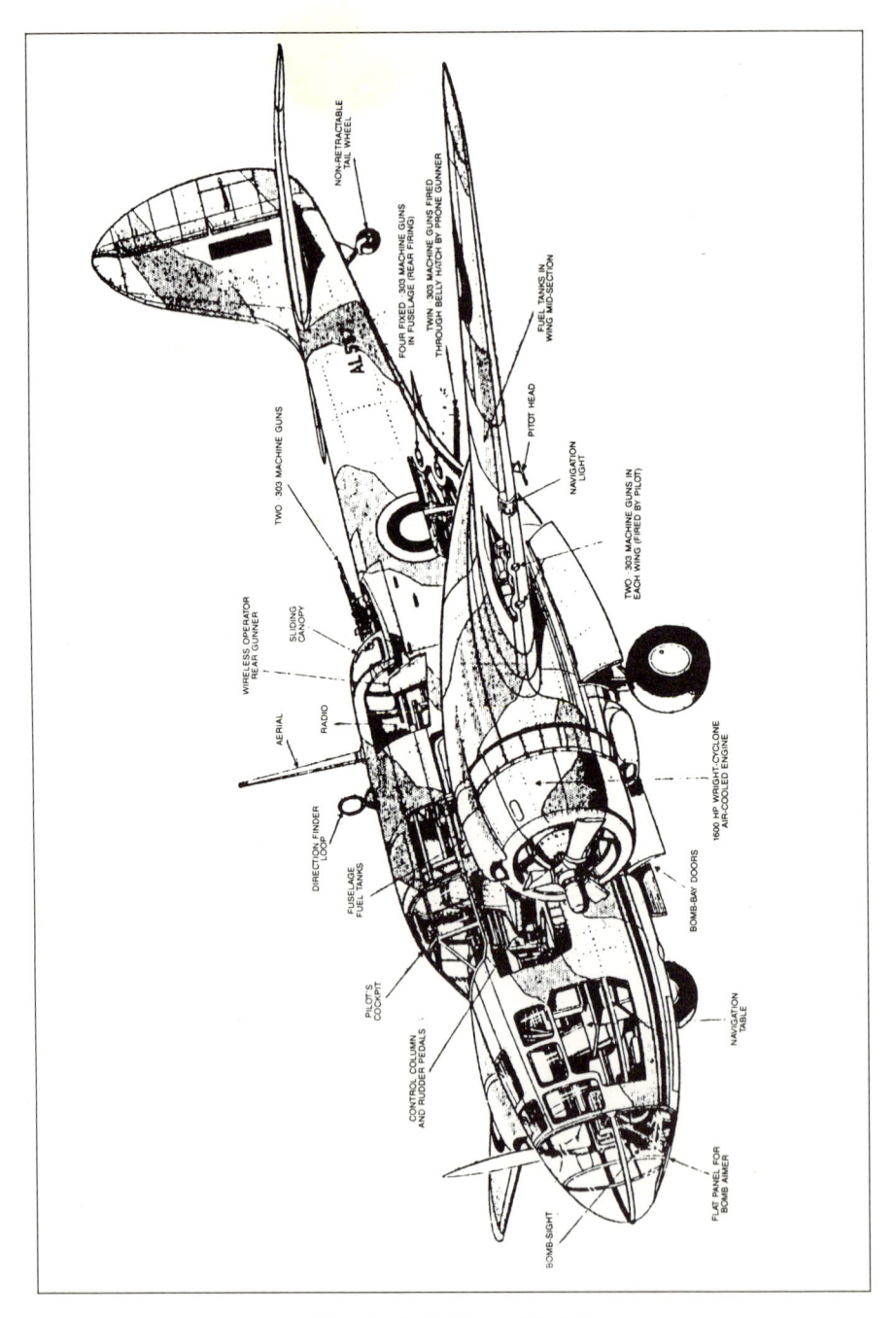

The Martin Baltimore Mark I.

"Yes Sir." quoth Les putting in appropriate actions to emphasise his story, "They were certainly pissed on from a great height!"

He had everyone rolling about in uncontrollable laughter. He did a good PR job for the RAF.

* * *

We slept through until 0700 hrs, shaved with borrowed razors, breakfasted and then to meet the Major for ground inspection. The storm had passed presenting us with a truly lovely morning. We had landed not a hundred yards from the east/west coastal road and quite parallel to it. The road was quite unsuitable as a temporary runway. Should we be able to have the camel thorn torn up, taxi back to the tentage, we would just about have enough take-off run. Soon, with a couple of suitably modified tank transporters, the Major had his men were ripping up the camel thorn and levelling the sand. A party had already left for Bardia, 121.MU to collect 200 gallons of fuel.

We inspected the aircraft, not a thing was bent and we climbed aboard after much voluable thanks and very firm handshakes. The engines snarled into life and I taxied, with some difficulty, to our take off point. I opened the throttles slowly and firmly against the brakes. The whole airframe shook in protest and I released the brakes. Major and his men stood at the far end near the minefield. Stick forward pressure and the tail came up. 60 ... 70 ... 80 mph. Hell it was bumpy and the soft parts of the sand were evident. 90 mph and she smacked a bump. I caught her on slight back pressure. Major was now coming up at an alarming rate. 110 ... 115 mph. I whipped up the undercart and we were off. I climbed to 250 feet and turned at 250 mph, depressed the nose and at 300 mph whipped over our hosts about twenty feet up. It was 1050 hrs and we all felt good. Some forty-three years later, when putting this book together, I felt it would be nice to express my thanks again to Major Austin. I forwarded a letter to MOD for onward transmission. On answering the telephone some days later I was delighted to hear a voice say,

"Hello Carruthers, Austin here..."

"I must say a very belated thank you," he continued, "for those two excellent bottles of beer hidden in your aircraft, of which you were quite obviously unaware."

It was intended that after the bombing trip we land at our forward base, Baheira for refuelling. The tips of our propellers were, for some six inches, painted bright yellow. The ground staff at both bases would write messages to each other on these tips. Apparently when the Major paid the aircraft guard a visit, he noted a current message. 'George, there are two bottles of beer in the tail. More next time.' Major, knowing we were not now dropping in at Baheira, had taken advantage of the situation and the taste had lingered since. What lingers clearly in my mind is the vigorous and enthusiastic way those gentlemen of the 15th Company waved their arms in farewell as they stood by the edge of the minefield as we almost whipped their hats off.

I landed at the base.

"The old man's waiting for you', I was told.

"Carruthers, you've been having fun. Tell me what happened. You're the first man back," which surprised me. All the others were safe with some of the aircraft bent and Scope was obliged to force land, through flak damage, just within friendly territory.

A Night in the Blue
(*from Desert Diary. 1942*)

The 'Heavies' droned their weary way west,
Shalufa 'Wimpies' seldom took a rest,
The ships and stores and Moles on Cyrene coast,
The harbour of Benghazi was the toast.

The Delta airfields sighed relief, when sun
Below the Western Desert sky had run
As 'Wimpies' laden to their maximum
Would heave their weight from ground towards the Hun.

The German might of armour men and stores,
Intending Allied forces then to crush,
In growing volume on the Sirte shores,
Would through this 'Samlung' of Benghazi push.

The haul for Axis ships was short compared
To that which British round the Cape had dared.
The threat Unterseeboten did present
Was sinister, – danger to our convoys meant.

Malta, though still resisting Axis below
Did all within her power to stem the flow
Of ships from Italy, Benghazi bound,
And kept her vigil all the clock around.

The tonnage safely passing through was still
Too great, and must not be allowed to fill
Or strengthen Axis ranks in Cyrene now.
Destruction was imperative, but how?

The only choice it was the Allies left,
Increase the bombing of the port with weft,
The nightly schedule was, however, tight,
Additional raids then must be done by light.

It was the choice our Squadron take the air,
No fighter escort would we have, to bear
The weight of Waffen of the Luft. But still
The element of surprise could fill the bill.

To eighteen thousand feet we'd climb to bomb,
But keep quite low en-route until we come,

By devious track, within the reach of port,
And bomb with noses facing our way home.

On daylight raid no need to carry then,
The usual flares in chutes provided, when
The rear gunner found a use, and trunked
Them full of bottles, tins and bricks and junk.

Agreed it was the privilege he should take,
If opportunity good should come, to make
His private bombing show, carried out with fun
If fighters nil. He'd still have a crack at Hun.

Terminal velocity for these weapons crude
He'd have us calculate, and then he made
Adjustment to their weights with liquid foul,
And laughed at thought of hitting 'Plappermaul'.

Baltimore in action in the Western Desert - the author's own aircraft taken through the hatch of the lead aircraft (Imperial War Museum).

A cloudless sky, our hopes raised high as we
Took off in Vic formation, one-two-three,
And forming now tight box of six on track,
Our gunfire concentrated, Hun to crack.

Odd though it be in African sun so bright,
There ice appeared as target came in sight,
There, forming on the wings it seemed so strange,
But minus round six centigrade the range.

The bombing run well aimed took toll,
And bombs fell all across Cathedral Mole,
So soon the trip worthwhile had been it seemed,
The element of surprise of which we'd dreamed.

Even on turn the flak bursts jarred the air,
Black acrid smoke puffs – forward, seemed to flare
In groups of six, or eight, or ten and then
Straight on we flew through these dispersing them.

We turned and weaved and dropped a bit, to catch
A warmer clime, where frozen limbs we'd scratch,
Until we felt more normal, thank our stars
That oxygen flow, through frost, had not been barred.

With flak crews now experience would pay off,
They picked us up again with accurate stuff,
And squarely hit old Scope amid the fray,
But on he struggled, airborne hoped to stay.

Baltimore leaving a trail of bombs accross a concentration of enemy transport, Western Desert – note the flak burst (Imperial War Museum).

OF PLOUGHS, PLANES & PALLIASSES

Nav Paddy up in front called out to Gunn,
"I see some Jerries down ahead, here's fun"
"I'll give you count-down for your private show,"
"Get ready now, Five-four-three-two-one-GO."

Gunn pulled the levers of the Chutes with glee,
And down went bottles, tins and rocks as he
Emitted squeals of pure delight, and said,
"Take those you Krauts, I hope they bend your head."

That night in strangers' mess, as you will learn,
Gunn sat there, pint in hand, and out he churned
The most incredible stories you could think,
How Krauts with foulest liquid strong did stink.

The sky assumed a darkened threatening look,
As east we flew to gain our safety nook.
Ahead we then saw what we'd learned from past
Was sandstorm, thick and wide and high. Oh blast.

On must we go our territory to reach,
Sand was so thick, formation must we breach
And go alone. Decisions now to make
For safety of our craft – no piece of cake.

On instruments then, but where to aim for best?
No turning back, and round the storm was last
Of all decisions now, over the top
Was my pet scheme, with safety height on clock.

The cockpit filled with choking dust. A trap
From which escape was nil. This awful crap
Abrazed the engines, airframe, props and screen,
And stripped the paint from leading edges clean.

Fifteen thousand feet and yet no break,
O'er friendly land towards the coast we'd make
And hope to get a glimpse of sea, from where
At nought feet on to land we may repair.

"We're well to sea now Perc," said Paddy who
Worked hard on course and track, the edge to woo
Of stubborn storm. Said I, "We must turn back
Or out of fuel we'll be 'ere land we track."

Increasing pressure? No check had we to seek,
Trust altimeter at five hundred feet,
With land three hundred feet above the sea,
Two hundred feet twixt us and destiny.

There was, apart from mark-one eyeball nav,
No other aid to hand. For us to have
A Q.D.M, just now to us, would be,
The very height of extreme luxury.

Around at this mere height we clowned, without
A trace of ground, which differed not one clout
To eye, from airborne sand, except by mass,
To lower fly would have been madness crass.

Yet I would sneak a few feet further down,
So, what the hell, we only had our own
Necks to preserve or break, and we were claimed
A crack crew on this flying lark. How famed -.

"TENTS – just fifty feet," screamed Paddy weird,
As from his lower nose compartment peered,
Reporting ground, "With thorn bedecked but flat"
I steered four square, o'er tents once more to track.

By God's good grace they came once more in sight,
Two Very lights shot we, to mark the right,
Track we had sighted on the previous run,
Then pitch and undercart and flaps I done.

"Watch for those lights in case they all get muffed".
Called I to crew, and feeling really chuffed,
Did one smart circuit, tight as hell would dare,
And put her down to earth. Who could care where?

We had been lower more than I had dared,
But now it did not matter, we had made
Some solid contact, which we'd keenly sought.
Who ventures not – as aye – comes up with nought.

We stopped. A jolting jogging run had we,
But everything intact appeared to be,
When up ran Major Austin and his men.
Detachment R.A. Service Corps. Ye ken?

I chose to leave the aircraft where it stood,
When Major Austin said, we certain would
Have been in little pieces, few yards on.
A minefield thick, lay wait for straying Hun.

Our passenger invisible Paddy thanked,
As he from bended knee 'neath wing I yanked,
So we could sing St. Peter's praise in mess,
Where lubrication loosed the words, no less.

They welcomed us as ne'er we'd known before,
And opened up the bar-tent, drinks galore.
We had no doubt a lot to celebrate,
And Major shouted out, "Bring one more crate."

Advised we then our base of our good fate,
And said, that evening we would hardly rate
As fit for flying duties even should
The weather clear and make conditions good.

Next morn the storm had blown itself to rest.
To get the aircraft off the ground would test
My skills, – and prick my bubble sore if I
Did fail to get this poor old crate to fly.

The sand was medium soft, I'd need a long run.
I'd also need this camel thorn agone.
Two hundred gallons of aviation gas
I'd also need, – before the test I'd pass.

Like rabbits from a hat, the Major brought
Earth movers strong, and camel thorn was wrought
Like magic out of the ground, as I stood hands
On hips, and watched the moving of the sands.

Bardia, close by our private strip,
Allowed the Major fuel and oil to trip
Along to us. The major's men then poured
'Bout fifty cans of fuel quick aboard.

Strong hands we shook, sincerely with our thanks,
For shifting camel thorn and filling tanks.
We climbed aboard, and stirred the virgin sands,
As engines leapt to life with whirling fans.

I taxied gingerly and found a lot
Of power was needed plane to move, to what
By me considered was, to be a spot where I
Run long enough could get, this crate to fly.

The Major must have thought me most unkind,
From billowing sands he was completely blind.
Where 'e're he stood or moved, he seemed intent
Of getting in the cruel slipstream vent.

By minefield now stood Major and his men.
Good seemed the distance as I turned to wind,
And smartly opened up the two long taps,
My trust in boost, St. Peter and the flaps.

Full power then brought us slowly to the roll,
As if reluctant would she pass the stroll,
Then suddenly as though she were aware,
Forward she bounded, eager for air.

Then, soft sand sought our progress to impede,
The soft rifts dragged, the firm bits helped the speed,
There was a moment almost when too late,
The props and flaps appeared to take some weight

Less wheel drag. Oh a moment of relief,
When one last effort seemed the call to meet.
The minefield and the men we're sure to clear,
When twenty feet below we saw them cheer.

I kept her nose down speed build to complete,
I thought the whole darned show had been quite neat,
And just to show our deep appreciation,
At nought feet came we back, – full motivation.

Along their ranks bare ten yards out we thundered,
As we passed by on clock we had three hundred,
They waved to us a vigorous good-bye.
I yanked the stick and shot into the sky.

A little apprehensive landed I
Expecting C.O. frowning, asking why
Last night I'd said I was to fly not fit.
"You're first man back." said he. I'd scored a hit.

In a few days time we were again told of tons of goodies being unloaded at Benghazi and we were asked to scatter them before the convoys of trucks could pick them up. I led the second vic in very rough convection conditions, which thrashed us the whole 900 miles. I felt we would suffer the same fate as Icarus. Bombing results were excellent from a lower altitude, and a more comfortable temperature. The flak caused us some twittering but no serious damage, and again, on this run we did not meet one enemy fighter. Les once more had a trip of much hilarity.

Attacking enemy aerodromes, the primary objective to destroy his aircraft whilst they were still on the ground, was a most unpredictable exercise. On occasions we would be able to sneak in and out again without a lot of opposition whilst sometimes the story was very different indeed.

We were asked to reduce the very large number of aircraft said to have recently arrived on Derna aerodrome. We had just been to Derna the previous week and had it all our own way. We had destroyed a lot of aircraft on a quick in quick out run before they could get any opposition arranged.

This next trip was one of the different ones. 109s were intent on letting no-one get to Derna. Our gunners engaged the enemy with vigour but the gun stoppages let them down badly. Bangley and Horsefield were both shot down. McLure went down but got away with a forced landing, and the fourth casualty, Leake, also force landed. This was no doubt one of the occasions when the 109 pilots realised we had stoppage problems. They were coming to within fifty yards. Someone however pressed the scatter gun button and shot one down.

It was on that day that one of our aircraft was peppered with no less than 400 holes. How did the crew survive – when we knew of cases where only a single bullet in an aircraft had claimed one of the crew? It was certainly true of wartime exploits that "one heard of things no-one but airmen would believe."

Staff up at forward base Baheira about 250 miles west were in need of some rather necessary items. I flew them up and as the enemy was now within 100 miles of that landing ground I would bring other essentials back. The fickle desert weather was playing its tricks and base confirmed, that since my departure they had become clamped in and that I was not to attempt to return that same day. Weather at Baheira was lovely. The night brought a brilliant moon with a scattering of fair-weather cumulus, a truly lovely night in contrast to the grot at base. It all started at 2100 hrs. After all the enemy aircraft we had bent and burned recently, one wondered where the Hun kept getting them from. Incessantly, right up to 0500 hrs he was over and around us, occasionally locating our 'drome, dropping bombs singly and in pairs throughout the night. We suffered no casualties but the maintenance area on the far side of the 'drome was hit square on. We spent the night in a dug-out over which had been erected a very welcome tent, the night was so very cold without any heat.

We brewed up continuously the night through and smoked a great deal. One of the aircraft at MU had a burst tyre and no replacement at ALG. Rather than fly one up I was asked to get the thing off with the burst tyre. This is an exercise I can recommend to be firmly avoided. Never have I had such a shattering experience on take-off, and the sleepless night did nothing to improve the situation. I got it back onto the ground at the other end, with one wing cocked up in the air and did a tight little pirouette when the burst wheel touched the ground. I shut down and walked thankfully away.

Just sign here, it's four o'clock straight up." said the Despatch Rider as with one hand he pushed a clip board and pencil under my nose and illuminated it with his torch. He disappeared through the tent flap. The chatter of his old khaki coloured Matchless receded as it broke the otherwise eerie silence of the desert night. It was dreadfully cold – again, as ever during deep night. It was hard to believe that within hours we would be perspiring profusely and the flies would be torturing everyone except those airborne.

> This land of arid waste and flies,
> Was surely set aside by fate
> For warring 'green-lush' powers and spies,
> Their forces to oppose and rate.
>
> The murderous blinding sun beats down,
> His daily rays on tender arm,
> The chilly nights make all hides frown
> But comradeship is welded firm.

The cooks had been up very much earlier having prepared for us tinned bacon sandwiches and very strong brown tea, as much as you would wish. It was about 0430 hrs when we shuffled into ops tent, shivering with hunched up shoulders, wearing any old woolies we could muster. I chatted with Johnnie who was to fly in vic-one with myself and Wallace. I liked Johnnie. He had qualities I admired. He wasted no words, he smiled reassuredly but did not laugh easily. He was devastatingly factual.

"Right gentlemen, we're going to have a good clean up on Derma this morning, We've all been there before and we know the score. Still more aircraft have been arriving there." There was a sinister silence. We all remembered the slaughter from the 109's caused by those feared gun stoppages. Wallace ran through the proposed tactics at length in an attempt to reassure those whose grimaces suggested some discomfort.

The C.O. had a few words of encouragement to add finishing with the usual question.

"Everybody happy about that?"

Les stood up without hesitation saying,

"No. Count me out. I've had enough of these guns and their stoppages. We're no more than sitting ducks."

The ops tent was stunned to silence but from the C.O. down all present knew just what he meant. The C.O. sidestepped the remark by not replying. He looked over to me.

"You and the rest of your crew OK for the trip if you take the stand-by gunner, Carruthers?" he queried, ignoring Les who was some yards to my right with some of the other gunners. No other gunner spoke a word. I looked at Paddy who was immediately next to me.

"Yes let's go." I said as Les came over and gripped my arm saying,

"Best of luck Perc."

Les was a great personality. We all loved him because of his brimming effervescence and clownish ways. He loved flying and was never far from my heels. I still have happy memories of the times we spent together and the larks he would initiate getting everyone involved. His bottle bombs and his mathematics on the trajectory and terminal velocity of his missiles will forever cause me to smile. Les in fact, I felt, had more courage than most, but I could not help thinking about those crews of 14 and 55 Squadrons who were still operating on clapped out Blenheims 100 mph slower than we.

Take-off was delayed. We were not off until 0555 hrs and the gunners were soon testing guns. Johnnie's gunner was obviously having trouble, so with jammed guns Johnnie peeled off and returned to base. The shoreline was beautiful as we passed over.

We were on the bombing run. The flak was devastatingly thick and close.

"Christ, look at Wallace's hatch," I said as his nose bottom hatch jolted open, hinged on it's rear edge and held at an angle of 45 degrees by its tension wire. Wallace raised his hand to me in acknowledgement, after we had bombed. He usually lit a cigarette at this stage of the party but today he had no chance with a 250 mph slipstream nipping through the hatch. I lit my pipe. We landed at forward base to refuel.

"I have often meant to ask you," said Wallace, "how you always manage to light your pipe, and fly the aircraft, immediately after 'bombs gone'."

He did not know until then that before take off I would fill the pipe and wedge it firmly in the cockpit geometry on the right hand side, along with a match box from which protruded a match. It was then a one handed operation.

✳ ✳ ✳

It often amazed me how quickly news travelled in the desert. The I.O. greeted us with congratulations on a good show. Lots of damaged aircraft which the Hun would be mourning, not on Derna 'drome but on the Martuba. We had clouted the wrong 'drome having over run Derna to our right, coming bang over Martuba which had been earmarked for attention by other squadrons.

"Do get it right next time gentlemen," was his advice. The 'Old Man' did not even mention the error, in fact he invited us to join him at the mess that evening and a jolly good time was had by all with stand down on the morrow.

Weather was not good for flying yet Stukas were hammering Bir Hacheim where the Free French were fighting for dear life. On the shifting front Army H.Q. were not able to give us a bombing line and our fear of bombing our own troops was even greater than usual. The enemy airmen were equally confused as we had in fact news that they had heavily bombed a detachment of their own troops. We would therefore keep 'harrassing the Hun' on his aerodromes. Enemy air activity was light, except for his Stukas, and he had assembled a very great many at Gazala keeping them on the ground until the weather cleared. Again his lack of practising the art of dispersal was to cost him dearly.

The Stukas, operating against our troops, were flying back to Tmimi landing ground to spend the hours of darkness. Four of us would go during the night in an attempt to bend them. Gidney, Bowley, Nicholls and myself, in that order, took off at five minute intervals. It was 2204 hrs when I lifted off. The night was pitch black, as only a desert night can be, and the cold rattled our knee caps uncontrollably. We would cross the coast at Mersa Matruh, stand off the coast past Sidi Barrani, Bardia and Tobruk and run into Tmimi from seawards. I was climbing through 5,000 feet at Mersa when the brilliance of the searchlights blinded me. I rolled right and left and the boys switched off. We passed Baheira and remembered the night in the dug-out. We turned for our run into the target. The night was so very black. I was expecting this show to be a piece of cake and have the bomb bursts of the other three aircraft to guide me in.

"We can't be far from the coast now Paddy. E.T.A. is almost up. Where in the hell are the other three kites?" I query.

"Perhaps stooging around trying to sort out the 'drome. It's so bloody dark they'll never find it without flares," said Paddy.

"Christ, I don't believe what I see," blurted I in disbelief, as peculiar chortling noises came over the intercom from Paddy and I held on some bank to behold the full glare of the Tmimi flare path.

"They're expecting us Perc boy, get in there quick and let's bend them up!" screamed Paddy, as only he in his excitement could scream.

"There's some bloody mistake here Paddy," said I, "Perhaps they're getting off a few night fighters quick." I reason.

"We'll lose the bloody thing entirely if they switch it off Perc. Go in now." Paddy insisted.

"Then where the hell are the first three kites?", I question. "We'll have to stand off a bit Paddy until they get orged."

"Be Jebus Perc, see those lovely fires, right spot on!" shouted Paddy. No.1 aircraft must have been correctly positioned for bombing when the flare path appeared. It jolly soon went out, I can assure you.

"There's No.2's bombs now Perc!" came the scream of delight. "They've clobbered something."

Curiosity caused me to bank over to take a look.

"Christ, look at that smoke against that far glow. Watch for bombs from No.3 as I stand off a bit." said I as I turned out to sea to prepare for the run-in.

"There they go," shouted Rick who was down by the bottom hatch by the dinghy.

I turned the aircraft back towards land. I was further from the shore than I had realised. The whole shoreline erupted with anti-aircraft fire in green and red and gold. It really was impressive but not exactly entertaining. It is funny how, when you see the tracer rising, at first apparently vertical, you may be excused for wondering at which poor devil it is being aimed. Then as the apparent trajectory continues and the combined closing speed narrows the gap, dramatic changes take place, and it becomes very obvious indeed that the poor devil is you, and as this was my first night op I claim that I might be excused from thinking,

"F – this for a lark, it's dangerous."

"The buggers have been caught with their trousers down this time Perc. What a bloody shambles." said Paddy, "The other three have left all that ack-ack for us to sample. I'll bet some heads will roll down there tonight."

"I'll go in on the glide Paddy, then level out about three thou with two-eighty on the clock. That'll get the gunners knotted up."

"What the hell do I aim at?" asked Paddy, "I can't see anything but glowing smoke."

"Hang on then a bit," I said, "I'll take a westerly course, and you Rick, get some flares organised. We'll drop them on the way, turn, then bomb on an easterly heading, then nip out to sea. How about three thou' and two-eighty indicated Paddy?"

"Yes, O.K. Perc we'll get a better look," came the reply.

"Did you boys get that in the back?" I queried.

"Yes O.K. Perc." came back Rick.

"What about you Gunn?"

No reply.

"Go back and give Gunn a jerk Rick, I think his plug must be out."

Rick came back.

"His plug's alright Perc, he's just frozen stiff with the twitters. The ack-ack's got the shits up him. I'll get him out of the turret and see how he goes."

"There's no time for that now Rick, we're busy. I want you down at those bloody flare toggles... Now, Paddy it's over to you now we're on the flare run, into wind, give Rick the countdown for release."

The flares were so brilliant that at three thousand feet I felt we would be illuminated as much as the target.

"There's Stukas by the score Perc, in that northwest corner" shouted Paddy "beyond that big glow."

"O.K. Paddy. A turn to starboard would bring us better for the run up."
I awaited Paddy's instructions.
"Bomb doors open and hard left-left."
I had over turned to starboard.
"S-T-E-A-D-Y," said Paddy slowly. Then quickly, "hold it," and in a deep guttural voice, slowly he said "L-o-v-e-l-y."
A few seconds of silence.
"Bombs gone. Bomb doors closed."
I banked to port and repeated Paddy's words.
"Those flak boys have gone mad down there fellows. I'm climbing, they won't have a clue."
"Rick, shake Gunn up now."
"Can I stay by the hatch Perc and watch for bomb bursts?"
Then, immediately and together, both Paddy and Rick started to babble.
"Right across those parked Stukas Perc. They won't harass the front line tomorrow, that's for sure," said Paddy. "We did a bloody good job there Perc and there's something more than just aircraft on fire. Might have got the pilots in bed at the same time."
"Good show Pad. I'm levelling at five thou. Give me a course when you're ready."

* * *

The 'Recco Kite' next morning got some lovely photographs of the Tmimi airfield scrap. I lit my pipe for a leisurely trip to base. Gunn was now re-composed and tension subsided.

Suddenly tracer shot past me from behind, over the port engine. Instinctively, nose down, throttles open and heaving turn to port.

"What in the hell's going on back there Gunn? Where's your eyes or your tongue? That can only be a one-one-o."

I watched the speed and throttled back at three-ten, heading out to sea, getting down low allowing for altimeter lag. The fighter boys did not like this diving to low altitude especially on pitch black nights. They had been known to get a fixation on lining up their target and before they could press the 'tit', the victim pulled up sharp at very low level, leaving the attacker with an excess of 'G' to handle, with disastrous results; either hitting ground or water without even knowing about it. Gunn was shaken. All he had seen of the fighter was the tracer weaving its way towards him and by the time he tried to say something I was already yapping. We were perhaps dangerously low and nothing more was happening. Gunn claimed to have seen a glow almost stationary, up 45 degrees. I just guessed it could be exhaust glow from the stubs, and he had headed off. Gunn was having a very bad night indeed. He never did have a lot of sparkling success, as his short operational period came to rather an unfortunate end just over a week later when cannon shells from some 109's shattered his legs below the knees. On reflection I feel sorry that I gave him a bit of a harsh time, but we were always good friends. I climbed back up to five thou' in the blackness and took up Paddy's new course.

Gremlin Goonery

When you're up there alone in the darkness
That's a hell of a lonely spot,
With a Messerschmidtt homing on zero,
The pace getting hotter than hot,
When you're frozen blue as the Monkey's,
When you've bombed the Jerries to stink,
And you're hundreds of miles from nowhere,
With nothing below but the drink.
It's then that you'll find the Gremlins,
Green and all colours but gold,
Male and female and neuter,
Gremlins both young and old.

It's no good trying to dodge them,
The lessons you learned on the link
Won't help you evade the Gremlins,
Though you turn and you dive and you jink.
Black ones will wiggle your wing tips,
Mauve ones will muddle your maps,
Green ones will guzzle your glycol,
And females will flutter your flaps.

Pink ones will perch on your perspex,
And dance pirouettes on your props,
There's a Kartoffeln gutted Gremlin
Who'll shake at your stick till it flops.
They'll freeze up your carb with the splutters,
They'll chew through your aileron wires,
They'll bend and they'll break and they'll batter,
And stick bayonet blades in your tyres.

They never would listen to flannel,
And swearing just makes them worse,
If they ever suspect that your rag's off
They'll love to hear you curse.
It's then that they'll jinx up your thinking,
And send your decisions all wrong,
To turn away from the Jerry,
Instead of ruddering on.
Steep turning when looking for Jerry
They'll sneak off your airspeed real quick,
And topple horizon right smartish,
And turn needle fully they'll flick. (STALL).

The little black ball from the centre, (SPIN)
In opposite corner they'll jam,

And you to the side of the cockpit,
With merciless force they will slam.
The tracer they whirl round in circles,
It always just curved before,
To pull on the stick doesn't alter
The height whizzing lower and low.
It's then that they'll all vacate you .
As though something's seriously muffed,
Stick forward and opposite rudder,
The problem is solved and you're chuffed.

That crazy gyration of needles,
Which winked in their luminous hash,
Now change to obedience and cause you,
A raspberry to Gremlins to pass.
But then they've got back before you,
They're waiting for you in the mess,
And smartly knock over your Whisky
Surprised to see you no less.
But out pops the Fairy Gremlin,
When the others find they have missed,
And guides you to Quarters through staggers,
Although you are thoroughly Pissed.

"Mersa ought to be coming up under our nose soon." said Paddy.

"Try them for a Q.D.M. Rick" I said half jokingly.

Much to my amazement Rick was back in no time with one. Base was only 30 miles inland so we decided that we had this nut cracked. The blackness of the night was not now so forbidding, but what was that down there? Surely it was a cloud which seemed to thicken as we went. Perhaps it was only some Katabatic stuff which would disappear when we crossed the coast. The slither of moon melted out of the blackness but there was no doubt that there was more cloud than we had bargained for and it was continuous.

"I'll make my way down through this lot fellows so 'all eyeballs peeled' and shout if you see anything."

"We ought to be over base in a couple of minutes." said Paddy.

We broke cloud base at 600 feet on the altimeter. It was darker now, the cloud blotted out the little bit of friendly moon.

"That surely looks like a blanket of fog down there Perc. Doesn't make sense to me." said Paddy.

"You don't get fog with this cloud set-up do you?" I asked. I never was a meteorologist, some of the theories baffled me. Why shouldn't they be just the opposite? But some forecasters have been known to be right.

I dropped a bit to take a closer look, only to confirm our suspicions.

"I wonder how thick that stuff can be," I said knowing full well that unless my altimeter was grossly under reading, it had to be right down to the deck.

"We're back again to Buys Ballot Paddy". I said once more. The situation was similar to the sandstorm set-up, in so far as the altimeter was concerned, we could trust it to be under reading.

"It's time I was circuiting if the E.T.A. is up Paddy." I said. I would do a square search, with two-minute legs. We calculated we had fuel for a further hour on economy settings. Paddy suggested that without delay we set course for the Delta area. We could make it on our fuel, and landing grounds were plentiful there.

"If there's fog as thick as this out here Paddy, I wouldn't give a monkeys for the Delta with their level of humidity." I reasoned. "I'll tell you what we can do, if after stooging around for an hour, there's no break in this fog and we can't inch our way down through it, I'll take the old crate up to about three thou' and you boys can hit the silk. At least you'll have a safe landing, otherwise there may not be a hope in hell."

"There's not a hope in hell for a few things in these conditions," said Paddy, "and one of them is me jumping out. You haven't said anything about you getting out Perc, and as long as you intend getting this old crate back on the deck, all nice and tidy, then I'm staying in," was Paddy's assessment of the parachute solution.

"So am I," said Rick. "We got down at Baheira and things were worse there."

There was silence for while. We had been searching for half an hour already. Suddenly,

"There's a light. Flashed on starboard bow." shouted Rick excitedly. "Another one, I saw them through the fog."

I heaved around. No lights. I counted down, 200 feet and gingerly down to 100 feet indicated. We were in the thick of it. I cleaned up the aircraft and climbed a bit.

"We can still keep prodding around for twenty minutes." I said. "Assuming we are where we think we are we can trade a few more millibars if those lights show up again. At least we know we are over activity and there were no hills sticking up when we went down to 100 feet."

There, dead in front of my nose, brilliant flashes. Obviously bombs and incendiaries. The brilliance lit up a ridge clear of fog, strewn with boulders. The land fell away into the fog. There was babbling from everyone at once.

"This is just like the land lay south of our L.G. fellows" I said "and my guess is that we're stooging around amongst a bunch of Jerry bombers."

Knowing what our Beaufighters did to Jerry bombers, I had to say,

"Let's hope there's none of our Beaus about because if one of them takes us for a Jerry, it's curtains for us."

I turned to fly north.

"It's decision time now fellows," I said. "Our fuel is stretched, so it's climb on what we have left and you all get out. Get your 'chutes clipped on."

"There's a glow on starboard bow again." shouted Rick. "Over there the fog has thinned a bit."

'More incendiaries,' I thought as I turned right. So there were, but it was different. It had a beam.

"It's a chance light." I said. "It's a landing ground." I banged on the pitch, undercart and flaps and turned to approach on three-four-zero, and if it happened to be our L.G. I knew we would have a good landing run.

"Watch that bloody glow fellows whilst I'm busy." It really is surprising how fast one is travelling when visibility is so limited. That was one hell of a tight turn I might say, to get lined up. 300 feet, 200 feet, 100 feet. There was the chance light. I went in hanging on the props and held off for landing.

"Oh Christ," I said with some emphasis, because there in front of me was a Blenheim taxiing across my path. I just had to hit him. I banged open the throttles, eased the stick forward, bounced the wheels hard on the ground just short of the Blenheim and pulled up sharply, bouncing clean over the top. Throttles closed, hold off, and we were rolling, into what I knew not. Severe braking and swing to the dead-side of the chance light. The intercom was deafening. I shut down the engines and thought that as we were amongst Blenheims we must have lobbed in on 55 Squadron 'drome.

We all got out quick to meet under the port wing as usual. Gunn and Rick were jumping up and down, shouting, "It's solid." There was much handshaking as some of the ground staff came running up. I recognised their faces.

"Christ I can't believe it. It's our very own 'drome!" What impossible luck. It was the Blenheim which was away from home. We had stooged around, above and in the fog for one hour thirty-five minutes. The time was 0220 hrs. We had been in the air 4 hrs 15 mins. The C.O. showed up with a very broad smile.

"See you after you have eaten." he said. "Jolly good show."

Paddy and I walked side by side with parachutes slung over our shoulders, to the mess. Our wonderful cooks were still on duty and had an apple pie as big as a cushion. Paddy said something about St Peter, our extra passenger for the night. Many of the boys had been out all night in the desert cold, listening for our engine note, and watching the Jerry bombs bursting. Gidney had arrived back before the weather closed in and had no trouble. Bowley had piled in near the 'drome and hit some boulders. He was unfortunately killed but Bignold his gunner was found, sixty yards away, still in his turret, and survived the ordeal. Nicholls crash-landed some fifteen miles away and fortunately they all survived. We had therefore something on the debit side but no doubt saved hundreds of lives up on the front the following day by reducing the number of those Stukas on Tmimi.

A NIGHT IN DESERT DIARY 1942

Pressed were our boys up front so hard, by thrusts of German armour,
Marred not one bit by effort brave of Allied Forces ardour,
It seemed the swing would once more turn to gain of Irwin Rommel,
The desert see-saw governed by supply and distance wobble.

Eastbound beyond Halfaya Pass no natural stand existed,
Tobruk was seiged, those troops were trapped, holding tight clenched fisted,
No rest was there for tired men, hounded by the Panzer,
Resistance strong retarded Hun no more than aged Lancer.

No sleep was theirs, just fitful naps in foxholes shallow lain,
The night long through the rumble and the flashes rent the plain,
The eastern light would herald yet another murderous day,
Mid battle scene, the cruel sun would bake their skins like clay.

The Stukas then would add their weight, cause havoc where they could,
As if in desperation screaming down, as though they could
Not one more single second wait to make their murderous kill,
Then back to base so hurriedly with bombs and fuel to fill.

A signal came, we must at once destroy this Stuka might.
Resolved we then this definite we'd do this very night.
Dispersed around their take-off run would they in darkness be,
The crews in mess tent celebrating their whole days kill with glee.

Should we be resolute, intent, to do our job real well,
And in the dark our target find, we'd blow them all to hell,
Aircraft and pilots, ground staff crews, fuel oil and spares
Would have to go the way we knew, we'd hunt them down like hares.

The flak thrown up we'd have to dodge, night fighters fool if we
Were bent on placing bombs square on, and making exit free
Without a crippled kite, so we may elsewhere fly again,
Our troops to save from punishment. The Hun we must contain.

But should we in this mission fail, destruction to complete,
We'd sentence hundreds of our boys, more Stuka deaths to meet,
And Teddar knew full well that he, had now the brunt of battle,
The 'Auk' was almost powerless, without the Air Force tackle.

The sun went down as though the string on which it daily hung
Surrendered had, to massive weight and heat, which swelled the tongue.
The Katabatic wind then flowed, across the coastal rim.
Our woolies thick we'd need tonight, to warm our pimpled skin.

The 'Shufti Kites' had brought the gen, that Stukas by the score,
They'd seen on 'drome Tmimi, close inland from the shore.
Three hundred miles to west it lay and found should easy be,
At briefing then decided we, approach it from the sea.

Knee caps shivering in the cold, calculations done,
Four of us at ten o'clock, would go off one by one,
We'd cross the coast at Mersa, and head out off Tobruk,
And make landfall at Bomba, if we had any luck.

"Have a good trip then gentlemen, make a real fine show,
And the very best of luck," was said at briefing by C.O.,
With C.S.C. and parachutes we jumped into the gharry
And bumped out to dispersal, much too cold to tarry.

Startling cold the clear night air, pitch black was the night,
On instruments over Mersa was, the blackness stabbed the light.
The brilliant searchlights got us full, blinding me full square,
For God's sake please don't open up, we'll never make it there.

When out to sea hard to believe the air could be so still,
When hours before in searing sun it threw us round at will.
Paddy's navigation keen kept us right on track,
And close on eighty minutes on, inland we headed back.

'Tis often said a battle's won, on element of surprise.
Of better example I can't think, slap between the eyes
Caught was he; with finger up – trousers down – and bending,
A costly error he did make. I'll bet there was some rending.

There below, 'twas unbelief, right before our eyes,
The flarepath on Tmimi 'drome, shone up to the skies,
"They're sure expecting us to call," said Paddy with a chuckle,
"Get right in there Perc old boy, and Stukas we shall buckle."

"Hang about," said I to Paddy, "is this some mistake?"
"Or are they getting fighters off, our tender ribs to rake?
Or do they think we're one of theirs, calling for the night
There's three of ours in front somewhere, we'll stand off in the night."

"Be Jebus. See those bloody fires?", called Paddy with a shrill,
"Number one has dropped the lot, straight into the kill."
Buildings burned some Stukas too, what a crazy pickle,
Who had thought the clever Hun, could ever be so fickle?

Flarepath vanished, served us well, fires now to guide us,
Pronto in went number two, dropping bombs like Midas,
Placing them so carefully, sorting out the target,
This is quite a tea party, strolling round the garden.

Fires more broke out to light the desert sand around,
Silhouetting objects new, potential targets found.
But heavy smoke now spoilt the view, very slowly drifting,
Out to sea I'd better go and see how things were shifting.

"Watch for the bombs from number three," I ask the boys each singly,
"There they go," cried wireless op, sitting by the dinghy.
Then decided fickle Hun, fireworks game to hold,
The whole shore line erupted, with red and green and gold.

Flak crews now awake from sleep, imagine Germans screaming,
Must to them a nightmare be, we had caught them dreaming,
So through that belt of tracer flak as number four we'd go,
'Twould be a bit ironical should we now collect a blow.

We headed for the coloured flak, its fascinating curves,
Would tell us at this point of time, number three they searched.
"We've got the height to do this right." said I to Paddy bold,
"You'll have to get your bomb sight set to lower altitude."

"We'll fool the flak boys with a dodge, go in on the glide,"
"I'll close the throttles till we do our bombing height decide."
"We'll level out, a short run up, with speed well up the clock,"
"And sort ourselves a target, if there's any left to knock."

"The fires have died down quite a bit." said Paddy wistfully,
"We need them stoking up a bit so we can better see."
"We'll do a double run," said I "westwards drop some flares,"
Then eastwards do the bombing run, and out to sea like hares."

"Bloody good for you Perc, can't go home unless
We've stoked up most considerably, this lovely Stuka mess."
"Rick and Gunner rear," I call, "did you get the gen?"
"Roger." came back Rick O.K. from Gunn there was no ken.

"Rick, check up on Gunner boy, his intercom seems duff."
"His intercom is O.K. Perc it's Gunner who is rough,
The fireworks seem to have him stiff, but just give us a wink,
He's frozen too, I'll get him out of turret in a blink"

Flares we dropped such brilliant glow, melting out the night,
There on northwest corner stood Stukas, what a sight,
Flak crews panicked shooting wild, thought we'd all gone home,
Quick turn round, flatten out, level in to bomb.

"Don't let's miss this little lot," said Paddy eagerly,
"Left – left – stead – eeee, now hold it there," he quietly said to me.
"Bombs gone." I turned and climbed a bit, a whoop from Paddy came,
"They'll bomb our troops no bloody more, that's stopped their little game."

"I'll bet," said Paddy with some glee, "There's not a Stuka left,
And even if there were I guess, of pilots they're bereft."
"Five thousand feet I've got on clock, I'll level out at this,
Give me a course for base," I ask "we'll travel back in bliss."

"We really stoked that little show, 'bout nine or ten we got,
There's one big fire on far northwest, perhaps his fuel's shot,"
Said Paddy as he made some notes of times and bombs away.
"If you go out on one-two-five, I'll get an E.T.A."

"Good on you Pad I'll light my pipe, and think of apple pie,
The cooks are staying late tonight to get us all a fry."
"What in the hell was that?" shout I as tracer flashed o'er wing,
I shoved her down and ruddered hard to get out of his ring.

That's all we need, a one-one-o, squirting from the rear,
"You get your bloody eyes peeled Gunn," I rasp and quietly fear
We may have something punctured, but be that as it may,
I was diving out to sea to get out of his way.

A dive o'er sea to fighter boys was really quite some nark,
An extra fear of sea they had should it happen to be dark,
Sighting up their prey 'twas known, they'd gone straight into sea,
When prey pulled out at slower speed and left them too much "G".

The gunner now had got an eye on exhaust glow of Hun,
Who couldn't get inside our turn to line us with his gun,
And then my altimeter showed if lower I should get,
We'd end up striking water and become extremely wet.

I levelled, asking Gunner what the hell was keeping him,
He said his intercom yanked out but now he'd got it in.
He'd seen the M.E. One-one-o turn port and head off back,
Then popped up Paddy smartly, "Steer one-five-o for track."

"You got your pipe Perc?" Paddy asked, "cos it just seems our luck,
That every time you light the thing, a Jerry then shows up,
Would it not a good plan be to save us from the brink,
To stuff it in the bomb bay and drop it in the drink?"

All systems working as they should we gained a bit of height,
And hoped that we could settle down and get home safe that night.
A silver slither of moon came up, and spread below we saw,
A solid mass of cumulus which was not there before.

Mersa gave us Q.D.M., they were from our L.G.
Thirty miles to north, so we should very easily see
Where base position really was, if cloud would only clear,
It was so low I dared not risk, the ground was much too near.

We stooged around for half an hour playing a waiting game,
When now for us can you believe a further layer came?
Of moonlight robbed and sandwiched in, what had we to choose?
I checked the fuel and set the taps to max-economy cruise.

At last a glow through lower cloud, twenty minutes on,
Could be chance light switching on, suddenly 'twas gone,
Glow upon glow, first here now there, just like a short burst,
Decided we 'twas bomber Hun, who had got here first.

"Watch it lads, 'cos if our Beaus are stooging round for Hun,
And take us for a Jerry, there'll be lots of fun,
If one of ours poops us off, down we're sure to go,
I'd rather say we got the chop from that darned one-one-o."

Over an hour we'd stooged around, looking for a chink.
"Not a hope in hell," say I, "maybe we could think
Of going up three thousand feet, and you three take a jump,
At least in safety would you land, albeit on your rump."

"You're right Perc not a hope in hell of lots of things tonight,"
"And one is me not jumping out, 'cause I am sitting tight.
So long as there's some fuel Perc, for me there's no great hurry,
It's when the motors start to cough, that I'll get in a flurry."

"I've got no height, five hundred feet, slight chances would we have,
We'd maybe hit a pile of rocks, and break the thing in half.
We've only got ten minutes fuel, and that's on God's good grace,
Prepare to go and best of luck, I'll see you in the mess."

"Fair enough" said Paddy cool, "you yet have made no mention,
Of you yourself a-jumping out, so it's your sole intention,
To get this crate back on the deck, all straight and neat and trim,
So if you are so confident, we may as well stay in."

"We don't want to jump from back, as long as fans are turning,"
Said Rick with confidence he'd got from Paddy, he was learning.
"Fuel says that I must go to find the ground for certain,
But if you three do come with me for all it may be curtains.."

"Baheira have we still in mind," Paddy reasoned sound,
"When in that sandstorm dark and thick, no hope seemed around,
We got down safe although it was way out in wildest Bundu,
And this is not quite half the hash. Once done – again can do."

"It seems to me then Paddy you're more confident than me,
I only have three hundred feet between the deck and we,
We've already tried one hundred assuming base below,
But then we could be five miles out and bend the so and so."

"Hey. There's a glow on starboard bow where fog has thinned a bit."
"Hell, so there is," say I alert. "Pin all your beads on it.
A landing ground it's got to be. I'm going in right down."
Full fine pitch and undercart, selecting full flap down.

Down through we went on three-four-o, hoping 'twas our ground,
And just as I was holding off, a Blenheim there I found,
Taxiing right across my path. – fully open taps,
Stick hard front – bounce the thing – leapfrog o'er their backs.

Throttle back – holding off – hope some run is left,
Touching down – screaming tyres – swing her to the left.
In to darkness – switching off – on to ground we leapt,
Meeting there beneath the wing, we four almost wept.

Rick and Gunn jumped up and down shouting out, "it's solid",
Ground staff then came running up, "Hell I don't believe it."
The Landing Ground our very own. There smiled our C.O.,
By ops tent where he'd said before. "Make a real fine show."

"See you in a while back here, it's now gone half past two.
Have a drink – a bit of grub – the cooks stayed late for you.
Number one got back safe soon, force landed number two,
Number three regret piled in, see you after brew."

As Paddy and I walked side by side, in silence to the tent,
He looked at me a knowing look, I knew just what he meant.
His forehead he flicked back and said "I can't fully believe it,
There's more to this than meets the eye, I just cannot conceive it."

"That extra passenger helped tonight," said I to studious Paddy,
"It helps a lot to fit him in, when e'er with us he'll travel."
"He's never let me down once yet." said Paddy fully knowing
To his St Peter I referred – a glistening tear was showing.

We ambled into mess tent lit, by swinging lantern hissing,
The cooks were smiling, calling out, "You just dare not go missing,
'Cos something here we've made for you, spoilt it would have been."
They then produced an apple pie, biggest I've ever seen.

Two feet long that apple pie, however did they make it?
In desert drum and tins on bricks, was all they had to bake it.
I cut huge wedges off as we talked turkey with the gang,
And learned that night that number three, some rocks hit with a bang.

"Jerry's been around all night, trying to get our 'drome,
He kept on dropping odd ones, could never get them home,
We didn't know if you were there, or were they all the Hun,
The flare path on we dared not switch, in case we started fun."

"Miserable lot he'll think you are, to us he's more obliging,
Not only did he switch his on, he put it on for guiding,
Exactly where we aimed to be, and left his aircraft standing,
So we could bend them all up nice, to save them further landing."

"He didn't even put up cloud, like you, to make it harder,
In fact when his old flare path fizzed, he worried we would scarper
So little lights, red, green and gold, he shot into the air,
That we would know just where he was, he showed us how they care."

"He even sent a messenger, in a lovely one-one-o,
To say to us that he would wish, back home we would not go,
Now he must think us very rude, you see we ran away,
So treatment nice we may not get, should we go another day."

For magic pie we thanked the cooks, 'twas little left for others,
And as a crew we walked to ops, as though we were four brothers,
I lit my pipe as we walked on, said Paddy broadly smiling,
"In fact you'll have a new one Perc, from now on no more riling."

For the record I got a corn cob.

· CHAPTER 6 ·

DOWN TO BRASS TACKS

The Luftwaffe pounded Tobruk. We pounded Derna, in fact we went twice one day, and we bent ME-109s at Gazala. We were led to believe that Tobruk was safe and secure so all the more shattering the news which followed shortly that Tobruk had surrendered with 17,000 of our troops trapped in there.

We were told to stand by to vacate L.G. 116 in favour of a more backward base. We could not just understand how the Hun was able to keep on pushing our ground forces further back. There seemed to be a new dimension to his tenacity. The ground staff had loaded everything moveable onto trucks. Our bombing target for the next day was given to us as a reference point where it was said we could destroy troop and vehicle concentrations in great profusion.

The scene was astounding, as from the air we witnessed the swarms of British heading east away from the rampant Hun. Along the desert tracks they poured in vast numbers and the established coastal road was spilling over with transport and vehicles of all descriptions. What an abundance of targets all this apparent confusion presented for the Luftwaffe. But where were they? Perhaps we had done more than we realised, in attacking their landing grounds, to contribute towards their impotence.

We crossed the familiar wire fence which marks the boundary of Egypt and Cyrenaica, running north from Fort Madalena to Sidi Omar, thence to Sollum. The enemy was pouring forward. He truly can be regarded as having had his tail up. Had his troops had the same support as did the British, then the battle of the Middle East would, for us, have been lost that very week. It was gratifying some time later to read: ''⸺ undoubtedly the Luftwaffe in North Africa was conquered on the ground rather than in the air.''

We sorted out a good concentration of enemy vehicles and scattered our bombs right amongst them. How strange, not a poop from the Flugabwehrkannona (FLAK) and not a Messerschmitt in sight, during the whole of the 2 hrs 45 mins. We were in fact out again two hours later to clout the spearhead and were back within 1 hr 50 mins dying for a mug of tea and something to eat. It was 1915 hrs and we'd had nothing since breakfast, with not much hope of anything for the remainder of the day, unless 'B' Flight dropped in from backward base to where the kitchen trailer had set out. We were so very hungry.

"Christ there's so many of them Perc, they'll eat us alive if we can't stop them." said Paddy as we wheeled over the advancing Germans not 15 miles behind our fleeing troops.

I lit my pipe to help stave off the hunger. I closed down the engines – hopefully for the last time that day – and as usual selected 'bomb doors open' to receive the next load. There was one ominous almighty thud which shook the ground beneath us.

"Christ!" I exclaimed. "A hang-up!"

Sure enough when we tumbled out, there underneath the aircraft was a 500lb bomb which had failed to release over the target. There was much laughter and speculation as to what may have happened had the extension-rod and nose-pistol hit the deck before the main shell of the bomb. My notes made at the time suggest that 'we would have thinly populated a very large area'. We brewed tea under the wing close to our wayward bomb, and gave thanks for our portable tea-making equipment. We sat under the wing until the sun 'dropped' out of the sky then moved on to the protection of our make-shift tent. We did not have sufficient water for a much needed wash-down so slept soundly in the fine layer of sand which clung to our sticky perspiring skin. At least we slept – which was more than the retreating army troops could do.

'B' Flight dropped in. Ah! Food at last... but all they had was mite-ridden 'dog biscuit' which just happened to taste really quite good at the time, although possibly Napoleon's leftovers. Wallace and myself took a vic of three each up to Garet El Kuresh on a rather spectacular exercise amongst the enemy covered-trucks, obviously bringing essentials up to their forward troops. We had extension rods fitted to the noses of our bombs designed to detonate the bombs before they actually hit the ground causing maximum blast, and fragmentation. What a satisfying spectacle to see those trucks being bowled over like bunches of tumbleweed and many of them being set alight. I taxied up for shut-down thinking of the hang-up of the previous day, selected the bomb doors open, when I almost hit my head on the canopy. CRUMP, went a second hang up, and for a second time we lived. There was to be no chancing a third one. I had the complete bomb rack changed. Paddy looked decidedly older as we walked away from the aircraft.

That night the enemy would try our tactics. JU88s were intent on destroying us on the ground. Wherever had they got the aircraft from? Like magic our fighter boys dropped in on the party, promptly shot down two right on the edge of our 'drome as we all stood around cheering wildly. There was a continuous and incessant drone of aircraft engines the whole night through as our Wimpies headed to and returned from enemy territory. We would take over at dawn. This was to be a big day. There were targets for everyone. How far can one stretch one's endurance? We were becoming somewhat fatigued. Daylight operations certainly sap your system. Lack of food does nothing but sap you further and the living conditions with the flies, the sores, the sand and the lack of water all contribute to your discomfort. Our losses, too started to grow. Macchi 202 fighters and ME-109s appeared in dangerous numbers. Flak crews had become established and more of our aircraft were returning damaged, and often some of the crew. It hurt to see your friends being carefully handled out of the aircraft, protesting against the pain with shouts and groans. We were flying low on one occasion on our way home, when fighters looked in. One of the vic had a propeller shot off and went straight down into the sea.

If yesterday was a big day, today had to be bigger. The bombing detail went up just after dawn. The foot note read "The enemy has to be stopped and it is up to the Desert Air Force to do it," then succinctly following a hyphen, "before darkness falls". This was a really big day. General Aukinlech had attempted a halt of the retreat on a line running south from Mersa Matruh. Whether it was a serious attempt perhaps he only knew, but it certainly had a delaying effect whilst he put his house in better order a few miles further east, where we were now witnessing the birth of the El Alamein line. This was a natural line of defence, 40 miles long, the southern end terminating at the impassable Quattara Depression.

Mischiefa was our 'important' target for today. We were now very soon over the front after take off. We passed Charing Cross, Oxford Circus, Picadilly and on to our reference at Mischiefa. There was some most uncomfortable flak. Rommel had stretched his lines some 500 miles in the matter of a month and would now desperately need supplies as quickly as possible, fuel especially. We were now within seconds of destroying thousands of gallons of his precious liquid.

"Christ," said Paddy with startling emphasis, "what have we hit? There are flames all over the place. Four huge fires and just look at that column of black smoke rising."

The black mass, climbing skywards, was still visible to us as we passed over the front on our return trip.

Sidi Barrani landing ground was reported to be crowded with both Italian and German aircraft. Someone had it right no doubt when it was said that a determined push was expected of the enemy. No doubt all the aircraft assembled were hoping to use a lot of that fuel we had just blown up. We then went for those Sidi Barrani aircraft. It really was quite shameful how we bent them. Some 109s took a look in at us, but stood off as though reluctant to engage.

There was some jockeying for position around the centre pole of the mess tent, on which hung the swinging board to which the Daily Occurrence Reports and other notices of various origins, were pinned. We read.

From Air Officer Commanding RAF Western Desert.
To Nos. 223, 24 and 12 Squadrons.
26.6.42

Congratulations from us all on a record day's bombing. Your attacks, which with the Wellingtons have been going on for almost forty-eight hours non-stop have been most damaging to the enemy and must be slowing him down. The ground work by personnel has been quite outstanding and I hope you are all proud the way the Hun has been hit. Well done.

The Desert Air Force was turning the course of events. Glasses were raised in good humour, and amongst much ribaldry, the boys were toasting, "To us", "To you," "To me," "To hell with the Hun." The bar tent was busy all evening.

The scene next morning however did nothing to bolster our confidence. "The Hun is just up the road." we were told. We were to pack up the bits and pieces which the main party had left for us when they pulled out. Take all you can in the aircraft was the mood, stores, kit, tents and fill fuel tanks to maximum and bomb-up fully. Get into the air as soon as possible. Occasions such as these would have been a wonderful opportunity for the Luftwaffe. We were to offload at L.G.24, only 40 miles east, lying just to the south east of El-Daba.

"By the way you have an extra passenger Perc." advised Paddy.

"Oh. Who?" I queried as I thought we may as well drop this load of bombs on the Jerries if they were so close as we were led to believe.

"It's the fitter. L.A.C. Parker." said Paddy.

"Now Paddy, you know the drill as well as I do. No passengers, and that's final. He would have no intercom or parachute and if he got clobbered I would take the can."

"He says other ground staff are going in other aircraft and that the Flight Commander has agreed." said the sage.

There was a flap on I agreed but no one had told me this story. Parker came over towards me. He had an extremely uncomfortable truck journey ahead of him if I did not take him. He was a good hard working conscientious airman, and I liked him.

"No one has told me that you are to go in my aircraft Parker." I said. "So don't ask if you can come, but if you stow away in the back there, with your arse firmly rivetted to the dinghy, I do not know anything about it. You'll have neither intercom nor 'chute."

Parker got in quick.

"Should Parker not come out of this in one piece Paddy, the 'Brass' will be on my back quicker than a Jerry."

Gidney and Davis were ready to start up, so the three of us taxied out and got into the air. I was first away, the others coming up loosely behind. Cloud base was low at about six tenths, (the jargon in those days), or five octas, as we levelled out just below it. Gunn was busy getting his equipment in order, whilst Paddy and I were chatting about the activity below and the hordes we could see. We were just contemplating doing a wide circuit and dropping the bombs on the first Jerries we saw. "One-O-Nines!" screamed Gunn. "They've got Gidney and he's going straight down!"

I immediately heaved over to starboard saying "keep me genned Gunn on their position!"

There was a metallic chatter which I took for Gunn engaging fire. I was swivelling my head from side to side.

"What's going on back there Gunn?" I shouted at the top of my voice. Then I suddenly realised that it was me that was being fired on from a blind spot. There was no reply from Gunn. I was not aware that he had been shot through his legs, and I continued to harangue him with revilement. I was heaving hard to port from where the attack had come, instinctively jamming on hard top rudder and holding off on ailerons to induce a confusing skid below the attacker.

"Two One-O-Nines jumped us from cloud," agonized Gunn. "They're now starboard ahead, up 30 degrees turning."

"For Christ's sake Gunn keep talking. Keep me genned on their every move." I called. "I can then either set them up for you or skid out of their bloody way."

Oil mist now streaked back in the slipstream from the port engine. Everything was all go. I was furious that we had been hit by One-O-Nines before they were even fired on. There was now smoke not just mist coming from the engine. Was it on fire or was this just oil on hot metal?

"One-O-Nines wheeling at eight o'clock high, 400 yards, closing!" shouted Gunn.

I knew then I was committed to turn towards the bad engine to get under him, and I would forfeit height. I was over quickly, almost vertical, in a slithering skid, and I heaved back on the stick into a very tight turn. They were not easily fooled and the stick started to snatch in my hands. They had got the elevators and the rudder bars kicked at the soles of my boots. The starboard aileron shattered in pieces, and one piece remained attached by the actuating arm. It fluttered in the slipstream. Hell how I needed that port engine.

"One-O-Nine going for Davis. They've got him. He's going down. He's hit the deck." shouted Gunn.

"One-O-Nines coming in at four o'clock Perc, watch it," It was Paddy's voice, cool and serious. "Five hundred yards, four, three..." I cut the motor, heaved over to starboard, hauled back, ruddering hard for a skid. Lucky my timing was good. I forced him over the top but he did get a bit more of my aileron, but that one piece was still fluttering, attached by the hinge. I opened full throttle in a vertical bank, looking out of the top of the canopy to see if I could locate his follower. No sign. I straightened immediately.

"No signs of the One-O-Nines Perc," said Paddy

"Gunn and Parker are both badly hit Perc," came Rick from the rear.

I was struggling with the damaged engine. It was losing power. The damaged fluttering rudder was shaking hell out of my legs as I tried to rudder onto the good engine. I was trying to hold on some bank to starboard with an aileron I no longer had. That little, angular, ominous-looking cockpit windscreen of the ME-109, stamped indelibly an image on my mind for a lifetime as it suddenly appeared again, as from nowhere, on the end of my starboard wing tip. The pilot formated on me for a few seconds not thirty feet away. He took a long straight look into my cockpit as I gazed at him in bewilderment. Was he going to flip my wing tip in the direction of my failed motor? I still remember his determined, serious facial expression as he glared out of the side panel. Either he wanted to have a look at those Englanders who refused to be shot down, or he had run out of ammunition, or both. He peeled off to starboard and left me alone.

Some forty years later, I was reading an account of air battles in the Desert, when I found this engagement described. The account named Hauptman Franzisket and Feldwebal Steinhausen as two of the German pilots. One claimed to have shot down Gidney and the other one, Davis. They both then concentrated on getting rid of me, but the report said that:

> '...a third aircraft, although badly damaged, succeeded in evading the pursuers and force landed at Wadi Natrune.'

I wrote to the Gemeinschaft der Jagdfliegers in Germany who advised me that Feldwebel Steinhausen, some three months later, following that incident, was shot down and fatally injured whilst in combat with Spitfires. Hauptman Franzisket however survived the war. They advised me of his address. He replied at great length to my letter inviting me to visit him in Münster. He advised me that he himself was shot down seven times, always landing in his own territory, and spending long periods in hospital. From a photograph, I recognised Steinhausen as being my wing-tip viewer. A report I read of him said that it was not known which one of two British pilots brought down "this brilliant young pilot" who was posthumously commissioned and awarded The Knight's Cross. He scored his fortieth victory in combat on the day he himself was shot down.

Oil pressure on the port engine had now disappeared. I feathered the airscrew. We were now down to 200 feet. The ground swarmed with troops whose faces turned skywards as we struggled and limped over them. The additional power I was now using on the good engine was torturing my right leg as I strained on the rudder to keep straight. I was hanging on at critical speed, where it would soon be necessary to reduce power to keep straight. This would mean a loss of height and I did not have any to forfeit. How had we survived with full fuel tanks? Rick said that Gunn was writhing in pain and that Parker was in poor shape. His bottom and bowel was full of shredded dinghy material which a shell had penetrated. We would be clear of ground troops when we could lighten our load by jettisoning the bombs. The old crate jumped noticeably when the bombs left her and so did my hopes. She would even climb a little.

"Rick, tell the boys we are taking the nearest route to the hospital."

I wished I had a fuel jettison tap to further lighten our load.

"Paddy give me a course to the nearest M.U., there will be a hospital close by."

"107.M.U. Kasfareet. We should make that." said Paddy.

"Oh no Paddy, it will take us an hour." I suggested to Rick that he give Gunn a shot with the morphine needle from the first aid kit, but as Rick said,

"He goes berserk when he sees this needle." We crept slowly towards a ridge which I was a little doubtful of clearing.

"Don't put the darned thing down here Perc, there's boulders as big as bowsers," said Paddy.

We were almost at our goal when the cylinder head temperature went off the clock and the engine tightened. I told the boys that our luck had run out. I would have to submit. I could not keep airborne any longer.

"Well we've nearly cracked it Perc. This is survival not submission." said Paddy.

There was a fairly level patch ahead. I selected undercart down and do the job properly but only one leg would operate. I cocked one wing up and wheeled in on one. Sand flew everywhere. When I saw my chewed up airframe I marvelled how we stayed in the air at all.

Gunn was now in a desperate state. We unloaded some bedding on which to lay the injured boys beneath the cocked up wing. Parker laid quite still not uttering a sound. He was in a serious condition and the pained expression I saw in his face and eyes, as we laid him on the shell torn blankets, told me the story of his discomfort. We cut the flying boots from Gunn's swollen legs to ease the pressure now building up, although he protested at every snip we made.

"Paddy, you and Rick look after things here, I'll go for help. We can't be far from the Alex road. I'll hurry like hell." said I as I moved off in my sweat-soaked desert clothing. The sand was so floury, it was similar to walking through deep snow, to run was impossible. I had not gone a mile when the going became much firmer and progress quicker, but my legs ached dreadfully. In the far distance I spotted what I took to be a scout car, far to my right heading across my path. I cupped my hands and called with all my power, but I realised their engine noise would drown my calls. I hurried to intercept them waving my arms and shouting. The car stopped, and the land fell away towards that position. Exhausted I reached the car occupied by two soldiers, British. The aircraft was not within my line of sight.

"I'm so glad to see you," I said. "I am the pilot of a twin engined bomber, force landed from fighter damage just beyond the lip of the ridge and two of my boys are badly shot up. We desperately need your help."

I was suffering from sun exposure and my tongue rattled around in my mouth like a piece of loofah. They kindly gave me water. However, the INDIFFERENCE THEY SHOWED to our plight was appalling. They were surely from a different army to that we were accustomed to supporting. They had an appointment to keep, and in any case that was a soft sand no-go area. My astonishment was utterly complete, and I babbled about the written report which I would be submitting finding its way to their C.O.. Reluctantly they agreed to try. I jumped aboard. We reached the soft sand area and they told me this would be their limit.

"We can't carry men with shattered bones without a stretcher." I insisted. "Two of us heaving on these rear corners and we'll make it, let's go!" I shouted, demonstrating. We were so glad when the truck drew up alongside our wounded men. The condition of the aircraft obviously startled the two reluctant helpers and drove them into action. The truck drive which Parker had so much attempted to avoid earlier, was now unbelievably welcome. The trip to Wadi Natrune was deplorably agonising, but within the hour we had the boys in hospital.

A DAY IN DESERT DIARY

The searing sun hung in the sky,
For weeks 'No mercy' was his cry,
There was no growth to turn to tinder,
Otherwise we'd all be cinder.

Flies by thousands milled around,
Our one escape was off the ground,
When we in search of Hun would go,
Which was the better, I don't know.

Awaiting 'scramble', sweating hot,
'Neath the aircraft wing some shade we got,
And thirst was quenched with tea we brewed,
Time upon time until it stewed.

Flour-like sand took to the air,
Danced upright pirouettes everywhere,
Swirling in face and hair and brew,
Sticking to sweaty skin like glue.

Cooks would work in heat and haste,
Flames from camel thorn and oil waste.
Magic meals they'd throw together
As though they worked in English weather.

Ground staff worked in heat of day,
Belting guns and bombs in bay,
Sand shields off, then fuel and oil,
Long hard hours did they toil.

Cheerfully we'd crack a gag,
A further crowd of Huns we'd bag,
"Take me," said Parker, airframe fitter,
"I'll keep watch without a jitter."

"Parker boy you are forbidden
Within my aircraft to be hidden
'Cos should you ever get the chop
Right down the line I'd have to hop."

Many a true word is said in jest,
Later I'll reveal the rest,
But Parker said with me he'd fly,
And brave the rigours of the sky.

Contorted by the shimmering heat,
Aircraft and crews, in distance meet,
The mirage blue, against the sky,
Though in cool waters did they lie.

Aircraft upper surface, scorched,
Skin to blisters, When it caught
Us unawares, as clanging gong,
To action bid us on, 'ere long.

Parker pleaded, "Sir, I'll come,
Then land at L.G.X. whereon
I'll find a place your tent to pitch,
And save me hours of gharry hitch."

"Parker this is quite some farce
On dinghy aft then park your arse,
But not a move, and out of you
No whimper make to any crew."

A circle round the desert 'drome
Formed by tall plumes of sand, now thrown,
Above horizon blurred, as streams
Of air belch back, and engines scream.

The whirling eddies now engulfed
In angry turmoil, as planes wolfed,
With snarling engines roaring keen,
To hunt the Hun in battle scene.

Gone are the flies, relief so sweet,
Cool slipstream sweating cheek to meet,
The groundstaff still those ills to bear,
Whilst we to different dangers tear.

Check temps and pressures, turrets, guns,
Check all before we sight the Huns,
Who would, with fighter, flak and shell
Destroy us, 'ere we give them hell.

But hell to him will come we're bound,
We planned it all whilst on the ground,
Some aircraft sleek hit though he may,
Low shall his tanks and crews we lay.

Ahead the desert scene is rent,
With tanks and trucks and armament,
By far outnumbered they our boys,
Who we flew o'er like soldier toys.

"There's One-O-Nines at eight o'clock,"
Shouts rear gunner in state of shock,
But 'ere he brought his guns to fire
They jammed. Torn rims, – oh what a mire.

In flames they shot down number three,
And then they'd have a go at me,
Without those guns my one defence
Was jink, if I had any sense.

I stood the aircraft on one wing,
And pulled her hard back under him,
But well aimed shot or lucky squirt,
My engine port, shells badly hurt.

One engine now out of Commission,
Would seem the end of this darned mission,
'Cos three of them were now hell bent,
Me to oblivion soon be sent.

Turning off, they, number two
Amidships hit, and cannon blew
Him straight to ground. And then they turned
More shells at me with aim they churned.

Again I'd skid beneath their aim,
My aircraft handled not the same
With engine out, I had to wrench
The rudder, beyond tests on bench.

Elevators now all tattered,
Starboard aileron also shattered,
Gunner shot clean through the legs,
And Parker's buttocks now in shreds.

They're four o'clock now, watch it Perc,
The navigator's voice all cool and terse,
I heaved her round with all my might,
If not we'd ne'er have lived the night.

"Good on you Pad you saved the day,"
But Hun returned into the fray,
Within ten yards he flew of me.
Exhausted his ammo be.

Admire their skills I really must,
Although I hated all their thrust,
Two planes with crews for us they'd lost,
To our small force, 'twas no mean cost.

We lumbered on, sick was my plane,
My leg was numb with rudder strain,
No trim to help. We clawed the air
For thirty minutes. No one there.

We needed help, on should we fly,
Some habitation should we spy,
But now some hills would threaten close,
'Twas hope too much to surmount those.

To open gills to decrease temp
But up the drag, which sadly meant,
More strain on our one struggling motor,
The temp must stay. I didn't oughta.

Critical speed was not per book,
With buffeting rudder, I now took,
A sad decision, though to make
Alternative, nil there was to take.

The plane's whole frame gave one big shudder,
"Blast and curse there goes the rudder,"
The throttle now I'm forced to close,
To keep control of her old nose.

I tried to get me three nice greens,
At times like these it almost seems,
Nothing goes right. I was a clown?
I only got me one leg down.

It wouldn't move. "It's real luck,"
Said Paddy "That it's firmly stuck,
Without this leg my bottom hatch,
In sand would firmly lock on latch."

"Oh God, I didn't think," I cried.
"Fate has St. Peter on your side.
Paddy my friend he pays you back,
For getting us out of that last wrack."

I put her down in swirls of sand,
At least we were on friendly land,
And wheeled her in cocked up askew,
Till wing tip dropped and round we drew.

Out like a flash in case of fire,
Paddy and I intent and dire,
The wounded now to extricate,
To save them both from further fate.

Parker said no single word,
Gunner mad with pain was heard,
As they 'neath upturned wing we lay,
With hypodermic, pain to stay.

With Rick and Paddy left behind
Gunner and Parker there to mind,
Off I set some help to find,
The gunner going off his mind.

Through miles of soft sand plodded I,
Until a gharry did I spy,
Soldiers two drew slowly near,
My story heard and thought most queer.

The trip to dock was hell for miles,
The bumping wagon bought no smiles,
The gunner called in agony,
In desert bare he'd rather be.

Brave Parker had no word to say,
Of what had happened on that day,
Until some months in hospital,
I found him talking to a pal.

I questioned Parker how he fared.
"No other thing in life compared,"
Said he, "With dodging One-O-Nines,
From now I'll stick to roads and lines."

"I'm sorry I asked not in vain,"
Said he "to fly in your old plane,
I wish that you had used your rank,
And stopped my silly bloody prank."

"My arse is almost well again,
But dinghy on it did remain,
Proof have I so, shall I be bound,
Torn dinghy up my arse they found."

"I hope they don't court martial you,
For taking me as extra crew,
But should they question me 'ere long,
I'll say that you deserved a gong."

To him I said, "You've been a brick,
Now get back to the squadron quick,
My plane I don't want on the blink-o,
You're the best fitter I can think-o."

So dinghy then his life did save,
Whilst rigours of the sky he'd brave,
He saved some time not riding gharry,
But lost much more in dock to tarry.

Ironical too though may it sound,
That Paddy saved us hitting ground,
One solit'ry shell mere five days on,
Our plane did hit, 'twas Paddy gone.

Every day we bashed the front,
Waves of aircraft, shunt on shunt,
Until at Alamein he halted,
Our reformed army, his wounds salted.

All proved that this was not in vain,
Egypt's land then to retain,
The Persian Gulf was him denied,
And saved the world from suicide.

From all this then, the labour force,
Of post-war Britain, should take course,
Enthuse in what you do today
And work as though you'd earn your pay.

It's proved that greed has done a lot,
For country not to care one jot,
If all would Parker's courage semble,
Why need good old England tremble?

Years later read I of this day,
Hauptmann Franzisket lead the fray,
Number Two shoot down did he,
Then pumped some shells straight into me.

Feldwebel Steinhausen said that he,
Dealt fatal blow to Number Three,
Then came determined both did they,
Intent to terminate my day.

'Tis true they did not see me crash,
Flew they away and left the hash,
With me, to struggle and to plod,
Protected thought they by some God.

Just three months on in combat fair,
Steinhausen with Spitfires tried his flair,
That day he was to meet his match,
'cos fate decreed his quick dispatch.

Franzisket, so the records said,
Survived the Combat, I was led
To Munster, there this man to find.
He wrote me letters. Very kind.

The pressurised JU-86-P Shufti Kite, came over regularly at 40,000 feet, taking pictures of extreme interest. We used to lay on our backs on the sand and view developments through binoculars. A Hurricane, and later a Spit, virtually hanging on their props, would attempt to gain sufficient altitude to knock it down but would stall from the recoil action of their own guns and come tumbling down as though they themselves had been shot. Then to try again all to no avail. The story was, that two Spits at 103.MU. were stripped down and polished up. They were fuelled to minimum requirement to get them high enough, and to save weight, armed to minimum. The engines were tweaked up and four bladed props fitted. The first attempt failed when the 'donkey' died a few hundred feet below the Shufti, with the pilot frozen as were his guns. He thawed out as he glided back to base for a dead stick landing. One skirmish was however eventually successful, and the Shufti was knocked down in perfect visibility, to cheers all over Egypt. More however were to come, some of which were pooped off, after which they ceased their visits.

I met my new gunner, Bob, straight from gunnery school, so we got into the air for some serious handling and deflection practice. We still awaited the new power operated turret aircraft.

Later that day it was confided to me that for my standard of flying on ops, and the scrapes from which I had untangled myself, I was to be recommended for the award of the D.F.M., the first on the squadron. This was really quite something as it was well known in the Desert Air Force that such awards were not made lightly. Had the wearer earned the award in the Middle East there was some measure of esteem attached. In the citation it was interesting to see reference to the Benghazi trips, the Tmimi night trip and the events of the previous ME-109 encounter. I also had a repeat of my trade assessment: 'Exceptional'. Paddy was in a state of great jubilation and so free with his congratulations. That evening we assumed the unmistakeable characteristics of the proverbial 'newts', and in the dim glimmer of the hissing mess tent lantern, drank and talked well into the night. It was however to be a further three years before I was able to visit Buckingham Palace for the Investiture.

"No, no, at ease gentlemen, take your seats. Good morning to you all, I've come to have a look at the colour of your eyes." said Air Chief Marshall Teddar as he came through ops tent flap. We had been expecting him. He displayed his well known infectious smile as he spoke. "I can see you are all in good fettle. My thanks for the hard work I know you have done." With a little more effort he assured us we could all move Rommell 'clean out of Africa'. He sat on the corner of a trestle table took out his pipe and invited us to smoke.

We took up battle formation right over his head on our way out to harrass the Hun. He was still there when we returned.

"I had to tell you that your forming up just went like clockwork, and your flying worthy of any Hendon." he said when we all assembled in the ops tent. He listened intently at de-briefing when mention was made of Panzer being overturned and trucks being fired.

"Today we're really going to have a clean up on a particular enemy concentration which we are sure will be on the move today." said the C.O. "In fact we have the responsibility of elimination as it is said that should we fail, matters could get very nasty indeed."

We had been up at 0400 hrs to ensure an early start to catch them before they could brew up. I was taking a box of six.

"Stick to me like glue fellows, we don't want any stragglers this morning, you know what happens to them."

The familiar faint hint of diffused light crept up on the eastern horizon. The sun would soon be up. The upper wing surfaces were so cold. Had I the choice of attacker I would take the fighter rather than the flak. One had the sporting chance with the fighter. At least you could usually see it coming in. Flak however was more sinister and churned up your stomach a bit, especially when you were committed to straight and level on the bombing run. My ageing process used to accelerate considerably when they had our measure. This morning one of my wingmen was hit, the flak so intense. Rick reported from the back we had a few flak splinter holes, whilst Paddy referred to the enemy below as

"Bloody hundreds of them Perc, – at least there was. We've really caused some havoc down there. Let them regroup and we'll call again."

We flew straight on into the sun, the gunners scanning for fighters. We felt vulnerable, the sun blinding us head on, and the heat was now pouring through the perspex. Gunners reported a gaggle of aircraft far distant, just discernable low down at nine o'clock.

"Look like Bostons on their way home." said Paddy.

"Gunn don't get a fixation," I chip in, "keep scanning. Paddy you can keep an eye on those at nine o'clock."

"If they're Stukas they're bound to have top cover." Paddy reasoned.

"Yea!" shouted Gunn with excitement. "One-O-Nines, 2 o'clock high. Thousand yards. Standing off."

"Hell!" I observed, "there's aircraft all around us."

"One-O-Nines coming in," reported Gunn with some urgency. Quickly continuing, "800 yards... 700... 600... broken off 3 o'clock ... 4 o'clock ... climbing."

"Funny bloody tactics. Sure they're not sprog Eyties in Macchis?" I query.

"Maybe a decoy. Look around the clock, One-O-Nines don't usually squirt and stand off like that, especially when they know we're not escorted."

"If they did squirt then they bloody missed us. May come in closer next time. Watch them."

"Five o'clock high." shouted Gunn.

"Watch them like a hawk Gunn." I urge.

"Coming in." called Gunn.

"Squirt early Gunn." I interjected as I turned off right to skid under their approach.

"Thousand yards, eight – seven – six – five." There was a sputtering as Gunn engaged them.

"They've got me Perc!" Paddy's voice from the front.

"They've got you Paddy? What do you mean? Is it bad? Where?"

No reply. I wasn't aware of any bullet or shell having struck the cockpit or nose area.

"Rick, how do you read. Is my mike OK?"

"Reading clear Perc." said Rick.

"Bastards!" I shouted and straightened up easterly.

"One-O-Nines broken off low. Now at seven o'clock" reported Gunn.

'Thank Christ for that, everybody seems to be flying. I'll bet Paddy's plug had yanked out. If he's been hit maybe he's jerked it. Maybe he's flaked out.' I figured. 'Give him a couple of minutes and he might surface.' I reasoned. These were the moments when I despaired of the segregation of the crew members in this particular aircraft. There was no way of even seeing into the navigators compartment.

"Keep scanning Gunn." I said.

"Roger" he replied. "No sign of them at all now."

"Paddy are you any better now?," I asked apprehensively, "Are you coming round a bit?"

No reply.

"Looks bad for Paddy fellows. We have an emergency. I'll have to get this crate back on the deck smartish. Break radio silence Rick and advise base."

I whipped on finer pitch, opened up the throttles and depressed the nose. We sped away from the others. Navigation lights and landing lights on I made a straight-in approach with a quick taxi to shut down. There was the senior Flight/NCO waiting for me. As I climbed out of the canopy to step on the wing, I called to Drakey,

"Paddy seems to have got it bad," as I pointed down to the nose section. I slid down the wing quickly and came square in front of Drakey, who, with a serious face was looking up into the nose section. Not daring to think what I might see, I too looked up with him.

"The bastards." I said quietly.

There was Paddy, slumped forward, supported by his bomb-sight, with his head turned slightly to his left, his face quite expressionless and his arms hanging limp.

My friend, with his arm around my shoulder, firmly pulled me around to walk away.

"We're too late Perc, there's nothing we can do, but I shall see that we look after Paddy with the greatest of care and respect."

I was torn with a feeling of extreme sadness and fury. I was cursing those Huns as I had never felt like cursing them before. It was now that the full impact of death hit me. This was my first fatality in my crew and it hurt terribly. Our squadron totals were 70 killed and 20 wounded – great sacrifices – but none greater than that I now experienced. I walked towards the ops tent.

"Tough luck Carruthers, I really am very sorry indeed. I shall see you later." said the Squadron Commander. "There's an aircraft awaiting test. Get it off the ground and have a look around."

"What ... now?" I asked, not a little surprised.

"Of course. Just what you need. Throw it about." he replied.

The boys were all back by now, but I was glad to avoid them just for a while, my mind benumbed with grief. I took off for this sham test, a good idea. If I proved anything it was that the aircraft was, at the least, very well bolted together. I yanked it in and out of very steep, vertical, tight shuddering turns. I dived it and climbed it until it almost fell off the props. I lined up the sights on imaginary Krauts and shouted curses at them, to take the blank numbness out of my brain. I felt the tension subside and I wanted to go back to Paddy and the boys. Drakey was there.

"Everything OK with that aircraft?" he asked.

"It's well glued together Drakey, I'll give you that." I said. "Where's Paddy?"

"He's over in the casualty tent." Drakey advised. "He's quite alone. By the way, one other navigator is injured, in the legs, he's off to hospital. Three of the other aircraft are battle-scarred from the trip." he continued.

"Really? Queer business out there today," I said, "all hit and run with the usual aggression missing. Today's bunch were from an entirely different school or different squadron, Drakey. Like a bunch of new boys might be, but they got my dear old comrade."

He drew the flap tent aside for me to enter, saying, "He's just right here." There was Paddy, on a high trestle table, all nicely covered over. He seemed peaceful and unmarked and I gazed into his face remembering in him the qualities I so admired. "There's no more to give my faithful old warrior." I said quietly, as Drakey touched my elbow. I did not resist. "Farewell my courageous old comrade." I said with some feeling and as I turned to go I was wracked with grief, as though mild convulsions, and was quite overcome. Tears welled up in my eyes as Drakey ushered me out, and as I fought my emotions the pains in my neck and head became more intense. We stood outside looking across the landing ground whilst I attempted to swallow the lumps which would just not go down. I wanted to break the silence and talk but the words would just not form in my mouth as though some paralysis had taken over. I had never been like that before.

"We all know how it is my old pal." said Drakey as he eased me forward, "Let's sink a couple of whiskies together, you've had enough for today."

"By the way, where was Paddy hit?" I enquired.

"You won't believe it," he replied, "But apart from a few flak holes in the rear-end of your aircraft, there was only one bullet hole, through the front end and it got Paddy through his neck."

We took a look. To my surprise there was the evidence. The attack I knew had come from 5 o'clock high and the fatal shot had entered my cockpit, without me even knowing, just over my right shoulder, passed by my right knee and down into Paddy's compartment. With such an injury as he had I have never failed to be amazed, that he had the courage and presence of mind to say as he did quite clearly, "They've got me Perc" and then no more.

* * *

Next detail was for mid-day the following day. It was the irony of it which intensely annoyed me. Paddy would have still been alive had such tactics been employed on our previous trip. We were to tie in with the Bostons who were always favoured with fighter escort. Such luxury was not known to us. The only fighters we saw were One-O-Nines.

I met Joe, a tall, lanky Aussie, quietly humoured with a wry smile. We seemed to be on the same wavelength immediately, so he would crack off as navigator on the next trip. The air was seldom empty of aircraft. We did two more sorties of six with the Bostons and were therefore escorted. The Hun must have taken punishment unheard of previously. The Daily Occurrence Report was printed as follows:

> Except for a period of four hours during the day when bad weather prevented operations, raids at hourly intervals were put on by 3 SAAF Wing. Bombing from six to nine thousand feet Bostons and Baltimores pressed home attacks on enemy formations, in most cases not well dispersed, in the battle area west of the El Alamein line. Bostons flew with fighter escort, and Baltimores unescorted, except when cooperating with the Boston formations.

This bulletin highlighted the anomalous situation regarding escort, which many crews considered ought to be rectified and which cost our RAF Squadron, so we thought, a number of avoidable losses.

It was still very dark, and cold too, as we ambled into ops on the following morning, after our Boston trips on the previous day. This was Joe's first trip. I was hoping it would be an uneventful one. 55 Squadron, who had just parted with their old Blenheims in favour of Baltimores would come along with us for our type of battle experience. One-O-Nines, stood off, one with a white spinner and one with a bright yellow one, skittered around our formation, possibly looking for stragglers. Soon the flak peppered the sky: there was much too much of it. The gunners anticipated our turn. I wondered why, how did they do it.   "There's an escarpment ahead, our target ought to be just at the base." said Joe.

The flak was extremely accurate and intense giving us a most uncomfortable and ring-twittering ride. I was sorry for Joe on his first trip.

"Wow," called Joe as we released our bombs, "Direct hit on a flak post."

Good friend Bluey McClure had returned from a spell in hospital following a previous flak wound in an arm. He had had it rough from time to time and he was popular, so it was understandable that there was great sorrow on the squadron when the climax of his bad luck was the complete disintegration of his aircraft over the target. Whilst we had learned to accept these losses with a certain subdued resignment we were fully aware that we were exposed almost daily to similar risks, partaking in a considerably dangerous pursuit. We would, however, never accept that we would be the next in line. Damaged or injured we would accept, perhaps because we had experienced just that, but total loss was foreign to our thoughts. This, no doubt, was the attitude of all RAF aircrew, with very few exceptions.

At this time of additional pressure it was really encouraging to see the C.O. in the airmens' mess, chatting informally, bringing them up to date on the facts of battle. They enjoyed it and deserved it.

For a target we were merely given a grid reference point, where at briefing it was said 'an obscure target lay', something buried? We would take eighteen aircraft in three boxes of six. This was perhaps the birth of 'pattern bombing' as we named it, to be known in some quarters as 'carpet bombing'. I was now elevated to leading a box of six rather than the usual vic of three. I now had almost thirty sorties behind me, but was still a hard grinding little Flight Sergeant with others of officer rank flying in the formation which I was leading. Perhaps promotion was just around the corner. Promotions at that time appeared to be going to the higher ranks. One we particularly welcomed was that of our respected Commander. He became Air Chief Marshall Sir Arthur Teddar.

The flak seemed to pour up in tons. It was all around us, in groups giving the impression that someone just had to be hit. On we flew as the fireballs burst and we flew through the black cordite smelling smoke puffs.

"They just can't get things right down there can they?" said I, by way of mock nonchalence. It sounded better than admitting my tension and my thoughts of 'how in the hell can they keep missing?' The run-up seemed longer than the usual 'three weeks', but we just had to get this one right, it all depended on our accurate flying with no visible target. The way it was being defended suggested it a was 'a plum'. What a victory that was for us. Eighteen of us got through that crazy screen of shell-fire and landed safely back at base. We must have caused some wild confusion and massive losses if the number of fires and explosions were any criteria to judge by. As used to be said at that time, 'the desert does not burn'. The previous few days, the twenty four hours through, must have been hell for those enemy troops along the whole forty-mile front, as one cannot imagine how they possibly could have slept – the Desert Air Force was over them continuously.

On occasions, when catching a glimpse of my reflection in the instrument panel, I remember thinking,

"Christ you look old Perc, for 23!"

I looked lined and worn compared with eight or nine months ago. I had an irritating ear discharge which burned my skin like acid and wearing a helmet in a scorching cockpit did not assist.

Oh for a cool wet day in England with a strong wind blowing the rain into my face. I would hold my face to the heavens so long as it came. Here in the desert we could not even get down to the nearby shoreline of the lovely Mediterranean, and its ink-blue waters, for a swim. The beaches were mined and decorated with all manner of little innocent looking things, which suggested they could be useful for various purposes. For example, one would blow off your head if you picked it up. Another would denude you of a leg should you give it a friendly kick. I was in fact, had I known it, somewhat battle-fatigued and ready for a break which was to come some four weeks later. Most aircrew I think experienced certain stages of attitudes as they progressed through their enemy operations. On daylight ops perhaps one could see too much. One saw the many boys flying close by to you being shot down or blown up merely yards away. Then the things which actually happened to yourselves. A few holes in the aircraft, or a bit shot off. A crew member badly wounded or, like Paddy, killed only three feet from you. You escaped the unpalatable possibility of death, by almost believing that the inevitable would only happen to someone else. Then after seeing the continued losses, one accepted the short odds, that it was now almost certain you would get the chop, but without apparent due concern.

So one continued with dedication, and a pride in one's own ability and expertise which one now recognised. A certain case hardening crept in, no doubt somewhat brittle, but under this case hardening, quite unnoticed for a while I think, health began to suffer. Of our original fifteen pilots in 'A' Flight, only Wallace (Flight Commander), Harland, Price, Collyer and myself were operational. So, in four weeks time we could relax.

We were called down to ops. I had just been giving my pet Chameleon some camouflage exercises by placing him on different coloured articles as I watched with fascination how he quickly changed the colour of his coat to blend with those of his immediate surrounds. I liked the little fellow as he squatted down, head on one side, absolutely motionless as I talked to him.

"Look how he listens to me Danny, so intently." I said as his little head froze with his big eyes looking at me.

"He's not listening Perc," said Danny, "he's just too bloody scared to move."

We continued our attacks on forward troops and against enemy airfields. The Wimpies kept up their nightly harrassment, causing some spectacular firework displays by catching ammo trains at Daba, Rhaman and Ghazal.

Our fighter boys put on some spectacular shows during the hours of darkness, knocking down the enemy bombers which sought to locate our landing ground. Six hundred German troops were taken and I recall flying over them as they were marched off to the Prisoner-of-War cages.

Again in the mess tent, appeared a notice of recognition of our recent efforts. A joint message of congratulations from A.O.C. Western Desert and General Aukinlech. The squadron rather enjoyed these significant psychological boosters. In fact, after some more days of troop harassment we got another one from General Auckinlech himself.

> Very grateful if you would convey to all ranks of the Royal Air Force
> The Army's deep appreciation of their magnificent efforts.

On one of the many two hour training trips, where I would take five other aircraft, crewed by our new replacement crews, brushing up on formation and navigational exercises, I routed via Wadi Natrune to see if there was any trace of my old shot up aircraft. The RSU boys had picked it up.

Squadron ops for the day were to be split. Desperate tank activity at Tel El Eisa was to be scattered and a most important ship which had got past the Beaufighters, and made Mersa Matruh harbour, was pouring stores onto the wharves.

"Rommell really desperately needs this particular cargo." we were told. "Please don't come back until you've sunk this ship and fired the stores." was said at the briefing. "Have a good trip."

S/Ldr Joel ('B' Flight Commander) and I would take three aircraft each, that is, a total of eight aircraft. There would be none of that low-level, mast-high, hero, gong-seeking, suicide stuff. We would do it on professional capabilities at safety height and 'guts for garters' if you get it wrong.

We had a lot of fun during training for shipping strikes, and when there is no-one shooting at you, you can have a giggle at your mistakes. Today there were not to be any. I remember whilst boring in onto target during simulated ship strikes, we would sometimes really get down to it, so low, to 'put one down the funnel'. It perked up the ego. Collyer followed me in one day on one of those 'split-arse' attacks, left things a little too late and 'took the funnel with him', bending his ego and his aircraft. I liked the rather fitting ditty to the tune of 'Elmer's Tune'.

> Bombing shipping, everybody here thinks its ripping,
> Diving, turning, look out for that mast 'cos it may be your last.
> And when you read in the papers that a ship has been sunk,
> And the rest of the convoy's a heap of old junk,
> It's not the season the reason the magical moon,
> It's just X-Y-Zee (Squadron number).

We headed off out out to sea where better stability awaited us, and which would contribute to our greater accuracy on our bombing run, heading from seawards to the harbour. On this wonderfully glorious day, the beautiful inky blueness of the Mediterranean seemed worlds away from war. This manoeuvre on which we were now engaged seemed totally incongruous.

A ship from altitude really can appear to be a very small object indeed. Precision flying now was paramount to ensure the accuracy of aiming the bombs. The navigator had to get his calculations right. Indicated height had to be computed to true height allowing for density and temperature. Indicated airspeed computed through corrected airspeed to true airspeed, applying known constant errors, and the atmospheric conditions. Under or over-shoot of the bombs was greatly influenced by these important factors.

The favoured approach on the bombing run was at sixty degrees to the fore and aft axis of the ship and it so happened that this was almost dead into wind. This minimised drift and assisted in lateral accuracy in placing the bombs. So really we had all possible errors buttoned up. Bomb doors were opened long before customary time to allow the pilots to absorb the drag in their throttle settings, so that when the target entered the drift wires it was just a matter of watching the bits fly off that ship. We hoped. We did not expect a great deal of trouble from flak initially, approaching from the sea, but we did expect a gaggle of crazed One-O-Nines to pick us up and disturb our tranquility. But not one showed up.

"Bombs gone!" and we wheeled away to port.

The results were fabulous. Bombs fell on the target ship and on the surrounding stores. We were jubilant. There were masses of explosions with volumes of smoke – or was it steam? – to be seen for miles. The spread of bombs was ideal, some falling on the other vessels. For crews on this trip this was the only sortie of the day and was rewarded by a printed message from Air Chief Marshall Teddar himself.

> To 233 Squadron, Western Desert.
>
> Congratulations on your bag at Mersa. That ship was most important. Please let me add my commendations to a first class operation which was outstandingly successful. Well done.

The sortie was mentioned on the radio news in the evening as we all sat having a beer in the mess tent. There was much cheering and banter about 'getting down the bloody funnels.'

"The radio only mentions our raids Danny, when you're on them." said someone teasing the droll Aussie, who spoke so slowly that every word claimed its own place in time.

"Rommell's – not – the – only – bloody – fox – in – this – desert." drawled Danny. I so well remember his musing saying if he was urging some action. "Quick – quick – like – the – fox."

The close cooperation between Army and Desert Air Force was something, I think, not before experienced. On one sortie the Army troops below had arranged to fire smoke puffs into a target area which they required us to attack. It really was a barrel of fun, perhaps just a bit hairy I might add, but gave one the feeling that together we had what it took to crack the Kraut. We were now getting rid of the old barrier between Army and the Brylcreme Boys, the pattern for the future cooperation between the Services where the shooting was actually taking place, was fashioned jointly by Teddar and the Auk.

Great jubilation, our Mark III Baltimores with the electric-hydraulic turrets arrived and we evaluated forthwith. I had just had some of the more advanced new boys up on exercises and we were discussing one of the flights after landing. One of the cockier type pilots admitted to me,

"I twittered a bit when I nearly hit you in one of those steep turns you put on," almost as though he were complaining. "You can have a better twitter tomorrow." I told him, "There will be some nice hair-raising flak to help you. I'm telling the Flight Commander you're operational."

His face drained.

"And you'll stick to me as never before, steep turns and all."

It was 0600 hrs when I saw him enter ops tent. By the look on his face I gathered he had not slept, but I knew he would be alright. The morning sky was overcast. We went motorised column cracking at El Mireir. A push at Ruweisat had been contained by the Auk who was pushing with some vigour. Rommell projecting some kind of aura, and being known for his quote, "Krieg ohne Hass" (war without hate), had at times been feared somewhat because some of the successes he had achieved had seemed quite impossible. But now this impression was changing, giving way to the symbol of the cool and steadfast Auk whose influence was obvious along the length of the Alamein front. The Auk was containing the Fox.

24. SAAF Squadron, who flew Bostons from an adjacent landing strip invited us over in the evening to help them celebrate their 1,000th sortie of the North African Campaign. What a fantastic spread. I had not realised how meagrely we of the RAF Desert Air Force were living until I arrived in their marquee. It almost seemed they had fresh food and stores specially flown up from the Union. The welcome they extended us was absolutely first class. We ate masses

of lovely food, of such variety we had not seen for a whole year, and drank too much cold beer. Our Squadron beer was always warm. The SAAF's were wonderful hosts and justly proud of their contribution to the effort to stem the Hun. I could not envisage such a party being arranged by the RAF. We drifted out into the blackness of the desert night, terribly inebriated, with a serious navigational problem. We were truly 'wandering in the wilderness' and I can offer no explanation as to how we arrived at our own landing ground, on foot.

By 14.42 hrs on the following day I had recuperated sufficiently to get off with the C.O. W/C Horgan. We took six aircraft each to attend to 'well concentrated vehicles' at El Mireir. When would the Germans learn to practice the art of dispersal? Such elementary basic tactics would have saved them an awful lot of valuable vehicles, just on our last trip alone, and surely well up in the four-figure bracket in just the past few weeks.

Excitement that evening grew as news came in of something brewing on the morrow. A very large number of JU88s were reported to have sneaked into El Daba landing ground and an armada of transport JU52s obviously loaded with stores. Were the Germans about to launch a blitz on the Allies the following day? We would have to be in the air that morning before the enemy was ready for engine start. W/C Horgan and I would go with a total of twelve aircraft again. It was said that the landing ground would be covered by One-O-Nines in profusion. It was on such ops as these where fighter escort would have been a wonderful asset, a necessity we thought, but such was not to be.

Visibility was good and we could see action over the northern sector of the front. Daba landing ground was soon in sight, but where were those enemy fighters?

"Christ Almighty!" exclaimed Joe as the first flak burst rocked us. Although you were expecting it it never failed to surprise you when it happened, that's when it's close enough to be felt. It was the suddenness of it all which crinkled your scalp, and galvanised your attention.

Air activity round the landing ground was more than we had realised. But flak still kept cracking about us. The guns were clattering in the back in bursts of three and four seconds, when Gunn called out. "We got a JU88. He's on his way down." I was sweating heavily, as I usually did when it was rough, then suddenly it was 'bombs gone'. We turned off to port.

"There's a One-O-Nine going down!" shouted Gunn excitedly. "It's all happening back here."

He was in good spirits because we were winning.

"Everybody had a go at that one Perc," he chattered. "It had no chance."

It was now noses down and head east. We could do the usual chatter about the target. We had started one large fire and wrecked quite a lot of aircraft. How furious must these Luftwaffe pilots have been. To have sneaked their aircraft into Daba, possibly from Crete, for a blitz on the morrow against our troops and landing grounds, and then we go along at dawn and scatter them like skittles.

It had been said at the briefing that on our return trip we may show the flag a bit to the boys up on the front. Morale boosting exercise. This we would be pleased to do, at low level, and show them how aggressive we could be when harassing the Hun. They would perhaps even wave and cheer. We came in at a cracking pace, holding on a spot of impressive bank, perhaps to draw from their smiling lips a few kind remarks of appreciation. But that was not to be. We were to draw something else. Our approach was from the direction from which they would expect a bunch of the Bosche and our intentions were very much misinterpreted. They smartly opened up on us. Much too close for comfort. It was very fortunate that we were so very low and so only in their sights for a very brief period. We immediately abandoned the exercise and cut through the front the short way.

We were to have eight days leave. Joe and I would favour Cairo first. On our programme we had a visit to poor old shot-up Gunn in hospital. We must also go in search of L.A.C. Parker and check what progress he had made over the past few weeks. Then there was Les my one-time gunner and master of the unique and 'wondrous strange' selection of bombing missiles. Would he be able to point us in the direction of dear old Ginger Adams? I do hope all, and many more of the boys mentioned in this paragraph, read this invitation and get in touch with me. None of them are members of the 223 Squadron Association.

Hurricane House was one of the perks, a rest house for operational aircrew run by the RAF in Sharia Soliman Pasha. It really was quite fantastic, not a Shepherd's by any means, but so lovely. Proper meals, real beds and people who made us feel that we were really somebody. It was heaven. What an impossible contrast to the conditions a hundred miles further up the 'Blue', to which we would return on the 23rd of August. To our tent on the wind-swept plateau, to the water ration, the flies, the heat of the day, the bone-chilling desert night air and the wind-blown sand.

To our complete amazement, an invitation awaited us on our arrival. There was to be a dinner at the British Embassy for operational aircrew on leave. Off we went in search of a haircut, the first since God knew when.

We were overawed. We were welcomed by Lady Teddar who introduced us to Lady Lampson, wife of the British Ambassador. We also met Mrs Were, wife of the British Consul, and many other dignatories. It was all so very wonderful after months in the desert. To see ladies and gentlemen in full evening dress for dinner in such sumptuous surroundings was something we had quite forgotten and reminded us once more just what living was all about, and to partake of such lovely food and wine was beyond our wildest dreams. This made the celebrations at 24 Squadron's 1,000th sortie party, with the greatest respect and reverence, pale somewhat. There was dancing to an orchestra and, although we did not know them, lots of lovely people. The hospitality was quite superb. Who could have believed that within a few days we would be clattering down the landing ground with a load of bombs aboard on our way to clout the Kraut to keep him away from this wonderful scene of very English living?

We were convinced, before we left the Embassy, that we were considered to be quite important people. We went along to RAF El Maza Transit Camp where we suspected Les might be. There he was, the same mirth-bubbling comedian. Head Quarters had taken no action on his refusal to fly on that operation some three months ago.

"Honestly Perc, I think the faggers lost my records, but I'm in no flap." said Les. He said how he would have loved to have joined us again, now that he had made his point on the inadequate defensive armament of the Mark I Baltimore.

We made our way to the hospital where we found our recuperating Gunn. His shot-up legs were still in plaster and he was quite immobile. I found a taxi for the remaining part of the day and we went exploring places he had not yet seen. Before leaving that area we also located L.A.C. Parker, our passenger whose life was saved by the dinghy on which he was sitting when the One-O-Nines shot us up. Parker had a good party piece about how the nurses, hand over hand, extricated the yellow shell torn dinghy material, yard by yard, from his shattered orifice.

We returned to the squadron to learn that General Auckinlech had handed over command to General Sir Harold Alexander and that Lt/General Montgomery was to command the Eighth Army. We had grown to like and respect 'The Auk'. He had personally taken over 'the army in the field' himself some short while ago and organised the troops to turn the tide against Rommell. What a shame he was not to be there to taste the fruits of his hard work and effective planning. He and Teddar together had cracked this serious situation.

Marauders and Mitchells were arriving. We were to pack up ready to move forward to a more advanced base. There was a general air of anticipation. The Hun was only going to be allowed to travel west.

Now that we had occupied our new landing ground and the Shufi Kite had taken note, consistent nightly raids by enemy bombers was the norm. The Luftwaffe however were never able to acquire the same night bombing expertise as did we. They were in fact quite ineffective, and more of a nuisance value. When the moon was up the drone of his de-synchronised engines would wake us up. When it was dark he would bedeck the sky with myriads of small parachute flares which were more decorative than effective. In either case he would drop incendiaries as though they were frightfully expensive. One here, one there, usually landing between tents or between aircraft and doing negligible damage. The expense of these operations was certainly not justified. Had he done something simple like dropping the incendiaries in sticks instead of singles, he would undoubtedly have caused damage by setting a number of aircraft on fire. Sometimes the anti-aircraft guns would become extremely busy and the enemy would disappear quickly. At other times the ack-ack would remain mute and the night fighter boys would join the party. A mere five or six hundred feet up one would hear the engines pass over. There would be gun chatter and a bomber would streak the fatal tongue of flame from the fighter's gun strikes. Heads would pop out of slit trenches all around. Screams of delight would rent the air, and naked bodies would run about in the warm dark evening emitting shrieks of joy.

A variation was for the enemy to come over in great numbers, dropping masses of 'spikes', but never really high explosive bombs. The 'spikes' were small metal objects, no more than about six inches from tip to tip with four spike protrusions, so that no matter how they landed, three spikes would form the base on which the object would stand and the fourth spike would be in the vertical plane. These were aircraft tyre bursters. Then he would drop masses of quite small delayed-action bombs which only exploded when compressed by a foot or a tyre. Then there were the 'cracker bombs'. These detonated on striking the ground, and when falling in our tentage area caused much confusion. These were anti-personnel devices with jumping-jack characteristics. They would explode at about five second intervals and with each explosion would jump about five yards, but one could never predict which way they would jump on the next explosion. We, I might add, did much more jumping than the devices when they fell amongst us. There were injuries but none that I can remember which were serious enough to require amputations. In order to clear the delayed action bombs and the spikes, the whole squadron would spread out, about arms length apart, along one edge of the landing ground and move forward sweeping the whole camp. We would pick up the spikes and the armourers would mark the positions of the bombs for attention by the bomb squad. Occasionally some of these sinister little objects would become embedded in soft sand and escape our notice until a vehicle or taxiing aircraft made contact. Leake once landed his aircraft on one of the delayed action contraptions and his aircraft was damaged. I was turning into wind for take-off when the sweeping tail wheel detonated one of the hidden unexploded personnel bombs which went off with quite a smart report. I stopped the fans and nipped out for a quick inspection. I was not impressed by the efficiency of the Kraut contraption. From the noise of the explosion I had expected to see the whole empennage unit amputated; instead there were only minor punctures in the body skin, so I wound up the fans and pushed off. The thing did not even have that vile objectionable smell which the 'jumping jacks' emitted. Being familiar with what appeals to German humour, I thought perhaps that here we had something hilariously funny. Oh how awful did those 'jumping jacks' stink. We had that morning just done a 'landing ground sweep' before flying commenced, removed many sacks of 'spikes' and forty unexploded bombs.

There was trouble reported from Rommell at Alam El Halfa. W/C Horgan and I took off immediately with our box of six each. We had been asked to 'get there quick'. The situation had been referred to as "...new thrust in the south sector. Large motorised concentrations reported to be on the move. Situation considered dangerous." For us that was no understatement. There was the danger, plain to be seen as we approached the target; which was also plain to be seen. The flak today was flak of a new dimension. We had previously had accurate, concentrated flak which rocked you about a bit, but this flak was in such liberal quantities that it was all around us, front, back, and sides and also right between the aircraft in the formation. It really was quite alarming and the barrage of explosions, "THWACK! – THWACK! - THWACK!" were clear to be heard above the thrashing of the engines. The black puffs with their brilliant centre fire-balls dominated the scene. The aircraft rocked to the explosions as I yanked the control column to keep level, and the formation became somewhat ragged as the pilots attempted to keep station on me. I felt this could not just go on much longer without someone being hit. It didn't.

"Christ Almighty!" I said, which seemed to be our usual exclamation when something extra surprising occurred. We were hit. The cockpit stunk of cordite, and the ring sight just forward of my cockpit screen, was clean blown off, right there in front of my eyes. 'Bloody funny,' thought I, 'why hasn't my perspex screen shattered,' being extremely surprised that the engines kept going, the props stayed on and the controls all brought response. I was bathed in perspiration, perhaps the product of concentration and fear. The other aircraft were rocking about like something crazy.

"We're coming up now Perc to thousands of the buggers," said Joe, "anytime now" as he lay on his stomach peering down through his bomb sight.

"Bomb doors open Perc," came Joe's voice of the concentration variety. "Just keep it at that Perc, you're coming right up the middle where I want to be." The flak was actually hammering and I felt if we did not get to 'bombs gone' soon, we may not arrive at all. A rasping bark exploded, it seemed, just behind my starboard wing and threw the aircraft to port. I corrected and looked out. My no. 2 aircraft was missing.

"Where's my No 2 Gunn" I asked the gunner who had obviously been keeping quiet because of the run-up.

"Bombs gone." said Joe firmly, "We just can not possibly miss." As I snatched up the bomb doors lever and turned to port Gunn came back saying our No. 2 had obviously got that hit in his port engine and was losing height and in a continuous turn to port. I did not like the sound of that. It suggested that the pilot had been hit, otherwise a straight course should have been possible.

"Wilson has copped it now Perc." came Gunn on the intercom. The flak kept pumping up as we turned first one way then the other. "He's going down Perc." added Gunn.

"Bastardy!" I said by way of reply and complete disappointment.

"He's not pulling out either." said Rick who was down at the dorsal hatch.

"Oh hell. They've gone straight in Perc." he continued. We were paying today, but as we later learned, this was the commencement of what was to become known in history as the 'Battle of Alam El Halfa'. Had we not turned the tide at Alam El Halfa there would never have been a 'Battle of El Alamein'.

"This is the roughest bloody ride we've ever had Perc." said Joe, "I'm surprised more of us haven't copped it".

And so it was proved when we landed. All the aircraft, without exception were carrying the scars of battle.

After leaving the battle area, I had kept looking out first one side and then the other. The flak had ceased but some of the aircraft were still wallowing. They would heave a bit, correct a bit, skid in or out, then steady. I could feel the pilots struggling. Perhaps they'd had enough at 'twitter stations' today. I know I had. It was after landing, that the reason for the wallowing became apparent. Three of the aircraft were declared totally unserviceable and the remainder all needed repairs to some larger or lesser degree. At de-briefing the standard of shooting by those flak crews at Alam El Halfa did not need to be emphasised. They certainly had something to defend and it was decided and agreed by all the navigators, who of course were the bomb aimers, that a fair assessment of the vehicle numbers was, give or take a few, about three thousand units.

Shortly after landing the wind freshened, the sand stirred, the dust quickly took to the air and within minutes our 'drome was totally clamped in. 'Stand-down' for the remaining part of the day was announced and welcomed, so we cleaned up and retired to the mess tent. The day was wearing on and we were enjoying the relaxation and talking of the battering we had just experienced and the misfortune of our friends who had not made it back.

We looked at each other in utter amazement. We could not believe what we heard, and no one spoke for a while as though to emphasize our disbelief. The scramble gong, for which was an old truck wheel denuded of tyre and hung on a gallows arrangement outside the ops tent, was vigorously being beaten by the heavy metal pinch-bar which was there just for that very purpose.

"Whoever it is bashing that thing in this grot, has got to be either an unmitigated joker or an idiot." said someone.

At ops we learned that the visibility over our last target area was still good, so we would go and give it some more treatment. Crews who were on the previous trip would be allocated new aircraft. We were to take off in tight vics of three, climb to clear air and formate en-route. It was suggested that after the trip we land at any 'drome where visibility allowed, should our own 'drome still be clamped in. It could have been said, and no doubt it was, that none of us were terribly enthusiastic about the errand.

I was second vic off and we broke to clear air at 7,000 feet, and levelled just above that brown choking dust-fog, which stretched as far as we were able to see. Unkind things were being said about Air H.Q. Ops. as we nipped along at about 250 mph above that airborne filth, under which no doubt the

Kraut would be hoping to sneak forward, unseen. I said that I hoped this crap would break soon, to give us sight of the surface, and the enemy, to make this trip worthwhile.

"It already is thinning Perc," said Joe, "could be a doddle this one."

"Message from base Perc," said Rick our wireless op, "we are recalled. Abort sortie."

There were some well-spiced comments which adequately delineated the mood. We were psyched-up for this skirmish by now and, as Joe said, 'it could be a doddle'.

Base was still firmly clamped in so we headed off for L.G.98. Here at least we could see the ground, so we reported to base and touched down. The purpose of our visit was of extreme interest to the boys in the mess, their squadron being on stand down. We were delighted to recognise some of the pilots who came forward to greet us, and they too showed pleasure in seeing us.

"Bloody keen types aren't you," said one we knew at Wadi Gazousa, "even the flies park up in this crap. Couldn't find your own strip, I know."

"Checking up on you civilised types." I countered.

There was some healthy ribaldry as we passed a couple of very pleasant hours. Base came on the air; the weather there had thinned a bit and we were to return, taking extra care on landing. We thanked the boys for their hospitality, bid them 'adios' and went to crank up. Base came on before we got airborne; we were not now to return until the following morning. It was a question of deciding whether someone knew if they were punched, bored or counter-sunk. There we were, no razor, no bed, no money and no 'all' other things you never had on your person when you set out to fly over enemy territory. The boys fixed us up with some kind of shake-down, and other items we could borrow, and we were on sympathy beer in the mess for the rest of the evening.

A knot of aircrew sitting clustered round one of the trestle tables just within the entrance of the marquee, had grown progressively noisier as the night progressed, eventually breaking into song.

> They say there's a troopship just leaving Bombay,
> Bound for 'Old Blighty' shore,
> Heavily laden with time expired men,
> Bound for the land they adore.
> There's many an airmen just finishing his time,
> There's many a runt signing on,
> You'll get no promotion this side of the ocean,
> So cheer up my lads fag 'em all."
>
> Fag 'em all, fag 'em all,
> The long and the short and the tall,
> Fag all the sergeants and W.O. ones,

> Fag all the corporals and their basket sons,
> 'Cos we're saying goodbye to them all,
> As up the CO's orifice they crawl,
> You'll get no promotion this side of the ocean,
> So cheer up my lads fag 'em all.

Weather had improved when we landed at base the following morning, but the target area was apparently clamped in so we would stand by. Meantime some of the boys went to attend to M.T. Vehicles in a clear patch, reporting good results and only mild opposition from flak. No fighters. Most encouraging.

Alam El Halfa weather was reported to be clearing. The C.O. and I would take a box of six each again to our previous point PP432-876 south of El Mireir with the hope that the battering which we experienced on the previous trip, when everybody was hit, would not be repeated. A similar barrage however awaited us once more as we approached the target. The glowing flame-balls were dead on our level just yards in front of our noses. We flew through the smoke. No one deviated, we were on our bombing run. The flak was dangerously close, we were committed to hold, the explosions shook the aircraft, and I knew it was too close to be healthy.

* * *

It was not until forty years later, when for the first time since those days, I met one of the few surviving pilots, that I made the effort to search out, at Public Records Office, what the official records of the squadron had to say about that raid and about so many others which we undertook in daylight. Some were relatively easy, but many left you with the feeling that perhaps your luck may not just stretch to many more like that. You would be shaken, of that there was no doubt, you would be soaked in perspiration from the heat of the desert sun on the cockpit combined with the concentration, nervous tension and fear, but you would have a wash down, a change of clothes, a meal, a few beers in the beer-tent, a couple of training trips with the new boys on the following day, and you were down at ops scanning through the battle order, scared in another way – that you may not be on it. Flying enemy operations was like being addicted to a drug. You were aware of the dangers involved, but they were a part of your life and you craved them. I read:

> Owing to dust storms the second sortie of the day did not take off until 1755 hrs Twelve Baltimores, target 1,000 M.T. P.P.432-876. Bombs, screamers attached, dropped 1849 hrs 3 fires started. All bombs dropped amongst enemy M.T. Extremely accurate and heavy ack-ack was encountered on the bombing run, and one of our aircraft piloted by P.W. Carruthers received a direct hit and crashed in the target area. The port engine was seen to fall away from the machine, which went straight to the ground. One member baled out. Eight other aircraft were holed but landed safely.

So, from the 24 aircraft on our last two sorties we had 21 either lost or damaged at Alam El Halfa, a casualty rate of 87½%, and three lost plus three write-offs, a loss of 25%, which must be some indication of the desperate attempt the Hun was making to crack the Allied stand, and of our resolve to prevent him from doing so.

✳ ✳ ✳

We kept on resolutely with the bombing run. The intensity of the battering did not abate. A sickening rending blast somewhere below my feet shattered the aircraft, admitting a force of air so violent that my eyelids were fluttered uncontrollably and the flesh on my cheeks and lips were rippling with the wind force. The control column, hinged at the floor between my legs, thrashed at me as though crazed. The port engine screamed then suddenly went quiet and clean fell off. Momentarily I caught sight of the formation above which I had just been leading, but they were leaving me and I was going down. I attempted to check the descent but I needed greater pressure. No one had yet come through on the intercom and I was too busy. I took my feet off the rudder bar to gain more leverage but my right leg didn't seem right for pushing although there was no pain. I was not aware it had ten shrapnel holes in it from thigh to knee. We were descending quickly. "Get out fellows. We've had it. I can do nothing with it. Get out. Get out." I remembered this situation before when Paddy was hit some weeks ago, he did not reply to me. I was not now getting any reply. They all could surely not have copped it. Could they have jumped already? No reply. Desperate moments indeed. We would soon hit the ground. I undid my harness, turned the canopy toggle and attempted to stand up, but the slipstream pinned me against the bulkhead. The force was stronger than me so for a few seconds I accepted that I was there to stay. I could not move. I found the force too great. I heaved with my good leg without success and stopped trying. I do not know what then happened to change the situation, but everything went quiet and I was falling, tumbling head over heels through the air. I felt around with my right hand for the parachute toggle. Now where could that have got to? I remember scratching the webbing hard to locate it and gave it a firm jerk. The wait seemed an age. I had in fact decided that I was going to make a deep depression in the sand when one dramatic jerk changed my fate. There, immediately below me, were the men and machines who had survived our bombs. I looked around for other 'chutes but could not see any. The formation had disappeared. I was torn with anxiety for the boys. The enemy armour and men were now only fifty feet below me, the men looking up at me eagerly.

I hit the ground and the 'chute canopy collapsed about me. Rough hands grabbed my harness and shook me violently. Something was stuck into my ribs and I was ordered to stand. My right leg would not function and I now noticed blood through my desert shorts. The thick crepe sole of my right boot was shredded by shrapnel and folded under as I dragged my leg forward. British shells were exploding at ground level, at twenty feet in the air, at fifty feet in the air, rasping deep into the eardrums. The battle was really on. I was a prisoner of war.

An extract from the London Gazette:

> THE KING has been graciously pleased to approve the following award.
>
> Royal Air Force,
>
> 546056. Flight Sergeant Percy Wilson Carruthers, of 223 Squadron.
>
> The above award is for gallantry and devotion to duty in the execution of air operations.
>
> The majority of the sorties in which this airman had participated have been unescorted raids on such targets as Benghazi harbour, and later on enemy ground troops. During these operations his flying was of an extremely high quality. His efficiency on the ground was only surpassed by his outstanding keeness to engage the enemy in the air. On one occasion after a successful night raid on Tmimi aerodrome, he arrived at base to find the landing ground completely obscured by mist. In spite of this he made a perfect landing through a break in the clouds. Later in the campaign Flight Sergeant Carruthers' aircraft was attacked and severely damaged by three enemy fighters. By means of skilful evasive action and superb airmanship he was able to make a successful crash landing, although two members of his crew were wounded. Throughout his period of service, this airman displayed the highest initiative, courage and devotion to duty.

DREAM IMBUO

Some things in life swell heart with joy
E'en just a wild daydream, as boy
With glassy eyes and far off stare
Would sit, conception all aware.
Escape to worlds of sharp desire,
Imagination strong to fire,
Where things of daily life are barred
An entry, lest the dream be marred.

The tinder dry of keen ambition,
Sparked by the flint of intuition,
With undeterred zeal and zest,
The dream, reality to quest.
The theory of aerometry,
To practice, test, to try and see,
How it did work on 'Tiger Moth'.
Eager to learn, to fail most loth.

Then six hours and half begone,
Of circuits and bumps and turnings, shone
Eyes with sapience, heart aglow,
'Twas my delight to go solo.
Surmounting tree-lined edge of field,

The urge to shout 'Yahoo', did yield
I to, and more expressive yelps,
Be heard by those in blanco belts.

The 'Oxford' twin then to aspire,
And one old 'Annie Anson', dire,
In need of reparation kind,
Did I for 'Blenheim' leave behind.
'Short Nose', spritely, three point sweep.
'Long Nose' lumbered, strained to reap,
Sufficient power the ground to leave.
Then 'Bostons', what a sweet reprieve.

Power and speed and fancy 'tryke',
An aircraft one just had to like.
But then came pencil 'Maryland'
With torque and swing, twin Wasps to hand.
Three points again, Then 'Baltimore',
Where operations saw galore,
Harsh strikes from One-O-Nines and flak,
Not always got her on the rack.

Oft she would fly with parts adrift,
But sometimes if hit in mid-rift
Would into little pieces blow,
And those inside would never know.
A short haul on the faithful 'Dak',
Which through all theatres forth and back,
Would fly, when others obsolete
Became. 'Twas slow but hard to beat.

'Mosquito', daddy of them all,
In embryo by brass hats tall,
Considered then would never be,
Of use to RAF – sadly.
It really was a Pilot's dream,
And had it first accepted been,
More tribute to de-Havilland
For helping save old Eng-a-land.

* * *

By the KING's Order the name of Warrant Officer P.W. Carruthers, Royal Air Force was published in the *London Gazette* on the 28th December 1945 as Mentioned in a Despatch for Distinguished Service.

I am charged to record his Majesty's high appreciation.

Arthur Henderson.
Secretary of State for Air.

CHAPTER 7

SCENERY CHANGE

I pulled up the right leg of my tattered shorts noting the jagged shrapnel gashes in my flesh. "How many parachutes?" I asked, with gestures. One of them understood and held up one finger. I felt utterly shattered, and they would not allow me to see the site of the crash.

From the time of landing my hopes of getting away were ever present. I was bundled into a truck and driven off with two guards. My right leg was now becoming very stiff and painful and there was also shrapnel in my left elbow causing pain with much inflammation and swelling. Something sharp irritated my right foot and I poked into the shredded crepe of the sole where the pricking was felt and extracted from there a cruel curled up piece of jagged shrapnel, absolutely razor sharp on one edge. Perhaps the sole had saved me the loss of a foot. I was to spend the next three months in hospital (Lazarette) in Athens mostly and later in Freizing near Munich, having shrapnel removed and poisons drained, much to my relief in view of the first decision by a surgeon, to amputate at the thigh.

* * *

For hours we bumped over the rough desert. Wimpeys in the darkness droned overhead a mere two hundred feet up, but could not be seen. The truck slowed to a halt when one approached.

I was so uncomfortable, and could just not get an easy place for my leg. The guards were totally uncooperative and distant.

We appeared to be heading generally north west closing with the coastline. In a shallow depression close to the coast was a collection of tents. A medium large one stood a few yards away from a very small type, into which I was bundled. The tent was completely empty but I was glad to rest, and I dug a depression for my hip but comfort avoided me. A new guard stuck his head in the tent, and said

"Sie mussen bald mit Offizier sprechen."

At least that was easily understood. I told him my leg was in bad shape and that I also needed a drink. He was not at all sympathetic and certainly not of the Arian Intelligentsia. With a wave of his hand he muttered, "Spater" and left.

I noted a rib in the tent and dug a small hole in the sand where it met the ground into which I placed the various items of my escape kit, compass, map, tablets etc, in case I was searched. I would have to take the risk of not being returned to the same tent. I had a feeling this could be Rommell's headquarters. The guard was extremely vigilant and insisted that the tent flap be laced up tightly. I tried to work at the back to raise the canvas, but the pegs were so deeply driven. I opened the flap and called him, squirming my way out, very obviously in pain, asking him for a doctor. "Halbe Stunde," he rasped, poking me back into the tent with the muzzle of his rifle.

I heard the thrash of an engine, surely a small aircraft. It was. The pilot cut the revs. I listened intently. It was slightly to the right, the engine tick over. It must be very close. The engine revved, he was taxiing. With heart thumping I forced my finger in the lace-up and got my eye to the slit. I saw it. A Fiezler Storch. The prop stopped, two figures alighted. I am sure one was Rommel. They made their way in the direction the aircraft was facing, seeming to lift their feet unnecessarily high for such a small gradient. The engine was warm, the aircraft uncomplicated. I would have it off the deck, light loaded, in fifty yards, once I found the starter. I unlaced the flap. The guard was about twenty yards to the left. I waited for him to turn away. He kicked at something in the sand, his rifle slung over his shoulder. He turned away. I squirmed out of the flap, making my own way on all fours, as it were, towards the Fiezler. I had only a further twenty yards to go and I would be hidden from his view by another tent, and I might not be missed until I was in the air. I was so excited, and in a manner a bit scared. It could only have been my trailing foot disappearing from view, that the guard saw. He came bounding over, screaming, "Halt Mensch. Zuruck." I just rolled over saying I could not wait any longer for a doctor. He may not have known I was a pilot, and so may not have suspected my intention. He was nevertheless furious, and rattled my ribs severely with the muzzle, so I slid back into the tent, deflated.

Almost immediately there was action. A truck drew up and I was driven to a field dressing station and placed at one end of a long queue filing into a marquee where anti-tetanus jabs were being dispensed. The doctor said he could not help me and that I needed hospital treatment.

I was taken to another tent where I met an English-speaking Feldwebel who had been a shipping agent in Newcastle. He searched me thoroughly and questioned me. I insisted on medical treatment and something to eat. Food was very low on their priority list.

A covered truck picked me up, in which I found some English soldiers. We were not allowed to speak or look out. Eventually the truck stopped and there we were not five yards from the loading door of a JU52. We were bundled in, made to sit on the floor, back to back, and no talking. This was surely Fuka landing ground. My word, how fortunes change. We were each given a lemon and the aircraft took off. I was as near to the front of the aircraft as was reasonably possible. If only I could get to the controls as soon as possible.

Total Allied strength on the aircraft was about twelve men. The aircraft had a crew of two plus three armed guards. The crew had holsters with side arms. All the Allied members appeared to be quite fit. I reasoned that if the twelve of them overcame the three armed guards, we could take care of the crew and I could get this crate back to L.G.86. I whispered this to the soldiers next to me, told them I could fly them to safety and to pass the word around, everyone to act when I shouted 'GO'.

The guards became very irritable, moving amongst us threatening us and forbidding any talking. I assured them we were only exchanging names and where we lived. They took an immediate and positive dislike to me, unfortunately, one of them motioning with a double handed swing towards the door, making it quite clear that if I talked again I would be on my way down, this time without a 'chute. They then moved me to the rear of the plane on my own, sat me in the middle of the floor facing the tail and hung a muzzle behind my ear.

We landed in Crete, I being taken away on my own and placed in some kind of stone-built cold store, very small, about ten feet square with stone slab shelves, the kind of place we had on the farm for curing and salting down hams and bacon sides. It could equally have been the local primitive morgue.

I was cold beyond belief. I had such pain that I will admit to having tears rolling down my cheeks. I told the guard who stood by the door of this isolated structure. I was taken to another JU52. We landed in Greece and I was taken to a Lazarette in Athens.

Soon I was in a ward with other Allied airmen, none of whom appeared to have two legs. Ginger on the right was waving a twelve inch, undressed, raw stump in the air, saying,

"They whip them off here at the slightest excuse."

He was a cockney with a great spirit and a marvellous sense of humour. Others were at various stages of recovery. It looked grim.

A doctor and a sister came to examine me, and from what was said it was clear to me that this was a surgeon and that this bluish greenish hard swollen leg was to be 'amputiert'. I was shocked and angry at such a quick and what seemed to be final decision. I shouted out quite loudly, which had the immediate effect of doubling the size of the doctor's and sister's eyes.

"Nicht amputieren! Nicht amputieren!"

Ginger said, "And you should be so lucky!"

I was taken away after injection to the theatre, and again protested before being anaesthetised.

I started to surface and remember where I was. I tried to raise my head to see how many legs I had, as I remember Ginger saying that I would not know if they had cut it off, because he could still waggle his toes on the foot that was not there. I was back in the same bed. Ginger had been watching me.

"You lucky bastard," he said, "you've still got two!"

I raised the single sheet and there I saw my damaged leg with rubber tubes sticking out of it, from knee to thigh, like skewers in meat. Into the ten shrapnel holes where he had been digging, the surgeon had inserted these tubes for draining.

My left arm was then very badly swollen. The surgeon came along to my bedside with his knife and the sister with a kidney bowl. He slit my elbow, and the relief, as the green-yellowish fluid poured out, was both immediate and amazing. I thanked them both.

The leg however actually smelled quite awful for a while, and was heavy and felt quite useless. When the six-foot orderly, Rudi, carried me out like a child to the bath, the leg would feel as though it were about to explode.

The food was terrible, mostly weak potato soup with the peel, or skins, floating on top. They never added meat or carrots or any other vegetable, and we were convinced it was made from the throw-away potato peelings only. If this were invalid rations, what could the conscientious objector expect? A bullet? A Greek decorator who was colouring the walls of the ward, aware of our plight, would plunge his hand into his bucket of colourwash, when the coast was clear, bring out tomatoes and other fruit, wash it quickly under the ward tap, and distribute it as quick as lightening. He even managed to pop in, at risk, long after he had finished our ward. He was wonderful. It was amazing what he had hidden in that bucket of colourwash, food he could ill afford to pass on, especially that his own life would be gravely at risk if his action were discovered.

After about eight weeks I was placed on a Lazarette JU52 fitted with three-tier bunks, and flown to Bari in southern Italy. There I was placed on a Lazarette train, similarly fitted with bunks, making the journey through the Brenner Pass to Munich. A short journey then to the hospital at Freizing, which was largely occupied by prisoners of war, many of whom were extremely irritating Frenchmen. Diet was, the same type of potato soup, with a slice of very rough bread, which seemed to contain a very generous amount of sawdust, and mint-tea. There was nothing to read except outdated German newspapers and magazines, but it was a wonderful opportunity to sharpen up my knowledge of German, which I could see would be extremely useful. I badly needed an English/German dictionary, which I was quite unable to obtain for many months.

It was now three months since I was captured and, with some difficulty, was able to walk again. I badly needed some clothing, it was now winter and I only possessed desert shorts and shirt.

I was moved to Mooseburg POW Camp 7a, a few miles out of Munich. That was truly a terrible place. Food was so very scarce and poor accommodation was in bare wooden huts, cold, draughty and depressing. Beyond the barbed wire fence was a Russian compound, the fence being lined all day long by those poor hungry miserable beings, clothed in all manner of rags and sacks, staring continuously into our compound. They had no footwear, the snow was falling

OF PLOUGHS, PLANES & PALLIASSES

I drew this cartoon in Alan Hamer's log book.

and they wrapped their feet in strips which they managed to tear from hessian sacks. They were dying in large numbers, the dead being thrown heaped up on ox carts, manned by other members of the Russian compound.

I was utterly appalled that such terrible conditions existed, and found it difficult to believe that a so-called civilized nation could stoop to treat other fellow humans with such degradation.

Soon I was taken by train, under armed guard, to Oberursal near Frankfurt-am-Main to an interrogation centre named Dulag Luft. Dulag being an abbreviation of Durchgangslager (transit camp). Here I was in a small cell with frequent visits from an interrogator, where the temperature in the cell was at times utterly freezing. I would complain and the heat would be turned on so severely that I could hardly breathe. I was advised that I only had myself to blame for the discomfort of the 'unpredictable' heating system, and that should I complete the 'Red Cross' (bogus) form and answer some simple questions, I would be moved. However should I continue to be un-cooperative, my stay in the cell could be very lengthy and uncomfortable and that the safety of my family in England could not be guaranteed when they (the Germans) marched into the British Isles.

The new insights into German behaviour nauseated me, and I was extremely glad I was born British. I was then taken to a compound where many other airmen were housed and where the place was very obviously bugged with microphones. We were aware of the location of one and used it frequently with much hilarity. Some said things like,

"Wait until these Kraut bastards find out about the new Crosse and Blackwell's super engine. That'll shake them."

There were three-tier bunks in this compound with straw palliasses, but actual cotton sheets and blankets. What luxury. In addition to all this there was reasonably good food, supplemented by food parcels sent by the Red Cross via Switzerland. Thank God for the Red Cross, it was only their food parcels which eventually saved many lives over the following two and a half years I spent in various camps or living rough or being force marched for months on end.

Then to Barth, Luft 1, Vogelsang, Stralsund by train coach – the last time we were to be treated as humans when travelling. From then on it was to be rough, bare, cold, uncomfortable cattle trucks, on occasions so crowded there was not even sufficient room for all of us to sit on the floor at any one time.

All three camps in which I was to be housed were similar in outlay and construction. All were built on sandy soil to discourage tunnelling, the light soil being prone to collapsing. Accommodation was in wooden huts erected on stilts, again to discourage tunnelling and to assist under floor inspection. Some camps were better or worse equipped than others, regarding books and opportunity for self-made entertainments, and for sport. The cookhouse and other facilities were manned by our own volunteers.

The overall camp was divided into compounds surrounded by two barbed wire fences. About ten to twelve feet distant, was a single strand of barbed wire, about three feet high, known as the warning wire, beyond which trespassers were shot. Guards patrolled outside the wire, where perimeter lights flooded the entanglements, and at intervals and on every corner were the Posten Boxes, roofed wooden towers about thirty feet high, equipped with hinged searchlights and machine guns. Guards also mingled within the compound, but were very closely watched by our security bods who happened to be on duty.

The Vorlager was a separate compound containing the German administration offices and accommodation quarters. Entry to the camp was via the Vorlager. Barth was the best of the camps in which I was housed, no doubt the better type of prison camp for initiation. Our compound was small having three huts only, with 156 men in each. A central corridor ran the full length of the hut, small rooms off to each side, containing two three-tier bed bunks. There was a space in the middle for table and chairs, and a cast iron cylindrical fuel-burning stove, for which it was a continual problem to obtain fuel. On the outer wall was a window fitted with heavily barred shutters on the outside. The toilets were in a room half way along the hut and consisted of a row of holes in a wooden construction over a cesspit which was emptied at intervals by an ingenious contraption, crudely known as the shit-cart, or as one of the members suitable described it, The sooper-dooper-schitzen-skooper. It was a very large steel cylinder on wheels drawn by oxen. A huge pipe was lowered from the cart into the cess. Some volatile fuel was poured in to a small appurtenance on the top of the cylinder and ignited. Everyone stood at a safe distance, but the oxen never showed any signs of concern. Almost immediately, one God Almighty explosion occurred, audible easily a mile away. This apparently caused quite a deep vacuum in the cylinder, and immediately the operation of quickly transferring masses of cess from the pit to the cylinder began. Amid much slurping, gushing and sucking a thousand gallons of the foul mixture nipped smartly along the pipe in a matter of seconds and if you happened to be down-wind and deaf, you would still be aware of the operation. The smell was vile. The cart would then distribute the contents, as fertilizer, over the nearby fields, so that over the following period of time we were committed to savour the aroma especially when a summer breeze was blowing on-camp.

We were reasonably well organised at Barth when a permanent Vertrauensman (senior British Representative) had been established. Tom May was, I think, the first, superceded by Jim Barnes, a stalwart New Zealander, later to become Sir James Barnes, Mayor of Dunedin.

Tom appeared not to like this, and declined to move out of Room 26 which was recognised as being the Admin Room. Jim being the gentleman we knew him to be, rode the situation with dignity and aplomb.

When we eventually left Barth I do not remember Tom and many others joining us. Those who stayed behind were reported to be forming the nucleus of the workforce for those who were to arrive. Our efficiency in organization went with us. What we did lose on leaving Barth was the direct leadership of Jim, who on arrival at Heydekrug took up deputy leader to Vic Clarke who was already there in A lager with Dixie Deans. On opening K lager, the Germans needed assistance in preparing for our arrival, and Dixie, who was Camp Leader sent Vic over to take charge of K lager. Vic was to prove a most capable man for the job, and for other not so pleasant tasks which were to follow. Jim's qualities continued to colour the scene.

Dixie was a very popular personality, remaining in that capacity until liberation. He was extremely diplomatic and could fool the Germans into thinking that they had him more on their side than we had him on ours. He could squeeze things out of the Germans which would never have come voluntarily. Everyone respected Dixie, including the captors. Many hundreds of British and Allied airmen benefitted from his efforts. Like most POW activators he spoke German well, which was always a prime asset. Why he was awarded recognition, on our return to England, no more generous than the MBE, many of us were never able to understand.

Prisoner-of-War life brought out in many men some superlative qualities, as did operational flying. It was a challenge to 'beat the system' and to 'get one up on the enemy'. Such activities could fully absorb the energies, enthusiasm, and the arrogance of youth.

Some of the boys undertook adventures beyond what was considered reasonable provocation; what could be termed to be acts of daring or foolhardiness, where the enemy was provoked to releasing the safety catch on his rifle and engaging his trigger finger. The heat would then be taken out of the situation, and no one was hurt. Regrettably many of our boys were shot, others were shot at, and on occasions bullets whined low over our heads and splatted into the earth about our feet.

On the other hand, prisoner of war life proved to be too much for others. They would sulk and mope, they would see no hope for the future, become extremely depressed and irritable, generally not helping themselves and burdening those around them. There were cases where the nerves collapsed and sanity was forfeited. Thankfully such were in the minority. Suicides were known.

An escape committee was formed, to which all ideas on escape were submitted, and by whom all escape attempts were organised and coordinated. A great many activities were over-seen by the escape committee, which were directly or indirectly associated with escape. There were the forgers, quite expert in their field with very limited materials, who would turn out some wonderful identity documents and permits and passes (Ausweis). There were the expert tailors who, from blankets dyed with all manner of substances, would turn out a German uniform or a worker's coat and hat, to fool the most observant. There were the German-speaking members who would be responsible for 'cultivating' the guards; a terrific asset to escape activities. 'Converts' would be compromised eventually, which led to many arrangements where all manner of goods from hacksaws to electrical components would find their way into the camp. Advance information regarding searches was particularly useful, helping to protect much escape work which included actual physical tunnelling.

Look-outs were on rota, checking times of all movements of guards, so that movements could be anticipated. All movements of guards entering our compound would be made known by the declaration, "Goons up!". 'Goons' was our name for the usual German guards, and 'Ferrets' was our name for the German staff dressed in overalls who would carry out under-hut inspections, and any activity connected with tunnel investigations.

'Goon baiting' was the art of rattling the Goons, guards and ferrets alike, sometimes to the point where their tempers were stretched to breaking point and the situation began to take on a rather ugly countenance.

Some of the more bizarre incidents I think were connected with 'Appell' - the twice-daily parade where we would have to assemble in ranks, five men deep for counting. These incidents were on occasions highly amusing. Our Parade discipline was deplorable. Dress was appalling, simply because some of us did not really have any other, and because others dressed ridiculously as another form of Goon bait.

Appell was one day terribly slow to form up and German agitation was reaching the point where action was almost sure to commence. Small knots of men came shuffling lazily along. The guards who had been hounding men out of the huts looked quite distraught, fearing the parade officer should burst

There were some very daring escape attempts made...

a blood vessel. Loud drumming sounds and a clattering of cans came over the breeze from behind one of the huts, whereupon prisoners and guards alike all turned their gazes in that direction. What scene of madness were we about to witness?

Around the hut came a bizarre gaggle of Kriegies, marching in step, believe it, to the beat of the drums. This squad of broadly smiling Kriegies masquerading, unmistakably as boy scouts, with nobbly knees and long shorts, advanced upon us under the firm direction of their leader, Lord Baden Lofty Maddocks. Lofty's legs looked so long and spindly. The whole parade broke forth into a state of convulsed side-splitting laughter. Some of the Germans caught the mood and smiled weakly at this ridiculous cocophany, others grabbed their rifles in the on-guard position and moved towards the entertainers. Von Muller, in charge of the parade, who was perhaps one of the less repulsive types of German we met, smiled and excused the interruption.

During our Kriegsgefangenenschaft it was necessary on occasions to cover up on Appell for missing Kriegies. Perhaps they had escaped or were hiding up to escape, or a snap Appell had been called and some were still down a tunnel, and of course obliged to stay there.

The sick were a useful means of cover-up. They would be allowed to stay in their bunks in the huts and counted there. Some of the sick were of course stuffed dummies with their faces to the wooden partition. In one case a trap door was discreetly cut in the wooden partition so that the Kriegie could be counted in one room and before the guard arrived in the next room, the Kriegie had nipped through the trap door to be counted again on the other side. This was apt to go wrong however if the guard approached from the wrong direction. Then would come a recount, both inside and out, perhaps a double count where one guard would follow another round the huts, both counting. Outside there would be two in front of the parade and two at the rear. They would all keep their totals to themselves until they stood stiffly to attention in front of the officer. They would then smartly step forward one by one and declare their totals. The officer would write them down and do his arithmetic. He would perhaps check his totals again, time after time, the guards becoming increasingly anxious. At times he would erupt in the familiar violent manner, when much screaming would take place. Faces would turn red, veins would become prominent, spit would start to fly, guards would be recalled to a heel-clicking halt before the officer, figures would not tally, and at times even face slapping took place in front of the parade. Our Camp Leader would intervene and would assure them that no one was missing. The counting would probably take place all over again and would perhaps confirm that no-one was missing, in fact perhaps they now had two too many. They would give up in sheer desperation and we would be dismissed. Being counted in parade in one position was possible, then in a crouched attitude one could nip along between the rows and appear upright further along to be counted again.

Red Cross parcels were in reasonably good supply at Barth, which supplemented the meagre German rations, so that it could be said that for POWs we ate, at Barth, fairly well.

The camp was large enough to permit space for a rugby-cum-soccer pitch, and a league was drawn up. Johnnie Griffiths would draw up the fixture lists, neatly prepared and displayed. With the compliments of Bill Higgs, I still have a copy. There were some extremely hotly contested matches at Barth, with much loud barracking and shouts of, "Hang him on the wire!"

We were also favoured with numerous energetic theatre enthusiasts. Fred Cullen and Frankie Taylor I well remember producing. Bob Bell and Harry Leary and others, knocking up scenery out of Red Cross boxes. There were so many others, too numerous to mention, whose ingenuity, acquisition and improvisation were stretched beyond what could have been believed possible. Both Kriegies and Captors reaped the benefit of their dedicated fanaticism. Morale was boosted beyond limits undreamt of and was a sterling example of the tenacious will of all the workers contributing. *The Man Who Came to Dinner*, was one I particularly enjoyed. G. Douglas took part in that and was later, sadly shot dead by attacking aircraft. *The Wind and the Rain*; *Love From A Stranger*; *Dover Road*; *The Rotters*; *Hellsapoppin*; *Symphony in Sea*; *Cameolette*; *Love in a Mist*; *The Ringer*; *Boy Meets Girl*; *George and Margaret*; *Honeymoon Hotel*; *French Without Tears*; and *Death of a Salesman*, are those which most easily come to mind.

The football pitch at Barth.

Tunnel activities were continuous at Barth, radiating around the compass, and well organised. The Germans fitted seismographs around the perimeter, buried in the ground, beyond the warning wire. I do not think that they entirely trusted that arrangement and suspected we were still tunnelling somewhere without our vibrations being registered on their machine.

One day we were amazed to see a huge tractor-like machine enter the compound and commence to slowly follow our well trodden path round the camp, the 'Circuit', our exercise track. There were cheers and much ribaldry, and many not too kind RAFisms expostulated. The Germans, generally, could never understand the British cheering like mad when some incident occurred which was much against our own interests. They surely thought we were quite mad. Boys stopped bashing the circuit, bodies appeared at doors and windows to witness the spectacle which came literally within minutes. The surface supporting the machine at one point, surrendered. The tunnel, because of the light sandy nature of the soil, had collapsed under the weight of the machine.

More and louder cheers rose from the compound as the huge machine took up an entirely unfamiliar angle of repose. It seemed that either the Germans had lost a machine or we had won one. If they could not move it then they had better guard it well, because I am sure we had enough expertise in our midst to employ it well to rip a hole in the fence.

The Germans were thrilled to have collapsed our tunnel, but their worries as to how to straighten up this drunken monster were only beginning.

Bill Baird attempted a somewhat daring escape by having himself concealed in a container which was to be removed from the compound. Timing was not to Bill's advantage, and besides being wracked with pain packed into such a restrictive space, into which no human was designed to fit, Bill was well on the way to suffocation by the time he was extracted. In fact, had Bill not been quite the physical specimen he was, the odds are he would not have survived the experience. He didn't do it again.

There were some very daring escape attempts made. Some of which demanded a great deal of courage in the face of rifles, machine guns and dogs. Some attempts were preceded by a very great deal of work. In some cases, twelve months and often more, concentrated study, and verbal practice, of the German language. This really was of immense value. Vigilance too over a long period of time, which is the basis of all freedom, was practised regularly and consistently. There was an awful lot of expert work on the false documents, the clothing to be prepared and concealed, detailed maps to be acquired and copied, train times to be noted, currency to be obtained and a host of other essential matters to attend to. Grimson's spectacular and daring escape in the disguise of a German electrician fixing the perimeter lights, fell into the category of an expert exercise. In contrast we had the Jack Axford skirmish, where no planning whatsoever was done, but the opportunity was firmly grabbed with courage and Jack got clean away from the camp. It took place immediately after a whole day search, where

KNOCK-OUT COMPETITION!

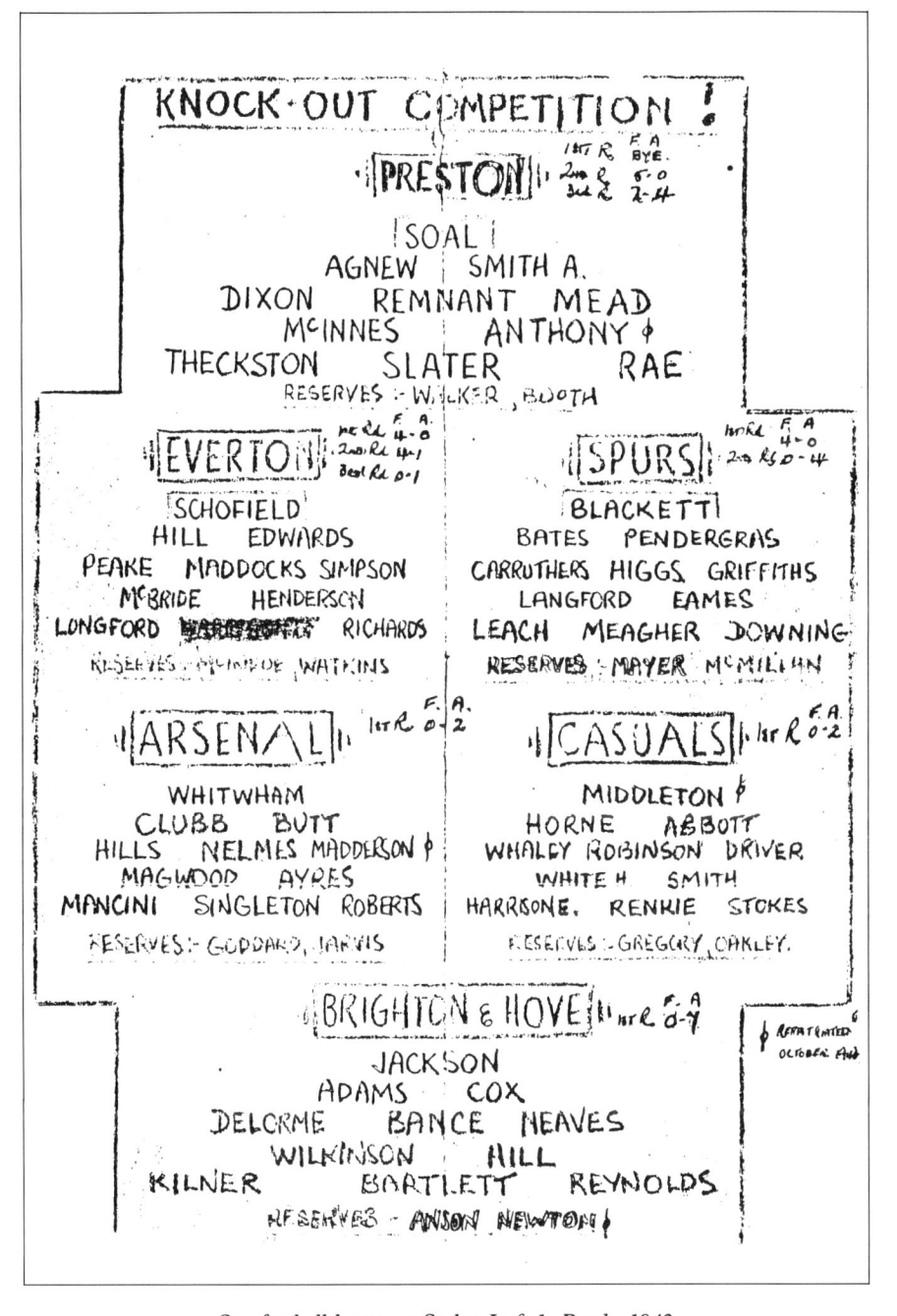

PRESTON 1st R. BYE. 2nd R. 5-0. 3rd R. 2-4.

SOAL
AGNEW   SMITH A.
DIXON   REMNANT   MEAD
McINNES   ANTHONY
THECKSTON   SLATER   RAE
RESERVES :- WALKER, BOOTH

EVERTON 1st R. 4-0. 2nd R. 4-1. Semi R. 0-1.

SCHOFIELD
HILL   EDWARDS
PEAKE   MADDOCKS   SIMPSON
McBRIDE   HENDERSON
LONGFORD   ~~~~   RICHARDS
RESERVES :- MUNROE, WATKINS

SPURS 1st R. 4-0. 2nd R. 0-4.

BLACKETT
BATES   PENDERGRAS
CARRUTHERS   HIGGS   GRIFFITHS
LANGFORD   EAMES
LEACH   MEAGHER   DOWNING
RESERVES :- MAYER, McMILLAN

ARSENAL 1st R. 0-2.

WHITWHAM
CLUBB   BUTT
HILLS   NELMES   MADDERSON
MAGWOOD   AYRES
MANCINI   SINGLETON   ROBERTS
RESERVES :- GODDARD, JARVIS

CASUALS 1st R. 0-2.

MIDDLETON
HORNE   ABBOTT
WHALEY   ROBINSON   DRIVER
WHITE H.   SMITH
HARRGONE.   RENNIE   STOKES
RESERVES :- GREGORY, OAKLEY.

BRIGHTON & HOVE 1st R. 0-7.

JACKSON
ADAMS   COX
DELORME   BANCE   NEAVES
WILKINSON   HILL
KILNER   BARTLETT   REYNOLDS
RESERVES :- ANSON, NEWTON

REPATRIATED OCTOBER 1943

Our football league at Stalag Luft 1, Barth, 1942.

Two cartoons by J. W. Barnett – a talented artist.

we had been herded into the other compound and kept there for hours. The authority to return to our own compound was given, and a knot of us headed the mad scramble, we were in fact running quite quickly, Charlie Harrison and myself amongst others, were only yards behind Jack Axford. Jack was vigorously leading the van and sped straight through the door of the hut, re-appearing within seconds with a sort of over-night bag, and headed straight for the wire in the far corner of the compound, immediately below the guard's gun tower. We had arrived back in our compound before the guards had been able to take up their positions in the gun towers and man the machine guns. Jack was up that wire in a flash, and scaled it as though he were a stick insect negotiating a bunch of twigs. It must be appreciated that the interwoven barbed wire fence was about eleven feet high, and a similar fence about ten feet on formed the enclosure wherein large coils of wire were arranged to make a very formidable obstacle. If Jack had seriously torn his hands, feet, legs and arms one would not have been the least surprised. He sped away with great agility towards the woods beyond the clearing. Charlie Harrison called loudly to him that he had been seen by some civilians who walked by the creek, but Jack was only intent in concealing his torso from view by getting into that wood as quickly as ever possible. The cry however was out, and Jack was back inside the 'cooler' within a few days.

I had been brushing up on German each and every day for months, plus gaining lots of conversational practice by conversing with the goons who came into the compound. The three months in hospital had already given me some valuable conversational practice.

Two others and myself would try a wire cutting job from the far compound to the Vorlager. We waited ages for the right conditions. We needed a very dark, windy and wet night. It arrived and we let ourselves down to earth through a trap door. The boys above replaced the trap door and would monitor our progress either by visual sight, so long as that were possible, or by searchlight or guard activity. It is amazing the degree of tension one experiences during such an exercise. It was similar to the run-up on a bombing trip. We squirmed our way, on our stomachs to the first wire fence. It was pelting with rain and the searchlights were particularly active. My heart, I am sure, stopped a few times as the searchlights hesitated as though they had found us, and one almost expected a spurt of soil to flick up into the eyes from a near miss bullet. No voices came however, and no shots, and the light moved on. My heart started to beat again, but it was so loud, pressed hard against the earth, I felt sure the seismograph would pick it up.

I cut the wires of the first single stranded woven fence with the wire clippers supplied by the Escape Committee. The snip as the cutting edge snapped through the wire was like a rifle shot to our over-acute hearing and we kept watch for the patrolling sentry. There were no loose patrolling sniffing dogs, but there appeared a dog patrol sentry not twenty yards to my left front. I dare hardly breathe, but I found I must. The dog had nose in air, searching for a scent. He would not go away. This was the end of his patrol stretch, he had a hundred yards the other way to go, and we would be through. The wind direction, I so well remember, was favourable, all we had to do was get through this particular wire and the next obstacle, a dozen feet away, and walk with heads down against the wind, to freedom, perhaps.

That sentry would not just simply turn left to face into wind and rain, to walk the other way. He played with his torch, he talked to his dog, he kept pulling up his collar, stamping his feet and driving us mad. I was confident the dog was not going to pick up our scent, but I either thought it discreet not to do any further wire cutting because of the noise it made, or I did not have the courage to do so.

Time wore on. We were so very wet, and the light would be filtering through exposing us to the sentries in their elevated posten boxes. We either chickened out or wisely chose to return another day. Reluctantly, and yet in a way gladly, we wriggled our way back over the sixty yards to the hut, cursing what we thought was pure bad luck. I had felt so confident of making good progress once we were away. One of the new guards to whom I had recently spoken had boosted my ego somewhat when he asked me how it came that I had a south German accent. I wasn't aware that I had, but perhaps I had picked it up whilst in the Freizing Lazarette.

I favoured escaping by any other method in preference to tunnelling. I did not really like tunnelling, it was a hard gruelling undertaking with not a good success rate, but at least we felt we were doing something towards escape and no doubt it was a form of mass goon-baiting. Psychologically we came out on the top side.

For a relatively short quick-build tunnel, the minimum of soil was extracted, firstly to reduce the amount for dispersal, which was usually carried out by the circuit bashers dribbling the sandy soil from some point in their clothing, and secondly to discourage collapse of the tunnel which was not uncommon. It would also avoid the use of shoring-up materials. This of course made for extremely uncomfortable working in a very confined space. Wriggling flat on ones stomach was the only means of movement. Crawling on knees was not possible, the tunnel was too shallow. As the tunnel lengthened more men were needed down there, head to feet, to pass the excavations back to the entrance. At first it was terribly cold and there was no means of altering position for comfort. The air became unbelievably foul and it was black dark except for a slight glimmer (if you were near the head of the tunnel) from the Kraut margarine lamp with the pyjama-cord wick.

The smell was nauseating and I was almost glad when the air in the tunnel became so foul that there was not enough to keep the flame alight. I preferred the ensuing headache which was usually a splitter. How Ed Corcoran and the rest of the face diggers up front stood up to the torture I do not quite know. One great spin-off from tunnelling was the sheer ecstasy of surfacing after a few hours down below. The light was fantastic with its blinding brilliance, the air was so sweet and pure one wished one had the lungs of an elephant to gulp more down.

Surprisingly as I sit here writing I have just received a letter from Bill Higgs, quite unsolicited, which in one part reads:

> ...one of the very short tunnels we used to dig down below the hut at Barth, in which we lived, I was digging with Wally Oakley. We were sitting with our backs to the hut one day, in our cut down long-johns, minding our own business, when Wally suggested starting to build another tunnel. We dived under the hut, along the doggie channels, and commenced to dig. It was one of those crazy spur-of-the-moment, browned off-efforts; cheesed-off with waiting, and for Christ's sake let's-do-something holes. Wally had dug about three feet when a voice from the rear said, "Come on out George". I thought it was one of those bloody nosey not-with-it Kriegies who couldn't keep out of it, so, without even looking around I said, "Shut up you clot, do you want the bloody goons to hear us?"
> The voice came again. "Come out here with your friends and put up your hands"
> I looked round, right up the wrong end of a rifle, with two very large angry German eyes on the other end, and his hands were shaking very nervously.

"Goons up, Wally", shouted Bill. Wally disappeared. Bill shuffled backwards catching his legs and arms on every protrusion under the hut, whilst the goon was yelling that he would shoot the nearest man if everyone did not come out. Bill was then marched, in his cut-down long-johns, with a gun in his ribs, round the block, the onlookers shouting, "Where you going Shiner?", whilst the Theckston crowd were singing, "Me and my shadow".

Straight into the cooler went Bill. Within minutes, from a swinging piece of string from the next cell window, with some difficulty, he had been able to catch a fag, a match and the side of a safety match box. John Eldridge was in the next cell. Von Muller would not believe Bill that he was under the hut looking for a ball, so gave him seven days in the cooler just to keep him out of mischief. On the recommendation of John, Bill collected all the dust and fluff possible from the cell floor, made it into a sort of pellet and jammed it into the peep-hole in the cell door. The guard thought he had lost Bill, so soon, and almost threw a goon-type hysteric, coming crashing through the door like a whirlwind, shouting and screaming "Verboten!". Walley reminded me that no one was aware that, at the time they were sitting with their backs to the hut that day, that he was already sitting on a hole where a tunnel had collapsed and he was hiding it with his bottom as repairs proceeded below.

Building of larger tunnels was much more acceptable. There was an air pump which we took turns to operate. A kit bag suitably fitted with a flap valve, being compressed horizontally in a wooden sliding frame arrangement, pushing air down along the Klim-tin-pipe-line, into the tunnel.

Bed boards were forefeited to shore up the tunnels to prevent collapse. The collapse was then transferred to the barrack.

At one time our Red Cross food which came in tins mostly, was emptied from the tins before distribution, so that we could not have the tins to assist our escape efforts. It proved to be a most unsatisfactory arrangement.

In the larger tunnels one also had a trolley arrangement for transporting the excavations back to the entrance. Shoring up was also common, and necessary, where every Kriegie had to forfeit a bed board towards the effort. This at one time was quite beyond the bounds of reason, and instead of having a continuous base to our beds of some twelve boards. Some of us were down to five, and it was a problem keeping these boards a suitable distance apart to support your palliasse and your body. To fall through the bottom of your bunk was certainly not an uncommon event, and if you were top bunk men it usually meant dire trouble for those below.

Tunnelling certainly kept the Gerries on their toes and indeed worried them a very great deal. The cooler was continually full of Kriegies being punished for their escape attempts.

With our fairly regular supply of Red Cross food parcels at Barth, our diet for Prisoner of War standards was good. Not only did we eat reasonably well, on occasions we drank rather well too. From the Germans now and then we would receive an issue of "Gerry Jam". The call would echo round the huts and the corridors, "Bowls for Gerry Jam". It was really quite a repulsive reddish brown concoction, of flavourings, colouring, turnips, crushed seeds, mangol wurzels and other questionables. When mixed however with raisins from the Red Cross parcels and encouraged to ferment it did produce a brew so lethal that it paralyzed your brain long before you were able to decide what it was you were supposed to be celebrating. One of our most difficult tasks was concealing the fermentations from the Goons. We had them hidden in the rafters and all manner of places. Even those in the rafters were on occasions uncovered much to our chagrin. To ensure the Goons did not partake thereof we would then be all too anxious to contaminate the concoction with some unpleasant additive, or ensure that it was somehow upset.

Barth being a Luftwaffe administered camp, was to house Allied airmen only, who were not allowed outside the wire for work parties as were the army. We did however have a few odd army bods with us, there being no known reason why, except perhaps some may have been connected with airborne troops. One was Bance, or Burglar Bill as we knew him. Another was Anson, known to us obviously as "Avro", from the old aircraft. He was at one time recognised as the camp barber; The Demon. Another was the unforgettable Bob Waddy, a Canadian of whom alone a book could be written.

Many of the boys at Barth of course were experienced escapers from other camps. Frankie Taylor and Jack Laing had escaped in Sudetenland in August 1942. They had changed identities with two army prisoners, L/C Bill Cochrane and L/C Howard, managing to get out on a working party to an *Eisen Grube* (iron ore mine), from which they crept away in the dark. They had covered over 150 miles in ten days, reaching Blansko in Moravia. Dreadful weather beat them, forcing them to take to the roads eventually.

Cec Room and Vic had fled a prison in Oslo picking up a Norwegian who soon linked them up with the Resistance. They had been guided to within 300 yards of the border to freedom. In that short distance Vic stumbled on a tent, actually stepping on the head of a German border guard. For their trouble, Cec and Vic were tied to a tree for the remaining hours of darkness. "Christ, it was cold," remembers Cec.

Jack Garland from Australia, Judy to his friends, was the first of 52 members of the 51st Highlanders, mostly Welsh miners, to escape from a tunnel at Molsdorf, which spewed out into a Thuringen ditch. From this attempt, Jack Hinton, VC (NZ), and his English soldier friend got through France to the Spanish border where the train they had jumped was involved in a collision. The two escapers were knocked unconscious and thereby ends their story.

Doug Grundy; Paul Winfield; Perry Magwood; Vince Mancini; Des Grealy; Don Goddard; Jimmy Walker; Wally Oakley; Alan Schofield; Jeff Longford; and Geoff Neeves, from Stalag V11.A. Munich, were all previous active escapers. Geoff recalls an escapade from V11.A of Doug and Paul. Pre-war Doug's Dad had business connections with a family in Germany, who used to invite Doug over for school holidays. Hence Doug's mastery of the Deutsche lingo.

Doug and Paul escaped with civvy suits and smakaroos, recalled Geoff. A few railway tickets later, Doug picked up the phone on Mannheim station, just down the road from his "friends", and announced, in his very excellent German, his arrival. They were "delighted" to hear him. "If he vud vait am ende der nummer vier platform, nach zirty minuten, vud they him come up to pick". Geoff remembers, there stood Doug and Paul in their best "Hepworth's", like ducks dressed for the kill. Later when they came out of the cooler at V11.A., no one was surprised to learn that in exactly zirty minuten, four well dressed gentlemen in long leather coats and well gloved hands showed up to see them on their way from whence they came. It only proved to Doug, that any friend is better than a German one.

Geoff also recalled how at V11.A. he started in bewilderment when he received some mail from a bogus aunt in Britain. Geoff was accused of hogging the mail van, but in fact to him the mail did not mean a thing. He merely handed it over to our top barrack boys for de-coding. Much information passed both ways between the RAF and Kriegies, much of it of vital importance and certainly all of it of great importance.

At Barth we had Dave Yardley from Little Sutton, who left a Lanc at twenty thousand feet without a parachute. Apart from masses of scar tissue, Dave was relatively unharmed. The terminal velocity of a free falling body is quickly diminished when clean stripping branches from closely growing pines and then bouncing on a two foot thick carpet of spent pine needles.

"Anyway," quoth Dave, "only cissies wear 'chutes".

Burwell dropped from thousands of feet also without a 'chute. He survived the unbelievable experience by waking up buried very deeply in a massive snowdrift. Der Adler, a German newspaper, reported one airman being found at daybreak, being suspended from the tallest chimney lightning conductor in the Rhur, by his parachute harness. His hair turned really grey practically overnight. He joined us at Barth. Rhys Roberts, who was on the same squadron as myself, was so badly burned that he was unable to close his eyes for two years. He was thankfully, repatriated. We had many other stories of strange and almost unbelievable events, which only airmen would believe.

I returned to following my usual physical fitness activities, once my shot-up leg was well enough and I encouraged many others who joined what turned out to be a series of regular very popular P.T. classes. The standard of physical fitness played a great part, for us as prisoners of war, in the six hundred miles march which was later to follow, towards our eventual survival.

Geoff was surprised, on arriving at Barth, to learn that tunnelling was 'nationalised', but it was not long before he was at it again in full swing. One of the tunnels collapsed at one particular point, so Geoff and Alan Schofield would go down below to effect repairs, by shoring it up. Vigilance was the other side this time however, and they were joined, down under, by a real live German 'ferret' and his real live Alsatian dog which was quite expert at making you believe that you wished you hadn't started this particular game. They both got fourteen days solitary, just to show there was no ill feeling.

Frankie Taylor, Somerville and Croft were going well with their tunnel, when the goons collapsed it, but no one fell victim to the cooler on that occasion.

Bill Higgs remembered the tunnel from the centre hut dug by Dusty Miller, Al Hayward, Ginger, the two Kiwi brothers George and Spike, when they got as far as the wire and then the seismograph picked them up. They were hopping mad, they really thought they had cracked it.

Pete Buttigieg, of Maltese extraction, was an avid escape artist. Von Muller dubbed him "The Maltese Eagle". He, Bill Higgs, Wendel Wilkins, and Dusty Miller worked hard on the cookhouse tunnel and were within feet of success when immediate evacuation of the camp was announced. The tunnel was within three feet of completion when an exit across the spare compound was to be made, then under the gate where the recently passing lorries had created two very deep ruts, then across the clearing to the creek where a convenient boat, with the bow pointing towards Sweden, would await their arrival.

Dusty and Pete would hide up in the blunt end of the tunnel whilst everyone else made their way to the camps anew. It was generally thought that they were shopped by some muddlesome Froggies. Pete and Dusty were tucked up nicely ready to dispose of the last three feet of earth separating them from freedom, when they were joined by the Chief Ferret and his snarling Alsation, in reverse order.

Desert scenes with fury raged,
Whilst Feint and bluff their part did play,
When Aussies and Kiwis boldly waged,
Destruction in the north each day.

At times, the front so quickly changed,
With parry and thrust the Hun would aim,
A weakness find in front, and ranged,
First north then south, in strength he came.

Round allied airstrips seldom did
Sand settle from a take off run,
Than aircraft from a previous bid,
Came into land, from striking Hun.

The air, electric felt with need
To pull out every stop we had,
Pilots and aircrews would not heed,
The strain of battle, flew like mad.

Ground staff round the clock did slave,
Willing and eager planes to keep
In order good, that they may save
Them standing there, success did reap.

Losses high did take a toll
Of planes and aircrew, as we pressed
The Hun, to stem and battle hold,
No time to waste, and little rest.

A thrust to east and swing to north
To Alam Halfa surged the Kraut,
Where major battle meant for both,
A turning point – advance or out.

Had Alam Halfa never been,
No Alamein would ever know,
Advance of Allied forces, clean
Through German lines, or winning blow.

This was the pivot of the war,
The Middle East for us to save,
And all of which followed proved for sure,
That Alam saved us from the grave.

We'd been o'er Alam to clout the Kraut,
Two or three times a day no less,
And marvelled he'd not taken rout,
From weight of bombs and shell to rest.

Again the Alam ridge we find,
In furious battle locked, as if
Survivors would be rendered blind
By blasts, as smoke and sand did drift.

Bombs bursting on the target there,
Great billowing plumes of sand did throw,
And giant mushrooms climbed the air,
To cover all beneath like snow.

The Flak came up ahead, in close,
More thick and accurate than before,
In quick succession blasts now rose,
With sinister threat, now more and more.

Cor. Why just there? Blast, fire and curse,
Where stark explosion rent the air,
A shattering, sickening, shaking burst,
Had caught us there, full fair and square.

Through gaping floor wind whistled free,
With objects flying here and there,
On looking down I could not see,
My eyelids wind did shake and tear.

My right leg numbed up from the knee,
And Johnnie's dead-pan face I saw
In aircraft no. 2 on me,
As slid we off to side and low.

From intercom not one small cough,
What had of crew through this become?,
From each the other was cut off,
Then nought to help could there be done.

Vibration beyond strength to stop,
Controls were crazed with shaking stick,
The descent quick one could not stop,
And ground was coming up so quick.

Right desert boot flapped in the air,
The crepe sole sliced clean through by shell,
Nose heavy trim was out of care,
I hoped the boys had left this hell.

Clean from the plane port engine came,
There was not now a hope to gain,
Thank God that there had been no flame,
Which oft occurred when mortal slain.

No news from intercom again,
Chop surely had they all not got,
They must be out and floating down,
If in I stayed I'd get my lot.

'Twas certain curtains, gone our luck,
The canopy toggle turned I full,
The lid shot off, I harness struck,
My left leg on to seat I'd pull.

My right leg must have helped support
My body as I stood full tall,
In slipstream was I firmly caught
Which pinned me to the bulkhead wall.

A flash of thought, this is despair,
As maximum effort seemed so weak,
And eyelids battered by the air,
No sight allowed. Then came the freak.

Some unknown force shot me o'er the tail,
For tumbling through the air was I
Head over heels, limbs all aflail,
Then saw first ground, horizon, sky.

Parachute toggle pulled I clean,
The following seconds seemed an age,
As though the thing had useless been,
And spun I on, it seemed so strange.

Astonished I, no ground hit me,
But violent jerk changed thoughts a bit,
And pendulum swing 'neath canopy,
Attempted I to stop forthwith.

I looked around for other 'chutes,
And thought I'd see them close around,
But all in vain my searching looks,
They must be down, I thought, on ground.

Below I saw but enemy troops,
And armour placed around the ridge,
No canopies white could I make out,
As down I came across Hun's bridge.

Allied shells were bursting there,
Some men looked up as down I came,
In seconds was I in their care,
And roughly handle was their game.

I asked where other 'chutes came down,
But soldier said, "Bloss ein heraus"
It saddened me, had they been hit,
Unable then to wriggle out?

With half a right boot and aching limb,
I was then dragged from Parachute,
And deafening bursts as shells did skim,
Above. Nought here remaining mute.

Into a bivvy I was rushed,
Where in the sand my aids I hid,
Compass and map and tablets pushed,
I in tin box and clamped on lid.

The sentry, rifle pushed in tent,
"Mit Offizier sofort sprechen",
Then Hauptmann anxious for me sent,
"How many Baltimore squadron?"

"Enough your forces here to rent,"
Said I, as searched he through my clothes,
But found he nil, they were in tent,
I hoped I'd there return once more.

His questions I edged round, until
He said, perhaps I'd later say,
A Fiezler Storch came over hill,
And dropped not forty yards away.

Pilot climbed out, went into tent,
I'd pinch that thing with slightest chance,
That rifle must I grab to rent,
That little crate, and off I'd dance.

But on the sand was forced to sit,
With rifle close to back of neck,
And leg was really not so fit,
I'd really welcome medic check.

I motioned to my swelling pin,
Punctured by shrapnel here and there,
The guard said truck would shortly bring
Me to a medic tent somewhere.

An anti-tet jab did I get,
Then off in truck was driven I,
Through darkness, long and bumping trek,
With Wimpeys stooging low nearby.

At dawn to Junkers fifty-two,
Was I transferred, with seven more,
But this one must I certain woo,
So well up front my way I'd go.

Guards did not like this, not at all,
Half way down and face the tail,
And speak no word, or turn or call,
I was a well attended male.

At Crete for pain I could not sleep,
So to field Lazarette go I,
Artz shook his head, back into 'jeep',
Then once more off again we'd fly.

To Athens Lazarette came we,
Where Artz examined leg and said,
"Wahrscheinlich amputieren," – Gee,
I had not thought of losing leg.

I called aloud at news from Kraut,
"No way could I agree to that,"
And said, "Just cut the shrapnel out,"
"I'll take my luck as desert rat."

Left elbow swollen, could not bend,
Said Artz, "Er braucht ein kleinen schlitz,"
With metal dish did 'sister' tend,
He sliced it open, two quick flicks.

Out poured greenish yellow puss,
It felt much better very quick,
With leg, I hoped as little fuss,
But there we'd need nick after nick.

Off to a ward, 'Pre-ops' to make,
Where there I met two pilots, who
Had legs of different lengths, like steak,
Who said "You're lucky to keep two."

"They whip them off here by the score,"
Said Ginger, who his left had lost,
I told him I'd complained real sore,
'Cause Artz had said a leg t'would cost.

On coming round after the 'Op',
Ginger called me, "Lucky you,"
Said he, "This time you came out top,"
"You lucky dog, you've still got two."

From holes in leg, drain tubes poked out,
It was a satisfying sight,
I thought the Artz a quite good Kraut,
And thanked him later on that night.

In days to come the flesh did stink,
Amazing how it mended up,
And ten weeks on 'twas in the pink,
Some weight it bore when standing up.

Through Italy by 'wounded train',
To Freizing Lazarette came I,
Close by was Munich, and the frame,
Of Mooseburg Lager, came to eye.

So here was what I'd never dreamed,
Captive of Hun was I to stay,
But take life then to me it seemed,
Day by day, the game to play.

A compound there with Russians many,
Crowded in beyond belief,
But food for them there was not any,
'cept weak potato peelings soup.

Starving they were, there was no doubt,
Their clothing tattered, thin and scarce,
Their feet they wrapped in dirty clout,
And stared thro' wire with haunting glares.

This was an insight to the fate,
Of allies fortune less than we,
Death in their ranks had higher rate,
Than ever we had thought we'd see.

Heaped up on carts the dead did go,
Obnoxious drill; each day the same.
To us it seemed appalling, though,
To poor Russians it was tame.

The folks at home could never grasp
The awful facts we witnessed near,
Where human dignity bounds were passed
Beyond belief of English here.

Hospital food was rough and poor,
Potato skins and sauerkraut.
We could not live that was for sure,
Unless Red Cross could help us out.

And Lager food was poor and spare,
Eight men to share a loaf per day,
And three boiled spuds in skins, to share,
Was all we had throughout our stay.

Our lot would much more serious been,
Had not the army of Red Cross
Sent parcels filled with milk to beans,
And many lives were saved from loss.

Then off to Allied airman's camp.
Three months had I already spent
Away from Rommell and Lili's lamp,
I'd choose the desert and my tent.

In desert shorts and jacket bush,
With bandages and limping leg,
I came with guards to Dulag Luft,
With better food and three-tier bed.

But first, in small unfriendly cell,
Where first I froze, then cooked with heat,
When threats were made my folks to beat,
If I did not cooperate.

"You havn't cracked old England yet,"
Did they, with anger, hear me say,
Then two weeks on the scene was set,
A further journey, – on our way.

Barth, in Stralsund, Vogelsang,
Stalag Luft 1 where there we met
Aircrews who formed a stronger band
Than anywhere we'd ever get.

This was the start of camp life proper
Where we would organise and plan,
Our plans did oft times fall a cropper,
But kept Huns busy to a man.

· CHAPTER 8 ·

ESCAPE

It was now November 1943, when about one thousand of us left Barth for Luft VI, Heydekrug, Königsberg, East Prussia. It was really just within the Lithuanian border, a railway journey of about 600 miles. This really was the beginning of the rot. The train conditions were appalling. Our boots, belts and braces were taken from us as we boarded. We were crowded into enclosed cattle trucks without food or water, and the only sanitation was a large oil drum, free-standing at the centre of the truck, which swilled the ever-increasing foul contents back and forth for the whole journey – which was optimistically forecast to take only three days and nights. There were some wooden racks at one end of the truck, the other was sectioned and occupied by the machine gun carrying guards. More guards were posted outside, between the tucks on wooden platforms so that their heads were about two and a half feet above the roof level. The only ventilation was an aperture in one side of the truck well up towards roof height. It was approximately twelve inches by eighteen inches, and covered by metal bars. I well remember the little weedy Hauptman Eilers before we left Barth, squeaking on parade, "Be good boys and do not attempt to escape". What utter nonsense. To live rough after escaping was infinitely more pleasant than to endure the conditions in those foul cattle trucks.

We were being herded here for checking identities and herded there for documentation, a lengthy and tiring procedure. Then to a building with kit for the inevitable search for escape materials and other forbidden interesting items. These of course were, as ever, well secreted, the radio having been dismantled and the components well distributed. It was some of the impromptu remarks which caused the greatest amount of merriment and this time the company fell about in hysterics. The name of Ross was called. Fred Simpson recalls how George reluctantly stepped forward with his little bag of belongings.

"Hello Ross." said Hauptman (Captain) von Mueller, "What have you got in your little bag? It's almost the shape of a baby." he ventured.

"Probably is," said Ross, "wouldn't surprise me if we all had one, the way you lot keep f***ing us about..."

The place resounded with uncontrollable laughter.

We were shunted back and forth by a ham-fisted engine driver, for what seemed to be hours. First we were sent rocketing to the front of the truck, and then to the rear, stepping on other feet on route. How true that we were treated not one bit better than the animals for which the cattle trucks were designed.

Humans were visibly associated with animals, as evidenced by the notice, in French, attached to the side of every wagon. "Eight horses or forty men." Forty men may have been quite an acceptable concentration for reasonably short journeys, but our concentration was twice that recommended, and the period half a week, and as we were to learn on this and subsequent occasions, a great deal of discomfort took place, especially when illness such as dysentery, vomiting and pneumonia was rife.

Whenever the song, *You are my Sunshine* is heard by many Kriegies, sickening memories of those cattle trucks will immediately spring to mind. Being in the same truck as armed guards made it extremely difficult to saw ones way out of the truck, even though we had, by devious means, succeeded in equipping ourselves with pieces of broken-off hacksaw. The noise which the blade made on the steel bars was of course unmistakable, and secondly the movements of the person operating the saw had to be carefully screened from sight. "Sing you bastards, sing!" was a loud and long familiar cry within the confines of those hell trucks. Being shouted at the top of their voices by desperate men operating the hack saw blades, these words, directed to the remaining occupants of the truck, suggested their singing somewhat lacked in volume. To drown the noise of the saw, the singing would have to be properly organised. A 'singsong leader' would have to be appointed. It was, to say the least, extremely difficult. Some of the boys were ill, all were tired, uncomfortable, hungry, thirsty, dirty and smelly, whilst those who were reasonably well were intent on caring for their less fortunate friends. Working frantically with the hacksaw was no pleasant task. The saw bit into the flesh, eventually making the fingers sore and dirty, and numbness crept on with the constant gripping. Hence the desperate pleas, "SING YOU BASTARDS, SING!"

In the truck where Wally Oakley found himself, similar activities were taking place, except that they were sawing through the floor which was a much more difficult task.

Eric Singleton, Harry Richards and myself were intent on getting out. Also in our truck, Johnnie Theckston, Bob Waddy and Jimmy Walker were equally desperate to make a break for freedom. We took our turns to do the sawing and shouting, and when you were not sawing you were either singing or shouting. The singing had to be done with suitable facial expressions which caused an amusing problem, were you able to see the funny side of a very serious situation. Thanks to Derek Woomack, who had previously serrated a piece of metal to resemble a saw, for which we drew lots. It was my lucky day. In Soggy Norton's truck it was a guard who was leading the singing, and making music on his harmonica. Soggy so praised and encouraged him that he became quite enthusiastic. Having so distracted the guard, Soggy removed the ammunition magazine from the guard's automatic rifle, and distributed it amongst the other occupants of the truck, who accepted a few rounds each, quite gladly; all except Bob Fee, who would have nothing to do with this insanity.

As the train pulled into a country siding, to halt, Soggy disposed of the empty magazine through a ventilator hole. A perceptive guard saw the wayward component come tumbling to the ground, and threw a category one hysteric, as only Krauts know how. He clamped the other guard under immediate close arrest, and demanded the return of the ammo. To calm the demented Deutschers, a handful of ammo was handed down from the truck, counted by the Krauts and found short, which was not altogether surprising. Even had it all been there perhaps the findings would have been the same. Following many evil sounding noises, accompanied by the usual gesticulations and gymnastics, where everyone down-wind got caught up in the spray of spit, a further few rounds were handed down. With their mathematical wizardry the Huns all agreed that one round was still missing. The Feldwebel decided that he would solve the problem by carrying out a body search. Everyone would remain in the truck until it was his turn to be searched. The first man they yanked out was the wildly protesting Bob Fee, who stood there on the snow covered ground, stripped starkers whilst his clothing was subjected to a most thorough inspection. Nothing obviously came to light, whereupon the Feldwebel ordered Bob to stand feet apart, knees straight and touch his toes whilst a squirming Kraut wielded some sinister looking instrument which assisted him in inspecting Bob's tonsils from a rather unusual angle. Witnessing such indignities, Soggy said that it was quite amazing how quickly the errant round came to light and how quickly he lost the cherished friendship of Bob.

The songsters did a great job, bless 'em all, the long and the short and the tall, and I poked my head, warily out of the newly made escape hole, immediately the last bar was severed. There in the semi-darkness only two feet forward from my saucer-sized eyes were the stomach-turning jack boots of a guard standing on a platform built onto the end of the truck. The toes were pointing away from me, the only morsel of encouragement I could find to prevent me from regretting I had ever embarked on this foolhardy caper. The train was rattling along at a frightful rate of knots just then, the wind whistling around my ears, lovely and fresh and cold. As I withdrew my head once again into the truck, the miriness of the oildrum contents convinced me I would be better gone as early as practicable.

We discussed the situation. Before dropping out we would have to wait until the speed decreased and then run the risk of the guard seeing us. We would have to get out quickly one after the other to prevent dispersal as much as possible. We would have to go out feet first, and with having no eyes at that end of the body, would just have to assume that we were not about to be shot at. I would go first and if bullets started to fly, any further attempts were to be delayed for at least an hour, provided the train did not stop. If all went well on landing, I would walk in the same direction of the train, Eric and Harry were to walk in the opposite direction until we met. Bad injuries on landing were to be read as bad luck and the fit were to flee. We had no boots but each of us had concealed a pair of thin-soled leather slippers which we tied on with string. Theckston, Waddy and Walker were to be the second party out.

The train was now running on an incline and the engine was labouring somewhat, the speed was dropping to about thirty miles per hour, so I estimated, and there was lots of lovely smoke and steam pouring back along the tracks. I even felt the gritty ash from the funnel on my cheeks, and hoped the clothing of the guards would catch fire from the sparks.

I quickly started to wriggle out. The aperture was smaller than I had thought. My clothes kept catching on the newly cut edges of the iron bars. I had reasoned that if I stuck my feet out in a sitting position, my legs could dangle from the knees, close in to the side of the truck, rather than stick out into view, the other way. The track on which the train was running bordered on an embankment which sloped away. What a bit of fortune, hurry. We could not see out of the other side, there were no openings.

I dropped. The gravel crunched under me and I rolled like a bumping log down the bank, coming to a halt with my back against the fence. Not even a bit of broken skin or a twinge, and fifteen feet above me the misery train lumbered on at a steady thirty miles an hour into the darkness. The guards were silhouetted against the sky, I could see them clearly perched on their platforms, as I sat with my back towards the fence. If only I could have picked them off with a machine gun. I hoped the others had all dropped out safely. I crept along the fence towards Eric and Harry and soon heard their scuffling ahead. No one was damaged so we mounted the fence and headed off north, where we could see the outline of the edge of a wood against the sky. We would try to put as much distance as possible between the railway and ourselves before sun-up.

Generally heading north west at the time, I was hoping to get near enough to a Luftwaffe airfield, to size up the possibility of borrowing an aircraft, a Junkers 52 for example, the cockpit of which I was familiar with, having become acquainted with a captured one we had on the squadron in Egypt. Now I dreamed of belting up the runway with the throttle levers being under pressure, to clout north at fifty feet above the Baltic waves, to Sweden, a little over a hundred miles distant. I might even catch some Kraut erks running up the engines on the apron. We could immobilise them with a spare spanner and take them with us. Mutti would be surprised. Failing all this there was the possibility of linking up with the Danzig railway, some Polish resistance and a Swedish ship.

We walked as briskly as possible so that anyone seeing us would be convinced that we appeared to fully understand the mission to which we were assigned.

Although the fear of being picked up was paramount in our minds, the feeling of comparative freedom was exhilarating. We were east of Stettin, and if we could meet up with the railway line running up to the coast, we would attempt to jump a goods train from which we could survey the scene for an airfield. If we were committed to conversation, I would do the talking, Eric and Harry being limited to Ja or Nein. We would shave every day and attempt to keep up appearances.

Little did we know that Johnnie, Bob and Jimmy had been picked up the following day after leaving the train. We would send them a funny postcard with a train on it as soon as we arrived home in England. How lovely that name sounded. They had been taken all the way back to Barth, tut-tutted by Von Muller, then sent all the way back to Heydekrug. Although we were to be free for a week we arrived at Heydekrug a short head before them.

Our disappearance from the train of course had been noticed. The train was halted and everyone was ordered out for counting. I should have thought that the boys would have welcomed this treat, fresh air, an opportunity to stretch their legs, perhaps a drink of water and a face splash and some time away from that foul smelling oildrum. However, the halt grew to be a very long drawn-out affair everyone becoming exceedingly fed up with the whole exercise, the Krauts knocking the boys about a bit, so we were cursed something shocking by both airmen and Krauts alike. Apparently our captors were unable to ascertain who or how many had escaped, and became extremely upset about our disappearance. Eventually they apparently went quite bezerk. Holding up their train and causing such chaos was not at all pleasing to them so they waded into our boys with rifle butts, with much shouting and cursing, making life a lot worse than it had been in the cattle trucks. To be in a state of physical discomfort through thirst, hunger and lack of sleep, with only hard boards on which to rest, should you be able to find a space, was the case for the boys we had just left behind in

The cattle trucks on route for Heydekrug, East Prussia, 1943.

those cattle trucks. Then to be rough handled and cursed by screaming irate armed guards was most unpleasant.

We walked until dawn, and continued until we saw a farmhouse on the hill in the distance. We heard voices from a nearby clump of trees, so we took cover in behind a grassy bank and found enough coverage under which to hide. The sun came up to thaw our frozen limbs. We were very hungry and decided, that although we had not had any sleep, we would shave first and then look for food and then finally get some sleep. It was lovely shaving in the cool early morning light. A helicopter thrashed its way over the hill and the farmhouse, straight for us as though the pilot knew we were there. We automatically crouched like hunted fugitives. Having picked up a few turnips we breakfasted and turned in to rest, the helicopter circling a patch of countryside about a mile to the south. We felt quite safe so long as they did not employ dogs in the search.

I felt more comfortable travelling by dark, and decided that we travel two together with the single one at least a hundred yards behind, so that should someone approach to ask questions at least someone could make a get-away. About every ten kilometres we would vary the arrangement. We came upon another farmhouse and in the half darkness made our way over to what appeared to be a large heap of straw where we could enjoy some blissful rest. The heap, in fact, was chaff, blown out after thrashing, as we found out to our dismay as we threw ourselves upon it in careless abandon. Hell, the torture was complete. The sharp prickly chaff was in our hair, our nostrils, our mouths down our necks up our sleeves, itching enough to drive us wild, and clung to every square inch of our clothing. This was something we could have well done without.

"With our present luck, if I sneak over to the shippon to milk a cow, no doubt I'll find they're all bloody bullocks!" was my mood. We heard voices approaching and found that a bunch of Russian workers with huge wooden shovels had come to bag up some chaff. I frightened the hell out of one of them, when I told him in German that we were on the run and we needed some food quicker than possible. He dutifully returned to present us with their ration of black German bread, all nicely dusted off with best quality saw dust.

We started out once more, passing down country lanes through a thick forested area. The moon got up and helped to light our way, we needed it, and we could pick out quite clearly the tall fire outlook towers built in the clearings. At least at a push we could use one of those as a refuge, they would only be manned on the air raid siren.

We came upon a beautiful lake, peaceful in the moonlight, stripped, had a most invigorating wash down, picked our clothes as clean as we could of the chaff to finally free ourselves of this most unwelcome irritant.

Once more we set out, in greater comfort, but Eric's feet were complaining badly and threatened to intervene totally. We had already covered about sixty miles which had played havoc with our thin-soled footwear and which irritated Eric's broken and bleeding blisters to the point where we discussed leaving him.

Opinion went against this, as it would only narrow the search area for Harry and myself. We would rather carry him. We headed to a village where perhaps I could obtain some kind of material which would act as a dressing for Eric's poor old feet. There may also be some food and drink to be had. As we came closer to the village, dogs started to bark incessantly, raised voices could be heard and a large fire broke out between us and the village. Harry reminded me when I met him quite recently, how insistent I was that we give the fire a nice wide berth in case we became implicated, and that by doing so we may rid ourselves of those yapping dogs. We successfully circumnavigated the fire and cut back into the village. Out of the frying pan into the fire; there, as we turned the corner, was the local Police station. We walked firmly on, heads high. Further up the street much singing was taking place. German troops were crowded into the local tavern, the door was open and they spilled out as they sang. The local band blared out the music as though under orders to blow their trumpets as straight as a yard of beer. We kept on, and I muttered something about "Gerade Aus", (straight on) in case one of them in his inebriation approached us. Clear of them, we were almost immediately in front of 'Gestapo Headquarters'. Whatever was such a place doing in a small village such as this? The opportunity to pick up some food would have to be made quite quickly as we were fast running out of village, and we could not stay in that hive of activity. I spotted a large old hand-operated water pump in the front garden of a cottage, boldly went up the path with tin in hand, pumped it full of water midst much clanging and squeaking, drank it, refilled it for the boys when the cottage door opened and a loud German voice enquired who was there. I jumped the wall to the right and rejoined the boys who gladly drank the fresh water.

A road led off to the right, with houses on the left hand side. A large German propping up the door post with his shoulder wished us, "Guten Abend". I replied suitably as we continued further down the road only to find, within a few yards, that we were in a cul-de-sac. There was no back tracking even though the big man may not have suspected that he had just spoken to an enemy pilot, so we surmounted the wire fence ahead into a clump of trees, where the ground fell steeply away and we stumbled through the undergrowth.

Again amidst much dog barking we continued down hill in the darkness and on reaching the clearing at the bottom of the descent, found ourselves ankle deep in mud. Our luck was certainly not in. We were wet-shod, uncomfortable, hungry, tired and wished for better fortune. We approached a type of Dutch barn hoping to find vegetables to eat and hay on which to rest. We found neither, but crawled into a heap of ferns and slept. We set out again and came to a farmhouse where we found some turnips and sugar beet which we eagerly devoured.

It was now Thursday, and we had continuously been on the move since Sunday. Eric's feet were causing us much concern, we had put about one hundred miles behind us, and to find either a railway or an airfield was now of the utmost importance. If only we could lay up somewhere near an airfield and watch developments, time would not greatly matter so long as we had some food. I approached the first farm which came into sight. I knocked on the door, leaving Harry and Eric concealed behind a wall. The door slowly opened about six inches, they eyes and nose of an old lady appearing inquisitively in the gap. I bid her "good evening", in my best German accent, told her I was walking to my home in the west, but had run out of food and still had fifty miles to go. I do not think she believed me, or perhaps she did not have food to spare. In any case she did not like the look of my clothes, the way she eyed them, so I thanked her for answering the door, hoping all the time she would weaken, and backed away empty handed.

Eventually we came within sight of a logging camp, where voices could be heard and we decided to investigate. Perhaps our luck was about to change. We could hardly believe our ears as the welcome sound of a chugging train came over the air, not very far distant, and the sound suggested it was pulling up an incline and heading in the right direction. This was surely our train, the line we had been hoping to contact in the next stage of our plan of escape. Perhaps we had better give the logging camp a miss and sort out ourselves with the earliest possible train.

It did not take us long to locate the railway line, and we walked along the track until we found what we considered to be a favourable boarding place. Eric's feet were festering, and so this new development in our progress boosted moral and gave us new hope. Not a lot further along we found a turnip clamp positioned so conveniently only yards from the track. It was partly used and at the business end there was a plentiful supply of nice dry straw and hay from which we could build a useful resting place. At least there was turnip enough for months. We crawled in and slept.

We awoke early, which is not surprising being in a heap of turnips, broke surface and surveyed the scenery. A farm to the rear, a wood to the right of us up gradient and a farm down gradient, on the other side of the track. There was no one to be seen in either direction so we could at least shave in the dew and generally tidy up in readiness for the first train to arrive to speed us along, at the expense of the third and last Reich, on a further stage of our adventure. We were just busy pulling the skin from a turnip when I glanced up gradient and spotted in the distance, a figure on our side of the line, walking in our direction. I hoped he had not noticed us. We dived under cover and waited. It appeared to be an age waiting to see him pass by through our little peep hole in the straw. Perhaps he had retraced his steps and our concern would then be unfounded. I would venture a peep out, as our peep hole only gave us a down gradient view. There he stood, rock rigid, not fifteen yards up gradient. I recognised his uniform immediately; Eisenbahn Polizei, railway police. He had seen us and was prepared to await us hatching out. "Guten Morgen," I greeted him. "Guten Morgen" he replied forcefully. "Was machen sie da?". I told him we were forced workers at the farm behind us, and that the farmer was quite unkind to us even though we worked hard. I said we were supposed to be preparing some turnips for lifting for cattle, but had been resting as the cart would not be here for a further half hour. We would start work immediately if he would not report us. He wished us good day and continued further down the gradient, crossed the line and disappeared from view. Harry and Eric had dutifully nodded their heads in agreement when I had looked their way.

"I think we got away with that pretty well," said Harry with a grin.

"We're sunk if he meets that bloody farmer", said I, "Let's get to hell out of it quick, up to that wood. Eric, take my hand, I'll help you along, 'cause we'll have to run for it." We brushed off the straw, turned up gradient and made good speed, Eric appearing not to notice the pain in his feet, and it did not take us long to halve the distance between the turnip clamp and the wood. Then the fun started. Loud voices behind us ordered us to halt, but we kept on running. I looked over my shoulder to see our Eisenbahn Polizei with reinforcements from the farm, giving chase, all brandishing guns above their heads. I felt we were out of range of the ordinary shot guns so I blurted out, "Into the woods fellows as quickly as you bloody can, split up and go like the clappers of hell". I yanked Eric along, and Harry was way ahead in no time. We could not abandon Eric now. BANG. BANG. BANG.

"Bloody hell, those are rifles not shot guns fellows," I said as I stopped the gallop. "We're beaten, we may as well face the bloody music."

We turned and faced the oncoming irate Krauts, who were screaming, "Hande Hoch!", and flicking the muzzles of their weapons up and down. More up than down it seemed. We put up our hands as they approached. They did not fire again, so luckily we came out of it quite unharmed. The Eisenbahn Polizei made straight for Harry in a half crouch, jabbing the muzzle forward in an excited manner, as though he were about to blow Harry's head clean off his shoulders. The others gathered around as the Polizei stuck the muzzle under Harry's chin, which action seemed to lengthen both Harry's neck and arms somewhat. My arms felt a hell of a lot longer too as the Polizei turned on me in anger shouting, "Er ist Rothaarig, fraglos Englander" (He is ginger haired, unquestionably English).

I confirmed that Harry was red haired as he said, but I explained that he was Welsh, not English if that made any difference. Goon baiting had become a habit, and this polizei did not like it. My humour was very obviously not appreciated and I was given one hell of a dressing down for telling the cock and bull story about working for the farmer. I was asked if we would go quietly to the local railway station with them, with no nonsense, otherwise they would have to take off our trousers and rope us together. We did not have to discuss the matter, we agreed. On our way across the fields to the village the Polizei showered us with questions and became somewhat less aggressive and eventually admitted that if it had not been for Harry's red hair he would have believed our story of working on the farm. Our captors however were not very sympathetic when I asked for some treatment to Eric's ailing feet. If we had walked over a hundred miles, a few more would not make a lot of difference, we were told.

We arrived at the local railway station where a mammoth photograph of Hitler adorned the wall opposite the entrance. It seemed that the whole population of the village were given instructions to come along to inspect us thoroughly, which indeed was the case when some advance guards came along and stripped us naked where we stood. This caused many of the village maidens to cackle, cover up their faces with their hands and peep through their fingers. Finding no hidden arms or dangerous weapons in our clothing we were allowed to dress, make our way to the village pump to drink and wash as we pleased.

An army Hauptmann arrived in a private car, with a spare armed guard, to take us to the military. Questions came thick and fast. How had we travelled so far? Who were our contacts? Where were we aiming to go? Who had helped us on the way? They were convinced that we were being passed along a series of contacts, and they were intent on locating some of the organisers.

Meantime the boys, in their cattle trucks had arrived at Heydekrug, and, as Harry reminded me forty years later, everyone was apparently in a filthy mood. It had taken them hours to return to their rightful owners, all the boots, braces and belts which had been taken from the boys when leaving Barth. After all this had been done they were of course left with some over, ours for example, but they had no means of establishing to whom these belonged. Little wonder then that we were to experience a very rough reception when we eventually arrived some days later at Heydekrug.

We arrived at Danzig station for onward transmission to Königsberg. Standing close by was a knot of Polish men who appeared to be taking a rather keen interest in us, and we kept their gaze for awhile without allowing our guards to notice. At a suitable opportunity one of the Poles turned up the lapel of his greatcoat to reveal a tiny neat RAF roundel. Here then, right under our very noses, were the resistance forces sought by the Germans; men who could probably have us out of the country by boat if only we could escape our guards. What an opportunity and what encouragement to escape again; all the allied airmen so much respected the courageous Poles.

On commencing our final short walk to the camp after leaving the train, we were joined by a Luftwaffe officer, who assured us that Heydekrug was a very good camp and suggested it would be even better for the three of us if we were to carry his luggage for him. We somehow did not think that he would realize that we were already deeply up to the neck in the fertilizer and so did not see why we should add to our agony by carrying his extra baggage.

Perhaps we ought to have carried his luggage. At least it could not have made things any worse and we may have stood a chance of at least ending up with one 'friend'. Reception was most uncomfortable. Interrogation was intense. Irrespective of what we might say, we were to be Court Martialled, possibly in Berlin. We had wantonly caused damage to Reich property, namely cattle trucks, were suspected of gathering military information when we were away from camp and that the usual penalty for such offences was death by shooting. Whatever our plea, no mercy was to be shown. It seemed they had it all cut and dried and when we were called in for interview, singly, I must confess that the officer conducting the proceedings left us in no doubt that we were very small fry, quite superfluous to requirements, and certainly quite simply disposed of. I had lost all touch with Harry and Eric. None of our boys would be aware that we had arrived at Heydekrug and knowing how the German machine worked, it would be quite easy for them to say that we had been popped off whilst resisting arrest or something similar.

I was lead off into a separate room where a full statement was typed out as I dictated it. I then had to sign it. I was then given the opportunity to give truthful answers to certain questions. I had been asked the questions before but this was the last time that I would be given the chance to tell the truth. This, I was told is final. What were my connections with Germany before the war? Who were my personal contacts? How could I possibly speak German the way I did without having lived in Germany? Who had supplied us with food and information whilst we were free? Was I aware that cigarette burns and finger nail extraction usually brought the necessary answers? I was somewhat relieved to be thrown into solitary confinement with practically not sufficient food to maintain life, at least I was on my own. I got two tiny pieces of bread, black, hard and dry, each day and some water. About every third day I was given a small bowl of coloured hot water, which the guard called soup. What flesh I had been able to retain was now disappearing extremely quickly, and not having eaten much other than turnips when we were on the run, hunger was now being spelled out to me slowly and clearly. I was delighted one day to be out in the exercise yard, to see Johnnie Theckston, Bob Waddy and Jimmy Walker. Harry and Eric I knew were not very far away. We spent thirty nine days in that state of solitary confinement, with no more quantity of food than I now feed to my dogs in four days. We came out of there like skeletons. Even our friends, when we met them again were somewhat shocked, but their lack of true sympathy was evident. They hadn't forgotten the inconvenience we had caused them on first arrival and many were now glad to see us back yet at the same time glad to say, "Served you bloody right".

During our thirty nine days we had our fun, and many incidents which one could never forget, occurred both within the cooler and in the exercise yard. The guards would peep at us in our little bare cells through the tiny peep-hole door. We would call the guard frequently to allow us to go to the toilet. Sometimes he would choose to ignore us, because he was fully aware that half our calls were hoaxes. As he would escort us down the corridor, we would overcome the no-talking ban by singing messages to our friends in other cells, tied up to familiar tunes such as *Auld Lang Syne* or *Abide With Me*. For example:

> Message from Johnnie, can you hear me Perc?
> Go to the bog, the second from your end
> There is a pipe which runs along the wall,
> On there you'll find a dog-end and a match.

None of it rhymed but who cared? It worked very well, and a good drag helped to allay the hunger a bit, even though it tended to send you a bit cross-eyed.

Bob Waddy (Canadian Airborne) was one of the most crazy and daring of our crowd. We were allowed out into the exercise area under armed guard. The instructions were, no talking and keep twenty paces minimum between each man. Bob would ignore this and close up to within half a dozen paces and blabber freely and even start singing. The guards would scream for silence. Bob would maintain his eyes front and would shout aloud, "Nicht Verstehen", and continue to sing or chatter, and keep station at six paces. The guard would run over to him, infuriated, screaming "Halt". Bob would stand there, hands on hips looking totally disinterested, whilst the tirade of German verbal ejaculations, rent the air. Bob would then turn on the guard, shouting in English that if only the guard would speak a civilised language he might get some civilised results. The guard of course would not understand a word Bob had said, and would start ranting again. Bob would twist this all up as though it meant something entirely different. Smiling, he would say, "Oh yes, now I understand." and stick up a thumb as he walked over to shake someone by the hand, or do something equally stupid. Why one of the guards never put a few bullets around Bob's feet I shall never know. They sometimes threatened to but Bob would shrug it off with a very cheeky remark and a wave of the hand, "Stupid bloody Kraut," or he would throw both arms in the air exclaiming, "Gott in Himmel!" I actually saw one irate guard smile at such a demonstration.

I remember at one time Bob shaved every hair off his body, except eye lashes of course, then found he could keep neither rain nor perspiration out of his eyes, and blamed the Krauts for the inconvenience.

CATTLE TRUCK CAPERS

> At Barth we made the camp go with a swing,
> Talented musicians, actors, singers who
> Hard work would do to perfect their own thing,
> Then culminate in concert – super do.

At rugger, soccer, cricket or frog leap,
What e'er the game enthusiasm was right,
A football league we formed, it was a treat,
When championship was fought with might.

Studies we formed of history, language, maths.
Societies for debates and county clubs,
And brews from raisins hidden in the laths,
Gave 'grog' more potent than in English pubs.

Escape committee worked with furtive fun,
Forged documents by artist experts made,
And out of blankets uniforms of Hun,
We'd fashion with great care, whilst plans we made.

Some radio boys with expertise did build
'Canary' out of odds and ends they 'won',
And sheets of news from BBC were filled,
And 'readers' round to eager ears did run.

Plans for escape were made and checked at length,
Tunnels at times like rabbit warrens ran
From various points, we dug to wire with strength,
And under surface soil passed man to man.

We really kept the Hun right on his toes,
Some days he'd turn us quickly out of huts,
All day we'd sit around in groups and rows,
Whilst Huns searched rooms, with stakes he poked the ruts.

If tunnel found, then fun would really start,
Mouths all afroth, arms working semaphore,
Gefreiter would be ordered down hole smart,
The narrow tunnel fearing to explore.

Hauptman would scream, "Sofort geh' runter mensch"
Reluctantly would ferret go to earth,
And where he would to surface come 'ere length,
Awaited eager was, as is a birth.

Great lusty cheers would then rise up from us,
As ferret gladly surfaced to the light,
But little did they know without a fuss,
We'd back to digging be, that very night.

For hours they'd keep us out there in the wet,
Or snow or sun, it did not matter what,
And if all day we stayed we would not get
A drink or eat a crumb, it mattered not.

Some always had their 'panic box' on hand,
Which took they with them daily on Appell,
So should we not return for hours on end,
Equipped with food and cards they were, quite well.

Das Oberkommando now had had enough,
Four hundred miles to east would have us roll,
And sixty men in cattle trucks packed rough,
Where forty men, or horses eight, was usual haul.

Huge metal drum was placed mid-truck as lav,
And arm-ed guards with us in truck would ride,
On platform 'tween the trucks more guards they'd have,
And those on roof would change with those inside.

No air or light saw we but one small ray
Through small square aperture high up in wall,
With iron bars and stacheldraht arrayed,
In dark interior trapped were then we all.

No food arrangements evidence yet bore,
We jolted back and forth, and here and there,
The contents of the lav splashed o'er the floor,
The stinking filth and squalor did we share.

Addressing us before we left the camp,
"Now good boys be and do not run away,"
To us the Oberleutnant Eilers loud did champ,
And Herr von Muller glad goodbye did say.

Derek produced a serrated metal blade,
Cross-talk and singing helped the guards distract,
And there on top of rack we made,
A platform, bars and wire to saw with tact.

A few hours passed, the sawing was complete,
And through small hole with difficulty we'd squeeze,
The guards outside, our object may defeat,
If saw us we, they could shoot with greatest ease.

Singly we'd drop, there'd be no talk,
The next would go if there were no alarm,
The first the forward way of train would walk,
The others in reverse if met no harm.

Hitting the ground at speed in darkness might,
Be risky, striking objects hard on track,
We hoped the noise of dropping in the night,
Would not attention of the guards attract.

Relaxed we fell and down embankment rolled,
By pine tree wood Eric, Harry and I did meet,
And hid up for a while and talk did hold,
On tactics now. We had no boots on feet.

Northwest we'd aim, by night we'd walk unseen,
In barns by day we'd hide and rest and sleep,
A Junkers might I pinch from airfield green,
To Sweden we would aim o'er Baltic-deep.

Food did we seek but barking dogs all round,
Would sniff us in the barns or stealing food,
And so by day to travel were we bound,
As foreign workers bluff our way I would.

Oft did we feel hard stares upon our backs,
Of Polizei, and youths and standers-by,
But with a few well chosen German cracks,
The boys I'd usher off again to try.

One night when stealing water from a pump,
Outside a cottage in a garden neat,
Der Herr popped out and threatened me to thump,
I leapt his hedge, an athletic feat.

On seventh day by railway gradient steep,
We would a goods train slow await to jump,
So refuge took we up in turnip heap,
And under straw became we part of lump.

At daybreak shaved and washed we in the dew,
When Eisenbahn Polizei popped up quite unseen,
Said I, we foreign workers were, and knew
We most untidy were and awfully lean.

Agreed he then to work we go, then went,
His way down gradient towards a farm nearby,
We took our leave to wood up gradient,
Walked we at first, then ran before the cry.

Gunshots whistled through the air, so we
The harder ran that we should safe to wood,
Come soon, where train we'd jump and still be free,
But shots now whistled closer. Cold ran blood.

Reluctantly we turned and held up hands,
When Polizei and farmer brandished guns,
"No redhead man in European lands"
"Was anything, but English" said the Huns.

To army depot quick then they'd take us,
So faded once again our freedom sweet,
And army Hauptman took us with great fuss,
And in the local cells said, "Cool your feet".

Scant slippers only wore we, full of holes,
In cattle trucks they'd taken all our boots,
And Hauptman said that we with such thin soles
A hundred miles could ne'er have done on hooves.

But so we did, though Eric's feet were sore,
And oft times would he stop in serious pain,
To give up would our pride have injured more,
Than being caught, with threats of being slain.

Co-operate we judged it best to be,
So sore were the Luftwaffe, their decree
Was, "Damage to the Reich's property,
Pure sabotage, with death as penalty."

"You've heard of Zigaretten burns to skin?"
"You've heard of finger nails pulled out by root?"
If S.S. take a hand in this, they'll trim"
"You right and proper, there's no doubt." said Kraut.

In 'cooler' cell for nine and thirty days,
Did they keep us in solitary mode,
The flesh from off our bones in no mean way
Did roll. Camp life we found a better code.

And so then, as the black-sheep bleach-ed white,
Returned we to our friends who then had been,
Installed in lager 'K', at Heydekrug,
Cold and hungry, tired and worn and lean.

In time we organised and planned,
And tunnels sprouted from unusual points,
Disguises many to escape this land
Did we contrive, with many aching joints.

· CHAPTER 9 ·
HYDEKRUG

Hydekrug (Luft VI) was situated out in the barren wastes of Lithuania. It was bleak and cold and inhospitable. We were to be there from November 1943 to July 1944. We were housed in 'K' Lager. By way of contrast, Barth had been comfortable but it was the ingenuity and resourcefulness of the Kriegie which soon injected some measure of organization amongst the inmates. 'A' Lager was adjacent, where 'Dixie' Deans was senior Airman or Lager Leader. Vic Clarke was our man in 'K' Lager, although he did not come with us from Barth. Jim Barnes of New Zealand, later to become Sir James Barnes, was our man from Barth, but Dixie had already installed Vic before our arrival. Jim, however, being the gentleman that he was did not contest the situation, but we were all very much aware of Jim's influence throughout.

Tunnelling was still a favourite activity, with the hope that contact could be made with the sympathetic loyal Poles leading to a boat to Sweden.

It was during our stay here that a fundamental change took place in German Prisoner of War administration. The Abwehr (security) as we had known it had disappeared. We learned eventually that it was dissolved at the personal directive of Hitler, because of his mounting mistrust in what was really the equivalent of our Military Police. Obergruppenfuhrer Gottlieb Berger, one of Himmler's henchmen, was given overall charge of POW Administration. It was later revealed that plans were afoot to execute all aircrew, commencing with the pilots (see letter) and there was some basis for our concern on some occasions. Increased Gestapo activities were also quite noticeable. We would be turned out without notice much more frequently and herded into the compound to stay there for hours, whilst every item of our possessions was searched. It was at this time that many of our personal items went missing. The searchers were taking items which could in no way have contributed to escaping. They were, in fact, thieving. Even some food went missing. Peanut butter sandwiches were next time purposely left for the goons to sample. The peanut butter content was of course obtained from the bog.

The Germans had also become much more trigger happy. One American escapee who had been recaptured was shot dead at close range, by revolver, outside the wire but within twenty yards of us. This was we thought a demonstration by the Germans of 'see we told you so'. One of our men was shot early one morning on his way to the ablutions just because he was out slightly in advance of the authorised time. A notice of warning appeared in camp, pinned up by the Camp Commandantur:

> To all prisoners of war. – The escape from a Prison Camp is no longer a sport. Germany has always kept up to the Hague Convention, and only punished recaptured POWs with minor disciplinary punishment. Germany will still maintain these Principles of International Law, but England has, besides fighting at the front in an honest manner, instituted an illegal warfare in non-combatant zones in the form of Gangster Commandos, Terror Bandits and Sabotage Troops, even up to the frontiers of Germany. They say in a secret and confidential English Military Pamphlet, *The Handbook of Modern Irregular Warfare*. 'The days when we should practice the rules of sportsmanship are over. For the time being every soldier must be a potential Gangster, and must be prepared to adopt their methods where ever possible. The sphere of operations should always include the enemy's own country and occupied territory, and in certain circumstances neutral countries he is using as a source of supply.' Engand has, with these instructions opened up a non-military form of gangster war. Germany is determined to safeguard her homeland, and especially her War Industry and Provision Centres for the fighting fronts. Therefore it has become necessary to create strictly forbidden zones, called Death Zones, in which all unauthorised trespassers will be immediately shot on sight. Escaping POWs on entering these zones will certainly lose their lives. They are in constant danger of being mistaken for enemy agents or sabotage groups. Urgent warning is given about making future escapes. In plain English stay in camp where you will be safe. Breaking out of it is a damned dangerous act. The chances of preserving your life are almost nil. All police and military guards have been given the most strict orders, to shoot on sight all suspected persons. Escaping from camp has ceased to be a sport."

Their licence was now to be applied practically.

> Every Bolshevist, every Englishman, every American on German soil is an outlaw for the Werewolves. Whenever an opportunity arises to extinguish his life we shall grasp it gladly without respecting our own lives. Hate is our Prayer – Death is our Password.

The Commandant however one day had something good to say to us. He was an ex-flying man himself and congratulated us on our sportsmanship and thunderous applause when a Heinkel 111 dived to its destruction quite close to the camp. He thought we had applauded because the pilot had managed to bail out, so we roared with laughter and applauded him even louder because he got it all wrong. He was never any the wiser.

It was shortly after the posting of the general warning that the Camp Commandant had something else to say in the form of a special announcement, on the morning roll call parade. He advised us that fifty RAF escapees from Sagan Luft 111 had been shot. We were stunned, and it was noted by the expression on his face and his demeanour that he was somewhat embarrassed to be making such an announcement. Three of those who escaped incidentally, finally reached England. Doug Moore told me, after our release, that he met an acquaintance after the war, who picked up Himmler and one of his henchmen in disguise, quite near the Elbe, and was awarded a Mention in Despatches for the action.

> The night was dark with cloud around
> The Merlins roared their thunderous sound,
> We rocked and swayed at angels ten,
> Our laden giant with bombs and men.
> At twenty hundred we were high
> Our fate no doubt to do or die.
> A thunderous crash a sudden roar
> We were on fire our hopes were poor.
> We jumped through holes and ports and door
> A long way from old England's shores
> Some 'chutes were burning, awful glow
> I landed heavy in the snow.
> Four days and nights I wandered there
> My state of health I did not care,
> Homesick weary and distraught
> Was hunted down and then was caught.
> Now here in Heydekrug I rest
> Hoping I shall stand the test,
> One day may be I'll lose this pain
> And with some luck go home again.
> *Jim Haskett (now in Australia)*

Illumination was bad when we arrived at Heydekrug, and Bob Hart reminded me of the long hours we used to spend playing Bridge with the assistance of the Gerry margarine lamp, ie. a piece of pyjama cord and some German margarine (after the extraction of the water).

Organisation pressed on. Harry Barber was i/c Intelligence in 'K' Lager, Ferdie Farrands, Fred Barnes and Brewster were librarians, Danny Horne, Bill Leech and Joe Musgrove were medical assistants to Dr Pollock and Dr Forest-Hayes. Denys Taaffe was the recognised expert on chronometrical creations, whilst during our time together at varying periods, such dedication as shown by Wally Oakley to stew making cannot pass unmentioned. Hundreds of hungry stomachs said their thanks to Wally. He was forever on the move, he was forever steeped in deepest hatred for the Kraut. I never met anyone who could quite hate our hosts to the extent which Wally was able to practice. It was one of Wally's many occupations, but one he could practice whilst following anyone of the others.

> This is the story of Wally Oakley
> Late of the village of Trent-cum-Stokely.
> Wally became a Kriegie bold,
> His sorrowful tale I now unfold.
> When Kriegie days were near the end,
> Walley started going round the bend,
> When hearing Gerries blowing whistles

His moustache became a mass of bristles.
Bellowing with rage, like thunder claps,
Would yell, "Get on parade you chaps",
First would plead and then would frown,
"For Christ's sake chaps they'll mow you down."
Afternoons some leisure hours,
Up jumps Wal, "For Christ's sake showers",
Evening comes – we think no more,
But up he jumps and takes the floor.
"Reference spuds and reference cooks,
Burn your names upon your books".
"Custard powders, piss poor stews,
Can't we have some stronger brews?
Seven tins for fifty, no five a man,
About this pissing in the can.
The fire bar's gone, another crime,
About this washing on the line,
Education block or not,
It makes no difference, you'll all be shot."
(Attrib. to W. Molyneux).

The mention of the can in the Wally verse reminds me of David Joseph telling the story of how Soggy Norton, the sixfoot-three Canadian, ex Mountie, overcame the tortuous cold experienced at dead of night when visiting the urinal can. The device he created, consisted of a number of suitably arranged empty 'Klim' tins, with the bottoms cut out. The vertical assembly commenced at a conveniently placed hole, cut to size, in the floor of the hut, and going up was attached at intervals to the bed-post, terminating at a comfortable height on the top three-tier bunk.

One evening after shutters up and lights out, a low flying aircraft could be heard hunting about as though searching for a pin point, but the engine note sounded very much like a German twin thrashing around. All attempts to see out were foiled by the shuttering and we imagined this infernal machine ploughing its way through the compound ripping up masses of barbed wire fencing, giving us a clear invitation to escape in droves without one moment's digging. Much to our sorrow, the following morning, there we saw standing, just beyond the 'K' Lager playing field, one ME110 all very much intact, even to the extent that later in the day a bright little Luftwaffe pilot climbed aboard and had the thing in the air in no time ... pity.

Word was passed around that some new and unusual method of counting was to be introduced, and that we were to resist it. It sounded as though it could be quite some fun, yet somehow foreboded some possible evil. We had been standing around in the playing field, in no particular order which was not surprising, when we were told that we were to be counted as we filed through between two of the barrack blocks. This sounded all too sinister, it even savoured of the possibility of the Goons getting the count right. This would never do, and as Bob Hart put it recently, "I remember we started to move around as though we were all going nowhere, which was the same thing as refusing to go through between those confounded huts." Moments such as these used to get the Germans totally bottled up. There was no clearly written instruction in their manual to cover such events as these, so the next move was the inevitable frenetic hysteria.

Instead of calling us to order in the usual parade formation they commenced to scream at us as we milled aimlessly about. Many threats were made in their attempts to coax or force us through the count but we were successful in fouling each new effort. The guards were called off and we were left to our own games for a while, but not allowed back into our barracks.

Then came a German officer, as Bob described, of some considerable military presence, accompanied by many evil looking aggressive guards. He called us to order and announced that we either conform to his command or take the consequences. He very obviously meant just what he said, so we naturally decided to conform. I think however that we had made our objectives quite plain, because it was interesting to note that similar tactics were attempted in the adjoining 'A' Lager, serious no doubt and yet amusing. These incidents were generally referred to as "The Sheep Counts".

There was a state of shambles where the boys had been on parade for what appeared to be hours and the count was still very unsatisfactory. The German officer was approaching a thrombosis, he was almost convinced there had been a mass escape. The incident was of course treated as a huge joke and the boys would start a game of footer in the rear, or some other form of distraction, which frayed even more the already tattered tempers of the Krauts. The officer would have some of the guards form up facing each other and in single file have the Kriegies pass between them. Each man would be counted the very moment he jumped over a horizontal ladder, held by two of the guards. In this way the Germans were convinced they would obtain an accurate count. The German language does of course not lend itself to quick counting. Imagine saying 222 (Two twenty two) in a hurry in German, Zwei hundert zwei und zwanzig. They would therefore allow fifty to jump the obstacle, stop the column, write it down and start again. The fun would start when a bunch of Kriegies would attempt to go over together or in quick succession. Then perhaps one would run up to the obstacle in a gallop, hesitate, walk backwards slowly preparing to take another run, with the pretence that the jump was beyond his capability. Someone shouted out, "First jump you've had in years Buster, and now you can't even make it". Many were falling about with laughter. Others would approach doing ballet steps on tip toe, finger and thumb on hips. Then crouching, as though on all fours some would come along like bleating sheep, when all the bystanders would call out, "Baa-Baa-Baaaa!" making a frightful din. The crowd would be in an uproar, the Germans being furious and confused. Those who had passed through the sheep count became restless, they would lark about and some even spilled over back into those uncounted. The operation was so ridiculous that had the lunatic charade been allowed to continue, the Gerries would have had so many Kriegies they would have suspected an invasion.

GOON BAITING

There came then yet a weary time,
A time most wondrous tiring -
When we were in a Kriegie camp,
All set round with wiring.

They counted – Oh they counted us,
By day as well by night;
Sideways, diagonally backwards -
But they never got it right,

At last they hit upon a wheeze
That seemed both cute and neat -
They fell the Kriegies in again,
And counted all their feet.

And when the feet were counted,
They divided them by two -
But still the answer wasn't right,
So they thought up something new.

They went and got excited,
And shouted with much Zest -
But it didn't do them any good,
For the Kriegies weren't impressed.

Then they lined up all the Kriegies,
At a time when most folk sleep,
And made them singly jump a pole -
And the Kriegies baa'd like sheep.

And when the count was finished,
And they added up the score,
They found they'd far more Kriegies
Than they'd ever had before.

For in a well-run Kriegie camp,
You can get lots of fun –
'Cos there's nothing quite so popular,
As baiting up the Hun.
Anon.

My friend Jack, from Auckland recently recalled an incident on one appel where all manner of diversions were being created to foul up the Gerry count which just had to be dragged out as long as possible and not be allowed to reach completion. The Gerries segregated a particular noisy bunch of Kriegies who became lumbered with the very real problem of having their names and numbers taken for addition to the waiting list for the cooler. The situation was serious and required some cool quick thinking to save them from the customary fourteen days 'zollitary'.

"Name und Nummer", demanded the guard of the first Kriegie.

"Smith, Whitehall 1212!" came the answer without hesitation. The guard wrote it down. He approached the next Kriegie now primed from No 1.

"Billy," answered the amused airman.

"Billy what?" enquired the unsuspecting guard.

"Yes" replied the airman.

"Yes what?" asked the guard impatiently.

"Billy Watt."

The guard shuffled his feet and tugged at his collar, this situation was a little beyond him, but he accepted the 'Watt' when spelled out.

"Next. Name und Nummer?"

"Billy." said another very amused airman almost bursting trying to contain his laughter. The guard looked very suspiciously straight into his face, then with anger looked back at the previous airman and enquired,

"Is this some Inklish Choke?"

He was assured it was not.

"Then I say again, Billy what?"

"Goat," came the reply without delay.

"Nummer?"

"Ein Nein Ein Nein" (1919). The guard threw a look of suspicion and approached a six foot airman with shoulders a yard wide.

"Name und Nummer?"

"Yura," he was advised.

"Spell it."

"Y-U-R-A ... Yura Koont!" came the lightening reply complete with spelling, whereupon the game was up for the next few minutes because no one was capable of conversation because of the laughter. The guards were furious and swung the muzzles of their rifles quickly from left to right, in an attempt to get the boys into some kind of order.

"Nummer?"

"Sechs-sechs-sechs-sechs" (6666).

"Vot iss yore name?" snarled the guard pushing his face a bit closer to that of the nearest Kriegie.

"My name is Bill Brewer," came the snappy reply.

"And mine," volunteered the next Kriegie "is Jan Stewar."

"And I'm Peter Davey."

"And me. I'm Dannel Widden."

"The little one here is Peter Gurney, and this is Harry Hawk, and over there could be Uncle Tom Cobley and all..." whereupon the entire bunch of airmen having got out of that trap rather well, all broke into song *Old Uncle Tom Cobley and all*.

One wonders if these names were explained to those particular goons whether they would appreciate the humour of the situation or be able to raise a laugh having received some measure of familiarisation with a brand of humour they found impossible to understand. I suspect the answer to be no, judging from the goon who later went round the barracks calling out these 'so called' airmen to assemble and who could not understand the hilarious laughter coming from the Kriegies within earshot, as he called out loudly. "Sechs-sechs-sechs-sechs! Yura Koont!"

One of the boys touched him on the arm saying quietly,

"You have the Christian name wrong. You'll never find him. His proper name is "I-Y-M-A."

The goon went shouting aloud the amended name, but without any positive results.

Space unfortunately will not allow mention of the names of all the wonderful characters we had in our midst from time to time during captivity. We had men of great ingenuity, of great creative art, of quite outstanding engineering ability who would create wonderfully effective productions from items we now throw away daily as rubbish.

Des Dunphy, who was forever busy in camp life of all spheres, has recently constructed true working replicas of the kit-bag air-pump which was used to ventilate the tunnels. Also a copy of the wooden rail system for transporting the excavated earth from the tunnel head to the entrance. Then again a working model of the 'blower' heater which was terribly efficient, working on the blow lamp principle producing unbelievable amounts of heat from a minimum of fuel, which was very often unwanted waste.

We had men of great courage, men of great organising ability, men of great tenacity, men of great public spirit, natural leaders, mathematicians, radio experts, comedians, actors, musicians, athletes, chemists, journalists, architects, artists and many other callings. One such, and who like a great many others was a pre-war flier, was Ferdie Farrands. Ferdie inspired all who met him and it was with great sadness that Geoff Neeves confirmed that Ferdie was killed shortly after the war on flying instruction duties.

Basil Craske well remembers, from the Hydekrug days, that when the Gerries discovered we were fermenting the fruit from the Red Cross parcels, and producing a rather potent home-brew, they forbid any further fruit to be allowed to individuals. Jock Barrett however discovered that the horrible mangol-wurzel Gerry jam would ferment quite freely even without the assistance of yeast and Ferdie fastened onto this with lightning dexterity. A small secret 'store room' was created in the overall admin block, by moving the position of a door and a window and a wall panel made from Red Cross chests.

Taaffe had his watch-repairing outfit by the window, the rest of the store housing odds and ends, sports items but mostly bed boards stacked neatly in a corner concealing a very large barrel of brew with a Gerry-jam base. As the brew progressed, so did the smell and this hazard was overcome by a tin-bashed outlet venting into the double wall then fed into the roof space.

All the ingredients temperatures, timing etc were scientifically determined and dictated by Ferdie. Then came the hour when the brew was ripe for distillation, not a process to be performed in public. Thus we were obliged to spend the night in the store with windows carefully blanketed against tell tale light chinks. The store contained one vital essential, a 'tortoiseshell' stove to produce the required heat. The Ferdie distillation plant consisted of a Gerry-jam tin, some 15 inches high and 12 inches diameter, surmounted by a wooden block bored out with two angulated holes meeting at the top and leading the condenser.

"One can imagine that being almost sealed hermetically in a small area with a red hot stove, the stench of almost pure alcohol, and the necessity to frequently taste for quality of product, we were left somewhat bedraggled by the time of the next morning appel," admitted Basil.

They did, however, have about eight bottles of the 'hard-stuff' to show for their labours.

"It was dynamite", said Basil, "as you no doubt remember we used it to good effect in our petrol lighters."

The bottles were to be left uncorked for a specific time to allow the 'aldehyde' to evaporate. The brew was finally dressed up by the addition of a lime essence of boiled-down sweets from Canadian Red-Cross parcels.

The metal portion of the still was discovered by the Gestapo during one of their snap searches, much to the annoyance of Ferdie, who, in high dudgeon and with his fluent Deutsche did succeed in persuading the Gerries that it was a dummy machine gun used as a stage prop in the theatre from the play, of all things, Journey's End.

Both Willy Mercer and Freddie Simpson took up the story at this point, remembering that evening when Room 3 sampled the distilled, stupefying

Basil's sketch of Ferdie's still.

product. Ferdie was Stube Fuhrer (Room Leader), and invited a few in to enjoy the samples. Now, this is delightful nostalgia, because that is what one inherits from an association with a character such as Ferdie Farrands, and to appreciate the high level of morale of combat airmen, even in captivity, in times of hardship, hunger, cold and oppression, is to recognise the true and genuine encouragement of those who would have their doubts for the future.

Such circumstances remind us of the true therapeutic value of a genuinely spontaneous bout of laughter in times of subservience when the enemy, being ridiculed, is bristling with rifles, guns, pistols and revolvers.

Stube 3 inhabitants had been imbibing sufficiently long enough for the party to have advanced to a very noisy state of a progressed condition of being utterly over-stewed, when a loud guttural "Achtung!" rang out followed by the entry of an irate Kraut officer and his retinue. They attempted, with much bawling and arm waving, to get in the inebriated Kriegies in to some sort of order and quell the deafening din.

"Zis iss a grosse inzult to a Cherman Offizer!" screamed the Kraut.

Howls of laughter and derision emanated from the Dutch courage of the entire ensemble.

"Zis iss an inzult to the third Reich also!" bellowed the indignant officer with protruding eyes and bulging veins.

"The third and last Reich!" chorused the Kriegies with more boos and demonstrative raspberries.

One cannot refrain from including the RAF parlance used during this incident otherwise the mood of the moment would not be fully conveyed and one cannot forfeit a story of such wonderfully humorous and courageous men just because of what might be regarded as a few superfluous expletives.

The mood was fast becoming somewhat overheated, as was the poor Kraut officer; and his retinue shuffled even closer. He in his rage would go one better than the Reich, and roared, with sprays of flying spit issuing forth.

"Ziss iss also a grossen inzult against dem Fuhrer!"

He was breathing heavily through bared tightly clenched teeth as he awaited the reaction of these insolent and inebriated Englanders. All hell was now loose as invectives and revilement flowed, when one bold, and cross-eyed Kriegie, in a very loud voice made a perfectly sensible recommendation.

"F*** the Fuhrer" he hollered.

The Kraut Officer was now truly aghast. His eyes protruded alarmingly, his arms became rod-stiff, his breathing became even more pronounced. For the moment he was totally perplexed whilst the Kriegies fell about in hysterics. Then to the astonishment of all present, noticeably his anger appeared to subside as he searched for a reply. He stuck out his chin forcibly, he stood with his feet astride and his hands clasped behind his back and leaned forward from the hips as he quietly stared the Kriegies in the eyes. There was a deathly silence emphasised as the Kraut officer moved his head very slowly from side to side. Then, very quietly, and almost plaintively, maintaining his stare, he said, "But I do not say 'F*** King George the Sixth!"

There were now howls of hysterical laughter, very loud cheering, much vigorous hand clapping with hands high in the air, and someone struck up *For He's a Jolly Good Fellow*. The German officer could in no way comprehend this strange behaviour and his retinue, who obviously did not understand English, looked at each other in bewilderment.

"If you don't say F*** King George the Sixth, then we'll say it for you!" shouted one of the Kriegies. "All together now...

F*** King George the Sixth too!"

The German was now totally perplexed and out-maneouvered, whilst the Kriegies continued to cheer having found a new degree of confidence. But again he erupted, obviously totally bewildered by these mad Englanders, and almost seemed to be on the verge of tears. He bellowed, as though by way of admonishment.

"How do you Englanders ever hope to vin der vor ven you say... (crescendo, with voice being strangulated into a squeak) 'F*** King George the Sixth?'"

The Kriegies were now beside themselves with glee and fell about in uncontrollable laughter. They had won this little bit of 'der vor' and danced the highland fling.

The German, not knowing quite what next to do, called for order, asking for 'der rezponzible room leader'. Ferdie had already taken up the horizontal palliasse having passed the bounds of conscious thought some time ago. He was dragged out on jelly legs and held upright by two less-inebriated Kriegies, in front of the German.

"Vot iss yor name?" asked the Kraut.

"Belt up" replied Ferdie.

"How you spell?" queried the Gerry.

"B.E.L.T.U.P" obliged Ferdie. The Kraut wrote it down, turned smartly on the right heel and left the room followed closely by his astounded guard.

At morning appel, Ferdie was 'sehr krank im Zimmer', when the duty officer on parade rasped out

"Step vorvard Sergeant Beltup, you haff bin avorded fourteen days zolitary."

One muses over the unforgettable scene when Ferdie was hauled off to the cooler, amid long uproarious cheers, still quite unconscious on a stretcher.

Ferdie had many names from time to time. Because of the shapely beard he once sported, the Germans called him Jesus Christ, and we couldn't improve on that.

From the moment Ferdie poured out the first shot of the colourless concoction, Cec Room's suspicions were aroused. Cec never could forget the potency of that deceitful brew. The smell was ominous and the air above the uncorked bottle shimmered like the tortured heat haze of a desert mirage or the quivering ejection from a jet-engine vent, and as you raised your glass, (in this case, as ever, the inevitable Klim tin), the raw evaporation of the volatile product somehow penetrated your sinuses, straight through your cheekbones it seemed, and you caught your breath by way of defence. The inner surface of your Klim suddenly became much cleaner than ever before as if purges with a swill of hydrochloric acid and you feared what was going to be the effect on your gullet, stomach, and entrails. Cec was soon to discover. He was suffering from some kind of poisoning which the Lager doctor found to be beyond the camp drug store capability. So off went Cec on some kind of primitive oxen cart transport to the local civil hospital with the customary armed guard in tow. He was ushered into a ward to be greeted by a lovely young nurse, whose beautiful and liberal appendages would have demanded space on page four to accommodate the overspill from page three.

From the greeting which the guard received from this glorious manifestation it was obvious that they knew each other. This was confirmed later that evening when the day-staff went off and the lovely one stayed on as the sole ward night-staff member.

"The prisoner is sleeping soundly." said the guard when she later approached Cec's bed, whereupon she moved gracefully to the foot of the next empty bed then tastefully removed her complete attire, (according to one of Cec's half closed eyes) as the guard propped his rifle against Cec's bedside locker, and concentrating on weaponry of a more personal nature, he nipped smartly into bed with her, to the accompanying oohs and aahs which suggested a target bulls-eye in one.

It was the small tent-like arrangement formed by Cec's bed covers which suggested he could be sleeping in a slightly knees-up format.

Such sensuality did not hasten a quick recovery from Cec's dreaded malady, so for yet a further seven days he feigned deep sleep at the convenient evening hour, enjoying the therapeutic movements of the young naked nurse and noted the advanced state of knackeredness creep o'er the frame of the guard as the week progressed. It was not often that Cec had experienced weaponry dilemma but in this case he did not know whether to lay the guard's rifle or rifle the guard's lay. That guard would never know that indirectly he owed someone dearly for that week of concentrated copulation. In any case Ferdie would not have appreciated receiving such thanks. Morty Vineberg well remembers Ferdie's brew not only for the electrifying potency and the stealthy paramnesia, but that it left his mouth effectively upholstered with rabbit fur.

Moving to a more moderate and palliative Kriegie brew, namely wine, the Mountain Brew of Spike Conolly was the first to be produced, according to Willy Mercer. It was brewed in a half-barrel, with a zinc bottom, which had at one time contained lime. Even so, the product was quite a killer and Willy, copying these experiments turned out some rather pleasant wine. But one batch went sour – oh disaster! Willy sought the advice of barrack 3 experts, two characters, Maddison and Maddox. One had his right arm missing and the other his left hand. They had both escaped from Amien by cutting their way through seven barbed wire entanglements after the repatriation they awaited, fell through. Apparently the Gerries insisted on having one of their U-boat Kommanders in exchange.

"Your sour wine is due to infection by a certain bacteria." was the verdict. The good news however was that the concoction was considered to form a most suitable base for a very good brand of 'whisky'. A still was required. Solder was acquired from melted down silver paper from cigarette packets, flux was from tallow traded from a goon, and stilling information, such as alcohol boils at 70°C and does not bubble like water but has its own nice little rustling hiss. All went well for Willy and his still and out dripped a lovely crystal clear liquid which proved to be totally unsympathetic to the drinker and devastatingly swift in operation. A creeping goon, quite unannounced, one afternoon looked over Willy's shoulder as he attended to his illicit still, enquiring how the product tasted. "Schmecht's gut?" To keep on the right side of the goon and hope to avoid possible confiscation, Willy kindly invited the Gerry to sample the precious product and before you could say 'Goons up', the poor square head was flat out, totally paralytic. Willy left him on his own bed to sleep it off and later saw him staggering away minus his cap, torch and prodding tool, not seeming to know whether he was punched, bored or countersunk. He returned later for his lost items, bringing pockets full of medicine bottles to house this mysterious grog, which precious stuff was later to become recognised by the name 'White Lightning'.

Groupy McDonald and Willy Turner came over to take part in the Bridge Tournament and on taking their seats were offered a fraternal welcome in the form of a glass (Klim tin) of Willie's wine.

"I just cannot understand," said Groupy, "how you fellows become so hopelessly drunk on this lovely tasting wine." as he enjoyed the savour of the bouquet. The levels in the 'glasses' went lower and lower and the levels of conversation climbed even higher. It was time for the 'glasses' to be replenished but of course it was a wee drap o' White Lightning which Willy now dispensed. Neither Groupy nor his friend even finished the first hand and had to be carried back to their barracks to keep the place tidy.

"Willie's White" could affect you in one of many ways. One imbiber was seen to be playing his guitar, with a glassy stare, under the communal shower. You could become drunk, being totally immobile whilst the brain appeared comparatively cool, or you were capable (in a manner of speaking), of perambulating but were best described as brain dead. There was, some years later, a very nasty situation on a flight in an old 'Annie Anson', where those concerned were fortunate to walk away from it. Pilot: G/C McDonald. Crew: Willey Mercer. As Willy observed it,

"My how those hang-overs could hangover."

He recalled how one of the Czech pilots (was it 'Tarbrush' Zebrowski?) who made a tolerable brandy from prunes. He would allow the mash of prunes to become slightly burnt at the bottom of the still, where an ingenious revolving, hand-turned arrangement allowed the prunes to be evenly burned ... Brandwein (burnt wine).

· CHAPTER 10 ·

THE BALTIC CRUISE

June 6th 1944 brought the Second Front, or 'D-day', and to my complete amazement the captors relayed the announcement over the loudspeaker they had installed.

> Das Oberkommando der Wehrmacht gibt bekannt (The Army High Command announces) In der vergangenen Nacht hat der Feind seinen seit langen vorbereiteten und von uns erwarteten Angriff auf Westeuropa begonnen. Eingeleitet durch schwere Luftangriffe auf unsere Kustbefestigungen setze er, an mehreren Stellen, der Nordfranzosischenkuste zwischen Le Havre und Cherbourg, Luftlandette Truppen ab, und landete gleichzeitig, unterstutzt durch starke Seestreitkrafte auch von See her. In den angegriffenen Kustenstreifen sind erbitterte Kampfe im Gange.*

Our airborne and seaborne troops were forming a bridgehead in France. We who understood German, had clung to every word, the non German speakers sensed there was something big, stopped in their circuitous tramp, and amid many shushes were asking, "What's the gen?".

We erupted with delight to tell of the newsflash, when morale took on a new and wonderful complexion.

Meantime advances on the Russian front against the Germans were very encouraging. The long hard winter had passed, we now had sunshine with us and more to look forward to, plus hope to sustain us. Within the next ten months we were to discover that we needed every bit of both which we could muster, and every ounce of food we could find, just to survive.

With the advent of the Second Front came an increase in German arrogance, a noticeably increasing iciness in their attitude developed, whilst they struggled to create the air of superiority, something they sought to achieve by instilling a certain measure of fear.

It was July 13th 1944 – we were told to prepare to move. There would be no transport, not even for our kit, so we were to take with us only items we could conveniently carry. Anyone approaching the incinerator to destroy surplus beyond our capacity would be shot. Jock Rae recalled how he concentrated on preserving that strongest currency on the continent, which could be transported the easiest of all – cigarettes.

---

*TRANSLATION. Last night, the enemy began his well prepared, and long awaited attack, on West Europe. It was preceded by heavy air attacks and at many points between Le Havre and Cherbourg. Simultaneously troops have landed from the sea supported by strong naval forces. Bitter fighting is taking place in the coastal defence areas."

We were wild with enthusiasm, not because we were leaving camp, as a very uncertain future awaited us, but because the news was good. We were heading west away from the advancing Russian armies. We had been able to hear the rumble of their guns for some time now and we knew the Hun was cracking. That pompous arrogance was perhaps now their strongest weapon. They were still top dog and they would let us know it.

Someone got into the store where the stock of camp toilet rolls was the target, and within what seemed only minutes everybody was celebrating. The whole camp was festooned with hundreds of fluttering toilet paper streamers. It streamed from the wire fences, it hung in crazy writhing snakes from telephone wire and from overhead electrical cables, from chimney roofs as though the Lager were some scene of lewd and grotesque carnival.

Edible items which could not be easily carried were hastily contaminated and rendered unfit for the Krauts to use.

Being outside the wire was a thrill we had long forgotten. To walk along a leafy lane or a tree lined path, to see the fields where the harvest was being worked, albeit in a manner not familiar to us in England, was stimulating and exciting, remembers Jock Rae. Rickety carts drawn by gaunt, lean oxen, swayed and creaked, surrounded by scampering ill-clad children, the oxen being driven by their mother in bonnet and long thick swaying skirt. The forced workers from other countries provided the labour required for the cutting, working and loading of the harvest, and they regarded us with inquisitive side glances as we shuffled along in a column a thousand strong. A young petite bride of some eighteen years was leaving the church with her burly Luftwaffe corporal groom as we shuffled past. She appeared to be quite genuinely upset at the sight of our plight – which she could not have been accustomed to.

> Behind barbed wire a world is known
> Comprised of men who once had flown
> Where tales are told of courage rare
> Heroic deeds done in the air.
>
> Men who have lived and fought for others
> Herded together more close than brothers
> Struggling along on Deutsch brown bread
> As tough as teak and heavy as lead
>
> Never a dull day but comes the news
> That puts a fellow in the blues
> A loved one married a Yank or worse
> Or back pay going in wife's own purse.
>
> The worthy host a jovial brute
> Takes our kit and calls it loot
> Stops our food at least pretext
> One wonders what or who is next.

> But all is not lost for these salvaged wrecks
> Who dream of back pay, booze and sex
> Soon will their ego be increased
> When they fly the skies of the far, far east.

We were loaded down with belongings in all kinds of ingenious rucksacks. The common one, I think, was the shirt sewn up at the bottom and along the button line, with the cuffs of the sleeves sewn to the bottom corners. Chas Harrison had one better. His shoulder straps were of the luxury brand, – a pair of real braces sewn on with some very colourful string he had received in a parcel.

We were herded onto a railway siding where stood, awaiting us, those ominous looking cattle trucks to which we had become accustomed on our trip from Barth. Perhaps, here again was the opportunity to saw our way to freedom once more and this time get to Danzig and those resistance workers, the Poles. Failing that one could always head east to welcome the oncoming Russians. The clanging doors were thrown open to reveal the bare internal starkness, staring uninvitingly.

We were pushed inside, the guards bustling and pushing, shouting, "Los, Los" (quickly, quickly), becoming increasingly irate as we struggled with our packs to climb in, when it seemed there was not just enough room for one more man. But there had to be the room for a further ten or fifteen or even twenty and more, until there were 76 to 80 in each truck designated to carry 40. Kit was so difficult to handle. It had to be taken off shoulders. One had no space to turn around. To bend down brought head and bottom into contact with other bodies and packs. To sit was impossible, even on your own kit because of being unbalanced by staggering bodies, and then trodden on. We would have to establish ourselves before the train got into motion otherwise there would be chaos.

The shunting started, doors having been forced shut and barred. If you were against the wall, down shunt, the breath was squeezed from your lungs by the weight of bodies thrown off balance. It was dreadful.

We arrived at Memel, the seaport on the western coast of Lithuania, the train pulling up on the dockside. It seemed we were to make a journey by sea. Speculation was rife. If they wanted to take us west, why not on the train on which we were packed, the same method by which we arrived. Surely that would have been quicker. "Were they going to scuttle us mid Baltic?" queried someone, "or have us walk the plank?" The dockside was crowded with Organization Todt, (Labour Corps), and hundreds of Volksturm, ill clad and dishevelled, carrying their usual tools of trade, picks and shovels. Had they fled the concentration camps to the east where perhaps they constituted the burial parties?

We were now in a quite exhausted state, having spent a long sleepless night, mostly on our feet, squashed up together in those cattle trucks, continually trying to keep balance and avoid tripping over kit when you would either have your toes stood on or you would be standing on someone else's. Thirst was especially bad, but the Germans reasoned that the less you drink the less you need to waste time urinating.

Clanging of doors could be heard. We were being disgorged. The drop from the floor of the truck to the ground was some four feet. The best way out was to shuffle over the edge on your bottom, then reach up for your kit and make your way from the mad house where the guards were urging everyone out, even by dragging. Oh for a drink and something to eat. In those trucks we could not even use our arms to organise a smoke. In any case the atmosphere was hot and foul enough.

Forming up on the dockside for a further lengthy boring count we were blasted and harangued by the irate Huns, whom we continually cursed for their arrogance and incompetence.

The column moved off along the dockside and the leading end turned up a gang plank leading onto a dilapidated, seemingly unseaworthy old and dirty coaster of about 1500 tons. The deck was soon crowded but the guards were continuing to cram more and more up the gangway. Frankie Taylor and Bob Galloway were together; Harry Pettie and Wendel; Bob Hart and Tommy Tomkins. Tommy had been prominent stockman in the education under Georgie Wood, Frank Hill, Jimmy White and Larry Butterworth and of course Ken Gosney. Who cannot remember Ken's maths classes? After each explanation or example, Ken, with his chin in the air, looking at the class, along the short length of his nose as though it had a ring sight fitted on the end, would query, "Now is that perfectly clear?" Most times to some of us it would not be, and to some it never was. Not that Ken was not a good teacher, it just took quite an effort to assimilate it. There were classes from 0800 hrs to 2030 hrs Included were; Bull fighting in Spain; Guernsey under the Germans; Rugby football; Spiritualism; and a host of academic subjects. I had classes on our solar system.

There was serious commotion on deck where we were to find the guards pushing the boys down two small square hatches which led, by two slender swinging ladders, to the bilge swilling hold of this filthy old coaler. Each man had to throw his pack onto an already mounting heap on deck, denying him any access to his food or belongings. The ship was a mere shell, the innards covered in flour-fine coal dust which became airborne at the slightest touch. The boys scrabbled and struggled in the semi darkness to get away from the foot of the ladder, stumbling over the ribs and the propeller shaft housing. Those already in the hold, numbering about five hundred, were shouting that there was no room for any more, but the deck was still overcrowded with hundreds more tired bodies being pushed around. The frantic Germans insisted that all men must go down into the hold. The whole operation was a nightmare, the boys were arriving at the bottom of the ladder with no floor space for them to occupy. They pushed along to the far extremities of the ship, to make room for those still descending, it was extremely difficult to see anything. There was not enough room to sit with your legs out, and to lie down was entirely out of the question.

Eventually, with cooperation, we all sat with our knees drawn up sitting back to back to give each other support. What a blessing that we did not know then that we were to spend half a week in those conditions becoming increasingly worse as the days went by. At the foot of the ladder by us, bodies were so clamped together that Harry and Wendel, last down, stood there all night until the following morning, when they at last got a knees-up sitting position near to Chas Harrison and Stotle.

Short of the usual coal ballast in the hold, the ship rode high in the water and one could detect, even at this stage, that if the sea were to be rough, we were in a for a very uncomfortable trip. To where we knew not.

What an empty vessel clatter, and what bone shaking vibration when the engines were bludgeoned into life. We lost all sense of direction. There were no portholes, no ventilation or light, except that afforded by the tiny hatch some thirty feet above our heads.

There were no toilet facilities at all, and bladders were now becoming uncomfortably full. So were bowels, some being desperate, but no amount of persuasion would bring the Krauts to allow anyone on deck.

A bucket was lowered through the hatch on the end of a long rope. It contained drinking water. It swung to and fro as it descended and slopped the contents over the sides, showering dozens of men clustered round the ladder area. How does one distribute a bucket of water amongst hundreds of thirsty men and preserve some semblance of order? The bucket was emptied and rather than have it do an empty journey it was promptly refilled for the return trip with urine. But what of the boys around the ladder area? The bucket was much too full as it was hauled up through that narrow hatch. Some boys of course could not possibly wait and had to relieve themselves on the dust laden floor where they sat.

Up and down went the buckets whilst the old *Insterburg* rolled and pitched, the slopping increasing from the ever swinging buckets as they clanged against the unstable ladder.

Danny, Joe and Bill, the medics, were allowed up on deck during the hours of daylight, to dispense the pills to the suffering who were also allowed up there in relays, in small numbers. We perched on the ribs of the hull in an attempt to gain some measure of relief from the crowded floor. Vic Hanks and his Otley friend slung a greatcoat between some spars as a hammock and by some odd quirk of fate it held.

One could hear the impact on the hull of every piece of driftwood, or whatever, as it rattled and clanged on the metal plates. With every sound we waited for the explosion of the mines which possibly some of our boys had "planted" whilst out "gardening".

We contemplated the impossibility of escape should we hit a mine, or should a sub put a tin fish into us. For a thousand of us to gain exit through those two tiny hatches was of course out of the question. Judy Garland reasoned it would be better not to hurry, it would avoid crowding the exit, but to keep swimming as the hold filled up, eventually floating up to the hatch for exit.

After the first two days and nights in the 'hell ship' we had really had enough. Men were indeed hungry, thirsty and filthy, with no indication as to what the future might hold. There was no way of knowing that there was yet a further two nights and a whole day to endure those barbaric conditions.

What a galvanising moment therefore when out of the darkness in the depths of the filthy hold a clear vibrant tenor voice broke the atmosphere and the strains of a well known aria rang with verve through the bowels of that rolling pitching shell. What a deep emotional moment to experience; one which cannot be forgotten in a lifetime, "My Wild Irish Rose", as Archie King recalls. One felt a new invigorating injection of hope into a very desperate situation.

The groans of some of the very ill pervaded the almost entirely dark interior. As a means of easing their own lot for a while, some of the boys volunteered to stand up, allowing more room on the floor for the sick to lie down and stretch their cramped bodies.

Meantime some gained temporary respite by a short visit onto deck, Jack Paul, with his station near the bottom of the ladder keeping some kind of order and standard of selection for exit. Vic Clarke, the Lager Leader, and other German speaking Kriegies, were up on top. I remember Jack Laing was there when I

The Insterburg, *shown obviously fully loaded, sitting very low in the water. Built in Sweden in 1919. Russian-owned until captured by the Germans. Finally sunk by RAF 3rd May 1945, now registered wreck (posn. 54.31.44N 10.21.08E).*

spent some time up top, and there was my Welsh friend Des Dunphy also a fluent German speaker.

What could be turning over in the minds of some of the armed German guards? Were they quietly hoping that here was an opportunity for them to escape from this madhouse Nazi dilemma? Sweden was not far distant to the north. They were in a strong enough position, had they been able to coerce or incite their fellows to overcome the crew and sail to freedom. Perhaps however they could not trust each other. As ever, amongst the Germans there was mistrust and fear. Is that then why one of the German guards, when in casual conversation with Des, laid his loaded rifle across Des's knees as though to suggest that he made of it what he would? Was he hoping Des would grab the opportunity of attempting to overcome the guards and give them the excuse to mow us down in order to quell the revolt or was he suggesting we plan to disarm the other guards, stick a pistol behind the ear of the helmsman and alter course to Sweden?

Surely his action was not precipitous. Perhaps had we been in better condition we may have done something about it. Did he know there was worse treatment in store for us?

Des, as one can imagine, was somewhat non-plussed. He did not handle the weapon whatsoever, and made no reference to the weapon in the conversation. Des was well known to the guards, and a respected Kriegie, so one could not regard this action as being entirely trivial.

Ian Watson-Jones recalls that he, Roy Stevens, and many others who were 'krank' on leaving Heydekrug (Ian had a broken ankle), were 'transported' to Memel, plonked on the deck of the *Insterburg* and covered with a huge tarpaulin. He remembered that the stench from below deck was terrible, and remarked how lucky they considered themselves to be, out in the open.

The boy next to Ian had a burst appendix, and Ian said that he was in one hell of a state and often wondered whether he survived.

A rather strange, incident occurred aboard 'that floating hell hole', wrote Ian. One late evening a German rifle was pitched under the tarpaulin which was stretched over us. It was passed from hand to hand a few times and eventually disappeared. Ian thought that we were, at the time, probably at the nearest point to the island of Bornholm and it gives rise, said Ian, to the thought that some Gerry, or Gerries, were just as browned off as we were, and hoped that one of us might have done something about it. But what could be expected, thought Ian, of the crippled and ailing? I don't quite know, reflected Ian. He never did know where the rifle went to eventually.

There was, that day, general consternation on deck which quickly spread through the whole complement on board. Lofty Minnitt recalled the wide eyes and the steely atmosphere when a sub was sighted, having surfaced close to our wake. If it were British or Russian, then there was no future.

"This bloody old crate is not worth a brass farthing", said a voice. "Who suggests we are any safer if that sub is a Gerry – They'd get rid of a thousand bods they don't want, at the cost of an old crate like this and a tin fish".

Everyone was ushered below and not allowed on deck again before disembarking.

We were nearing port after three nights and three days in those beastly conditions. It would, we cogitated, be heaven to be out of these slave-like conditions. Harry Pettie remembered, too well, the ominous scraping noise along the keel, just under his bottom where he sat, as the ship made contact with the boom to the entrance of Swinemunde harbour, but we were yet to spend a further night in those foul conditions.

> In days to come when I am free
> In looking back I'll sometimes see
> The *Insterburg* by Memel Quay
> Which borders on the Baltic sea.
>
> I'll smell again the stifling hold
> Where near a thousand prisoners bold
> Were stored as slaves in days of old
> In transit to another fold.
>
> Four nights I spent there sick and sore
> Huddling round that filthy floor
> Wondering would I ever more
> See once again old England's shore.
>
> But such is life in many ways
> Tempt not the fates it never pays
> "Roll on the boat", a common phrase
> I'll say no more in all my days."
>
> *Luft VI, 1944*

We were to spill out at last, to scramble up that weak and shaky ladder and emerge at last to eye-aching daylight. What a spectacle we were. Really, how could any decent, self-respecting human with any sense of values whatsoever allow fellow men to be in such a condition. To the Germans in charge of us, however, such was commonplace, so long as it was not happening to them. They behaved despicably, seeming to enjoy doing it. To allow, or even to think of such behaviour was entirely foreign to our British way of thinking. Times such as these really made us feel proud to be British, and that the Allied Forces were surely, within a few months to crush the breath out of this murderous Nazi machine; to see Hitler dead, and free the world from tyranny.

Under Nazi rule there would have been no future for British youth, or any other nationality, except the arrogant Arian chosen race.

The guards urged us to pick up any pack nearest to us, whether it can be our own or not, saying we could sort it out later.

Jim Haskett, as we docked, worked his way up to the front on deck with Andy. The gang plank was laid from ship to shore and Jim had a good view of all that was happening in that area. Suddenly two of the boys, obviously quite crazed, made a suicidal break for the gang plank, down towards the direction of some trucks. The metallic sickening staccato chatter of a machine gun rasped out from the Bridge without hesitation and mowed one of the boys down unmercifully. The German guards flew into a furore, pushing, shoving and threatening every one near to them. The victim died there on the wharf where he fell. Instinctively, as the machine gun chatter rattled out again, we ducked. One boy dropped as he ran. The momentum of his run carried him on and he fell between the side of the ship and the wharf, riddled with bullets. This precipitous action was all quite unnecessary and yet just another example of the characteristic butchery of these Krauts, and the typical over reaction we had come to recognise as part of German procedure in such situations which could have been contained quite adequately with a measure of typical British restraint and no bullets.

Once again we were faced with the now all too familiar cattle trucks. Many of the boys had been herded in, sixty to eighty per truck, roughly pushed with brutal rifle butt blows here and there to hurry matters along. Many of us were yet on the quayside being urged to enter other trucks, when to add to the chaos, the air-raid siren screamed. The Germans became wide eyed with confusion and panic, fearing we would break in all directions of the compass and escape. They motioned us to dive under the trucks for cover. The tension was too much for some of them and without waiting for us to dive under the trucks they dived under themselves motioning to us to follow suit. During the act of diving under the trucks some guards had lost their rifles, and some of us were kicking their rifles to them under the trucks. One of the boys close by to me was shouting to a guard who was peeping out from beneath a truck, urging him to get under. "Get further under you yellow bellied Kraut, there's hardly room for Kriegies", and he threw his rifle at him.

An immediate chemical smoke screen was released. Thick, acrid and choking, the smoke spread quickly setting off coughing bouts and blinding our visibility. Then the anti-aircraft guns opened up with ear splitting reports. I and those around me dived under the trucks without delay and laid flat. More German rifles came tumbling after us, with the guards flinging themselves prone, quaking and obviously shaken. The battle-cruiser, Leipzig, and the Prinz Eugen, anchored in the harbour loosed off their guns with thunderous reverberations to add to the already deafening noise.

Judy Garland, lying flat on the floor, locked inside one of the trucks, recalled how the bombs fell around causing the trucks to actually jump in the air from the blast and vibration. Judy said how it reminded him of the old RAF mess song, a *Bless 'em all* parody:

> They say there's a Lancaster leaving the Ruhr,
> Bound for old Blighty's shore
> Heavily laden with terrified men
> Shit scared and prone on the floor.

Bob Hart remembered being locked up, packed sardine-fashion in one of the trucks. Bob said that the trucks almost fell apart with vibration. It was quite dark in the truck and with every shattering salvo the roof boards would spring apart, momentarily admit narrow shafts of light and spring back into position again. Bombs continued to rain down and Bob said that they feared that many of them would be killed before the wave of bombers had passed.

Years later, Johnnie Theckston pulled out of his pocket an old photograph he had in his possession in one of those trucks. He handed it to me on the back, written whilst in the truck, I read; "Here we are off the boat and in cattle trucks again. An alarm has just sounded and a smoke screen spread out, and what bloody smoke. I can just manage to see with difficulty. We have three possibilities; we get bombed, we get choked or we get out of this nightmare – to what? They are now chaining us together."

The Germans extremely irate and shaken, turned their full attention on us, once the bombers had turned away. They stripped us all of boots, belts, braces, knives and matches and commenced to handcuff us in pairs. The guards had now taken on a new attitude of frigidity and arrogance.

Luckily there were not enough handcuffs to tether everyone in pairs, and I along with a few others just managed to dodge the guards who were busy detailing those for treatment by the gaolers with the sacks of handcuffs. There was great confusion. The whole scene was a madhouse. The guards were screaming at the boys, lined up handcuffed, standing by the trucks. They waved their rifles in the air wildly to encourage the boys to board the trucks, shrieking, "Einsteigen! Einsteigen! Los! Los!" The boys who were handcuffed, effectively only had one hand with which to handle their kit into the trucks, and then it was by no means easy hoisting themselves four feet up to the truck floor level. Some were handcuffed by that arm which had already been passed through the shoulder strap of the kit bag, which meant they could not free themselves from the pack. This was a great inconvenience causing serious problems. I being free from fetters, was assisting some of them with their problems, when a fuming guard attempted to hustle me into the truck. He did not wish to admit that I was helping to solve some of the chaos he had clumsily caused, and the situation developed into a verbal slanging match, which I claimed to win, albeit that I had the bruises whilst he had the bulging eyes and a chin covered in frothy German spit.

Eventually the train moved off with a very compact load of extremely uncomfortable Kriegies. To those who were able to stretch their necks long enough, to see out of the ventilator, the aircraft carrier, Graf Zepplin, was to be seen, anchored in one of the docks.

We were to spend the whole of that night in those conditions, again without food, water, a wash or shave, without sanitation, sleep or a sit down. This treatment, following the boat trip, had most of us on the point of exhaustion, but many were already quite beyond that point and were collapsed down amongst our feet. There was not enough room to bend down to render them assistance and we feared the worst for many who were being trodden on, quite unintentionally, there was no way of avoiding it. It is in such conditions as these that one realises just how long a really long night can be. Even when the train was brought to a halt, the guards refused to unbolt the doors to allow in some fresh air or to unload the very sick to gain some comfort and a drink of water.

Morning came with the hope of some relief. The German speaking Kriegies, and many others were shouting at the guards through the bolted doors to unlock the doors and let in some air. It was the 19th July and the sun rose hot in the early hours. The temperature in the trucks steadily rose as the morning progressed, until, for some, it actually became unbearable and they sank at last to their knees, tongues were parched and they breathed in gasps. Those who had fallen during the night were limp and silent. Were they dead or were they just fast asleep with utter exhaustion? It was so necessary that those of us who were able to stand remained doing so, just for the sake of those who had collapsed.

The hours came and went. Nine o'clock; ten; eleven; mid-day, and the sun became hotter and hotter. We could of course now see each other, although not very clearly, but gaunt faces and hollow eyes were all around. What we were not going to do to these bloody Krauts when the boot was on the other foot, was not worth a whisper. "Thank Christ for the English Channel," said Dave, "to keep these bastards off my doorstep". That was just what we had been fighting for, and so in these cattle trucks were still fighting, in a different kind of way. We were not going to give in to this brutality so easy as the Germans perhaps hoped.

In the heat of that July day the doors of those oven-like trucks were opened just after 1pm and with great relief we contemplated some moments of welcome respite. We helped out the sick and commenced to lay them down in the fresh but very warm air. The Germans busied themselves prodding everyone to their feet. No one was allowed to sit and no one was allowed to rest their pack on the ground, even when they were sorting out our boots, braces and belts to return to us. We were lined up in fives for counting and great numbers of new guards were milling around in a most aggressive manner. The greatest number of new guards were youths of the Kriegsmarina, equipped with rifles and fixed bayonets and were shod in sports type footwear. Men from the Luftwaffe Signals equipped with automatic weapons were present and it became quite obvious that something rather ominous was about to take place. Packs of very large Alsatian dogs, with handlers then came upon the scene and distributed themselves along our flanks. There now appeared to be approximately one guard for each two Kriegies.

Bob Bell and Fred Tees succeeded in getting their handcuffs off, were noticed by a sympathetic guard and told to keep them out of sight but to replace them immediately they saw the officer coming along. Magwood and Alan Schofield managed to unlock theirs with a corned beef key. Bob Hart leaned against a tree for a moment of relief and received a flogging from a very unsympathetic guard for taking such a liberty.

Bob Sharpe was handcuffed to Wroublewski, Vic Hanks to another Polish boy, Jim Smith to Ivan Ure, Frankie Taylor to Bob Galloway, Lofty Maddocks to Stotle, Eric Willis to Bert Law, Chas Harrison to Jock Davidson, Filliter to Cornish, Soggy Norton, at six foot three, to a very short Polish Kriegie, Jim Haskett to Andy Anderton, Bob Bell to Fred Tees, Bill Vine to Mitch, Wally to Harry Parkes and so were scores of others shackled together unable to handle their packs properly.

Vic Clarke came along the ranks telling us that the Germans intended the march to the camp to be uncomfortable, but not to hurry unduly. The Germans announced that we may abandon our kit now so that our forthcoming journey would be made much easier.

In the heat of the sun, in our extremely weakened condition, we perspired profusely and the thirst was tortuous. Lips and mouths were so parched that tongues felt like foreign bodies as with some effort they rattled around and were unable to swallow. In the Western Desert I had experienced some uncomfortable thirsts when lips and eyes were ringed and caked in dust, when one could not find enough saliva to help spit out the sand. This however was a different kind of thirst, born of days of lack of sleep of rough handling with neither food nor water. Everyone suffered the agonies. We were subjected to yet a further extended and farcical count before moving off in column of fives. The agonisingly hot July sun was almost unbearable in our condition. There was no escape from this punishment.

We were then halted on a road, slightly on the incline and quite straight as far as the eye could see. The road ran through what was obviously a heavily-forested area, the road being flanked by a fairly deeply dug-out ditch on either side, and perhaps a further twelve feet beyond that, were the closely packed pine trees. The atmosphere was torrid.

The young Kriegsmarina guards now became extremely active and excited, being paraded, with a great deal of raucous shouting, with their fixed bayonets at the ready. The guards with the automatic weapons also brought theirs to the ready. The situation now appeared to be quite sinister.

Suddenly there appeared a most unusual-looking character on the scene. He was riding on the running-board of a vehicle. A small somewhat portly figure, much overdressed, brutal eyed, fleshy faced and twitching with excitement.

This beastly little Hauptmann by the name of Pickhardt left no-one in any doubt that he was in complete charge of events. Sweat poured out. Surely this man was demented. Hate spewed from every expression. He commenced to scream and gyrate in a fashion one could never have imagined. We had many times witnessed the undignified outbursts by Germans, officers and men alike, with flashing eyes and spraying saliva, but nothing to equal this exhibition of what appeared to be totally frenzied madness.

He harangued the guards, told them that we were the Terrorflieger and Luftgangsters who had bombed their cities, killed their fathers, mothers, brothers, sisters, aunts and uncles, sweethearts, friends, wives and children. The Kriegsmarina now seethed with rage. He reminded the guards that we had, with evil intentions bombed the old and helpless out of their homes to cause widespread miseries to those who could not hit back, and that we were now to take the consequences. He further told them that they were not to rely on verbal orders to us. "Nur Waffen! Nur Waffen!" he shrieked (weapons only), as the veins stood out prominently on his features and neck, and his eyeballs threatened to vacate their sockets.

He grabbed his revolver from the holster and began to wave it high in the air as he bellowed at the guards, and, as he stabbed the air with his revolver, the whole frame jerked convulsively. He really did present a most ridiculous exposition, his voice winding up to a crescendo where it started to break, making hysterical swine-like guttural squeals.

"Make these Luftgangsters run! Make them run fast! Make them run even faster and faster! They must run! They must run until they drop!"

Many were dropping already. In addition to being quite demented he was also obviously quite vain. As more than one Kriegie was to remark, he looked like an overdressed Italian ice cream vendor. His clothing was quite immaculate, his gleaming white breeches were faultless and his knee-length boots were polished to a glass-like finish. He most certainly wore facial make-up which was much too heavily applied, and the warm July air appeared to accentuate the pungency of his acrid perfume.

Those of us who understood his actual words were able to pass on a potted version, but those who were near enough to see this lunatic display really did not need to have his words interpreted. His expression said it all.

The boys up at the front of the column and those at the extreme rear end, were of course too far away to know what was being said, and were therefore quite oblivious as to what was afoot. To those of us who were close enough to witness the physical exhibition and hear the verbal diatribe of this psycho neurotic, it was clear that a certain measure of restraint and discipline was essential if we were to handle this situation without anyone being very seriously hurt. How could these people be so despicable?

Pickhardt then waving his revolver high at arms length, ordered his driver to start the vehicle moving slowly along the flank of the column as he now stood higher in the vehicle scanning the whole length of the column frantically screaming,

"Alles laufen! Alles laufen! Alles laufen!" (everybody run).

The guards broke into immediate action, especially those in our vicinity, close to Pickhardt, as they were intent on putting up a good show in the immediate presence of their worshipful master. The guards, at the top of their voices urged us to run. There was nowhere to run. There were about five hundred boys in front of us blocking our path. They had not yet commenced to run and we were not going to push them. Many of our boys who had suffered on the boat and the train, were still very weak, and of those who were handcuffed it was very clear that we were to expect some casualties.

The guards commenced to become really angry because we were not jumping to their commands and the young Kriegsmarina charged into our flanks with their bayonets thrust forward. They aimed at our buttocks, and the blade made a funny little crunching sound as it pierced your flesh but you found that you could still run. Even though the blade would penetrate quite some way it did not render the muscle inoperative. It hurt a lot more if they missed your buttocks and got the blade in your thigh or hamstring. You were then apt to slip in a half step and a spontaneous remark, such as "You Kraut bastard!" Rifle butts then descended on our shoulders and packs in varying degrees of severity, but we had to ward off the blows as best we could, there was still no way forward. The boys on the flanks were getting the worst of the treatment and made their way to the centre of the column. Others, less physically handicapped with no handcuffs on, voluntarily made their way to the flanks in order to afford protection to those who had received some blows.

The guards were shouting to other guards further up the column and also making their way forward to get the head of the column moving... "Laufen! Laufen!"

The boys up front and towards the rear, at first brushed off the order to run as some kind of sick joke, not being fully aware of the situation, having been quite out of earshot when the initial ranting took place. Harry Pettie and Wendel at the rear of the column were amongst those being harassed to run but saw no reason why they should. Having kept the ranks fairly well closed up they thought they were just being encouraged to keep closer ranks which could be quite easily achieved without running. One of their number who was still very sore from the train journey, saw no reason whatsoever why he should hurry after all those wasted hours standing cooking in the trucks, and told the guard who was screaming at them to, "Wrap up you fagging excitable Kraut bastard". Not for a moment was it believed that the guard understood a word of this, but he must have sensed the interpretation and lashed out with his rifle butt so viciously that the Kriegie went reeling, quite stunned. The boys were quite taken aback at this treatment, being of the opinion that what they had endured over the past few days could not be escalated into something even worse.

Then, as Harry remembered, rifle shots rang out from further up the column, and the general din of noise was topped by the yelping and barking dogs with much angry growling and even howls of what appeared to be caused by pain. What could this confusion be?

Judy Garland and Barney Smith up front, Bob Bell and Fred Tees, were close to Chas Harrison and Jock Davidson. They had already quickened their step somewhat but resisted the increasing pressure to run. A Feldwebel near to Judy was goading a British boy on the outer flank shouting "Run, run, run!" There was no reaction from the passive airman, whereupon the Feldwebel motioned to a guard to use his bayonet on the hapless airman. The boy did not run and even parried off the bayonet thrusts as they came in, with a few appropriate remarks such as, "What's the bloody game, you irritating bastard?" Judy recalled that by this time the tempers of the guards were becoming frightfully raggy around the edges and the crescendo of the voices grew dramatically. Dogs were being riled and tormented, then being given a long lead to enable them to lunge into the flanks and take the first available victim. The Feldwebel was fast losing what little patience he had remaining. He drew his revolver, pushed it into the ear of the imperturbable airman, and with a beetroot type complexion and protruding eyeballs, squeaked, "Run English swine, run!" The Feldwebel would have dearly loved to bellow at his victim in his customary voice, but he had become so worked up at that his attempt at bellowing hatched out the weakest of tortured squeaks; one almost felt a touch of sympathy for the innate being.

The Feldwebel was now quite overcome with fury, as the dispassionate English swine just ambled along as before. The Feldwebel withdrew his pistol from the boy's ear and with a very determined expression on his face, firmly flicked the safety catch off with the thumb of his other hand, Judy felt sure that the sound of that flick was loud enough to travel the length of the column; disregarding the sound of rifle shots, barking dogs, bellowing guards and cursing, swearing Kriegies. There was something singularly sinister about that click, to Judy's ear, and to other ears around; they all commenced to run without further vacillation. Even the Feldwebel couldn't find the same ear again in which to stick his pistol; it had disappeared into the crowd.

At this time, those up front around Judy's area, could now detect a greater volume of noise from further back down the column. There were more rifle shots, louder and more hysterical shouting and greater savagery in the dog malversation.

Down mid-column we were still more closely packed together, and were not able to move as quickly as the guards would have us do so, but this movement which was now taking place up front eased the mid-column pressure considerably. We had taken quite some volume of punishment in those first few minutes, with the blows from rifle butts, the biting and tearing of the dogs, and the stabbing and slashing of the bayonets, but quite unable to move until now.

Pickhardt was touring up and down the column screaming his invectives, stopping now and again to bellow at the guards to be more active with their weapons. It was in the vicinity of Pickhardt where the guards were particularly savage and where many injuries were inflicted.

This was of course a very long column of about one thousand men, and by no means could I possibly recount the experiences of everyone, we would need a thousand stories and they would all be different in some respects. I was there in the thick of it, so I am able to record what I saw and experienced. I am also able to record the experiences of many others who had already become my firm and lasting friends, many of whom survive today some forty odd years later, and with whom I regularly meet up and correspond.

The pace of the moving column now gathered momentum, although the head of the column was not really moving at a fast pace. Vic Clarke who had attempted to reason with Pickhardt, but who had been dismissed out of hand, had made his way to the head of the column from where he could regulate the pace somewhat by shouting to the boys to simmer down the pace when he deemed it advisable.

"Burglar Bill Bance", a paratrooper, acquitted himself handsomely towards the head of the column, when the tempo of the harassment increased considerably. He was calling out aloud, as were many others,

"Keep it up steady fellows. Don't break the ranks. Keep in close and don't panic."

Many other calls of encouragement were to be heard above the hysterical voices of the guards and of Pickhardt. It was pandemonium.

Jack Laing was to be seen helping fallen boys to their feet. That was like Jack, being where he could help, disregarding his own safety.

The quickened pace, having brought a measure of relief to the centre of the column, now brought new problems as the guards now intensified their weapons activity. Stabbing by bayonets increased to an alarming level and became even more dangerous as the guards elevated the blades in an attempt to slash the shoulder straps of the packs, intent on cutting them free from our possession. Rifle butts were being rained down heavily on shoulders and packs, some guards attempting to free the packs solely through clubbing. The dogs were being goaded and encouraged which rendered them devastatingly aggressive, jumping, snarling and ravaging legs, thighs and hands. Guards were loosing off rifle shots and screaming, "Los! Los! Weiter! Weiter!"

Some boys dropped their packs, whereupon they became immediate obstacles for the boys immediately following. They tripped over them and other Kriegies then fell over the already prostrate bodies. The guards quickly moved in with bayonets and rifle butts, and the dog handlers encouraged the dogs to tear at the struggling Kriegies, with unbelievable savagery and fierceness.

Doug Moore, who was already suffering from an injured ankle, a left-over from being shot down, was helpless on the ground on the outer edge of the column. A large Alsatian was frantically tearing at Doug whilst the handler bawled encouragement to it from a half crouched position. I was placed quite handy in my line of approach as I came upon the scene, and with my right boot I lifted that brute right up the goolies, and immediately diverted its attention to more personal problems. Forty years later when I met Doug for the first time since that incident, Doug greeted me with the question,

"Got any Alsatians up the goolies recently? Thanks anyway."

One of the Canadian boys took a swipe at another of the ferocious animals, as it came into attack, with the banjo he was carrying. The crazed Alsatian howled and yelped, and as though losing all control of its actions, savagely attacked the guard-handler who was so alarmed and infuriated, and being obviously in pain, shot the animal dead on the spot. The banjo was of course ruined, but it had proved to be a useful weapon. It was rather surprising that the guard did not follow up the Kriegie to get even with him. The rifle butts continued to rain down upon us, more packs were shed, more boys were reeling and stumbling, dizzy and half stunned. The whole column now was running under the pressure, the guards now being quite incensed and infuriated. The Kriegsmarina seemed to be everywhere with their flashing steel bayonets as the steel glinted in the brilliant July sun. With each stab of the blade the guard would scream, "Hamburg!", "Berlin!", "Cologne!", "Frankfurt!", "Dresden!", "Dusseldorf!", "Essen!", "Stuttgart!".

"Christ!" said someone near to Harry Pettie, "I wish they would stop remembering these bloody city names!" Then Harry said how he remembered with delight, that a boy in the column near to him, with the usual British phlegm, would, with every stab, shout "London – OOOOH!", "Coventry – AHH!", "Liverpool – You Kraut bastards!"

Pickhardt, in his truck, would first accelerate part of the column and decelerate another part causing bunching and confusion, but try what tactics they may, they were not successful in getting us to fragment or break ranks.

I was now running in a bunch with Des Dunphy, Lofty Minnitt, Gordon Clubb and others, immediately behind John Sheridan. John was a big burly muscular Canadian, a wonderful character one could not help liking. Suddenly one of the more muscular guards took a seething dislike to John and crashed his rifle butt with such terrific force on John's head, that even the butt fractured. Such a blow, I am sure, would have put anyone else, but John, clean out for the count. John's knees buckled, blood spurted from his head spilling over Des Dunphy and splashing over many others, but miraculously John kept going, albeit somewhat unsteady, his face framed in blood.

Red-headed Wilf Flower, as we approached him, was stopped. He was being flogged by a couple of vigorous butt-wielding guards, who seemed to have taken a dislike to the colour of his hair. Instinctively I made my way over to Wilf, grabbed my old desert hat from my head and clamped it over Wilf's mass of red hair. Forty years later at Kriegie

Call reunion Wilf said how he recalled me slapping that old hat on his head and saying,

"Get down and stay down."

"The Gerries left me then, quite alone," said Wilf, "and you came back for that bloody hat. Have you still got it? I'd like it if you're for parting."

Some years later Fred Darycott and I were talking of Tychow and 'The Run'. "I was lucky", said Fred. "I was not chained. I carried my pack much further than most around me. I received the merest prick in my backside which I took to be a gentlemanly hint to dump my kit bag. Had it been my own pack I would have speeded up a bit but it belonged to a stranger. I looked to my right and saw a guard, and the way I placed the pack under his legs, he had no chance. He came an awful cropper and his own rifle butt may well have added to his problems the way he was astride it."

One dog handler who held his dog on a very short lead was noisily winding it up into a blind fury, ready to lengthen the lead for a vicious attack. At the moment of release a rifle waving Goon stepped in to deal a blow on a Kriegie target, but tripped, falling heavily, before he could deliver the blow, right in the path of the crazed animal. The Alsatian did however not differentiate between Goon and Kriegie, savagely attacked the Goon, tearing at him with utmost bestiality. The confusion was frightful and tempers ran high. I cannot say what injuries the Goon suffered, as we were not particularly concerned, but they would not be trivial. Other guards witnessing this skirmish obviously held us to blame, and with ugly, hateful grimaces, stabbed and clubbed at any of us who happened to be in range. They appeared now to be suffering from a loss of all reasonable thinking; they themselves were acting like animals. Thank heavens we kept our cool, because it really was us who were supposed to lose all our reason under the pressure, break ranks and die.

Some years later, when Bob Pegg (Canadian) learned that we in Kriegie Call were to hold a reunion, he wrote to me saying, 'I wonder if you will all chain yourselves together and wildly dance round a roasting Alsatian?'

Wally Oakley, chained to Harry Parkes, was following one of the boys who appeared to throw some kind of fit, falling backwards frothing at the mouth. He fell right across the arm of Wally, the one handcuffed to Harry, so pinning Wally and Harry to the ground. Some of the guards then turned their attention to this pile of very unfortunate Kriegies, and commenced to stab and flog them where they lay, whilst they screamed in their faces,

"Escape! Escape! Escape now you English pigs!"

Wally was always known as the arch hater of Goons, but following this exhibition his every waking hour was thereafter directed to cursing their very being.

Vic Clarke, who was still up front (remembered Bob Bell) dictating the tempo by calling out,

"Don't let them goad you too much, we don't want the column opening up or broken." The bayonets kept on flashing and the rifle butts continued to crash and dogs were being so provoked and encouraged to attack, that many in the column were almost too injured or exhausted by heat and exertion, to go any further.

Pickhardt still continued to rant from his transport vehicle, realising that even some of his own were weakening under this blazing July sun.

I received an even heavier blow than usual from a rifle butt, which totally wrong footed me. I am sure I would not have been writing this had it connected with my head. My pack took the severity of the blow, I was not really hurt, just badly off balance. In a flash I decided not to correct the fall, but directed the tendency towards the left hand ditch. I fell by the roadside and rolled down the side of the ditch into the bottom ending up in some grotesque position, intentionally face down. I feigned unconsciousness and lay there, all ears, whilst the boys in the column rumbled and clattered past. Where there were bodies to be picked up, as we had seen in the Russian compound, the Gerries would come around with the old oxen drawn death-cart and throw the bodies on. If such were to come around after this mad escapade was over, I would risk being thrown on, from where I would have the opportunity to come alive and escape. I kept 'deathly' still, almost too tense to breathe. I heard German voices in the ditch.

"Hier gibt's noch eine Heinz. Hole ihm weg." (There's another one here Heinz. Get him out). A heavy boot in my ribs made me take up a new attitude and almost vacated my lungs entirely of air. The two guards then beat and slashed at my pack, grunting with frenzied effort to free the pack from my back, but it was too well secured. They then attempted to cut through the straps, grunting and puffing with dire intent.

A prod in my buttocks almost called my bluff when I almost squawked aloud. I oft thanked good fortune for my knowledge of German.

"I think he's out for the count Heinz," said one.

"Then put a bullet through him just to make sure." came the reply.

Christ, I had not bargained for the Gerries taking such detailed precautions, and had no doubt that they would do just that, especially in their present state of mind. This was no time for make-believe, or playing silly little acting games where real live bullets were already whining about in the air, and now being suggested as a cure for my incapacity. Without further thought I chickened out, and with one high pitched, "AAAARRRGGH!", I leapt up in a flash, shot past both of them, knocking one of them off balance, and before they had time to realise what had happened I was back in the column lost from their sight.

I remember John O'Reilly recounting this incident, at Kriegie Call some thirty-five years on, and amid some laughter John quipped, as a parting shot,

"And don't I remember you banging their heads together on the way past?"

It became quite obvious as 'The Run' progressed, that the evil eyed, ranting Pickhardt, intended to denude every Kriegie of his pack of belongings. He bawled continuously that they should use their weapons more and more. The roadway was now strewn with packs which had either been discarded or hacked off. Dozens of men were in varied positions from totally prone, sitting dazed, on hands and knees to trying to help their handcuffed partner to his feet. It was vaguely reminiscent of a strafing trip on a supply column. As Judy Garland wrote to me later, "There now seemed to be shooting everywhere, all around us. Alsatians were jumping, snarling, snapping, barking. There was now more shooting up ahead. We could not really tell what was happening, (whether people were being shot or not) so our thoughts were many and varied, prisoners were discarding their packs and also having them cut from off their backs." Judy also remembered seeing cases where the poor staggering Kriegie could not undo his pack because of the restriction of the handcuffs, and even so in many cases when he did succeed in getting the pack from off his shoulders, he could not get it any further because of the handcuffs. One of the more mature guards was seen by Judy to stab his bayonet deep into the pack of one distressed Kriegie and hold it there, running along with him to help him to keep on his feet.

Twenty to thirty yards into the woods on either side of the road, Judy remembered how he saw other guards manning machine guns at the ready. Also at intervals deeper in the tress, were cameras, set up and manned, which, when operated, would have in focus the machine guns in the woods and a full view of the road and the ditches.

As Pop Kingdon said to Trapper Pegg, "Was it ever intended that we did not complete that run?" Pop in those few words was asking the question which hung in most minds on that blazing hot summer day. Generally we were all in very poor shape after half a week with no food, drink or sleep. In addition to the lack of those essentials was the discomfort, of the boat and cattle trucks with no sanitation. in this condition then, surely only a minimum of guards would have been necessary to contain us for these last few miles of journey to Tychow, Luft 1V. There was therefore some other, and more sinister reason for all those guards posted deep in the woods. There were guards enough on the road with us, approximately one to every two prisoners, to ensure our good behaviour and to be adequate for normal security measures. Then there were the cameras on the tripods. What was the purpose of those? Was it hoped that following the rough handling by guards and dogs, that we would panic when the shooting started, that we would break ranks to seek cover amongst the trees? Many of us thought just that, at the time, 'The Run' was taking place only to be confirmed eventually when we reached our destination, where in fact no camp existed as such.

The cameras would have recorded us running in the first instance without suggesting that the running had been forced upon us. Then, had we broken ranks and entered the woods it would have appeared quite convincing on a cinema screen that we were attempting a mass escape.

The local and national papers would have reported the incident as a "Mass break for freedom by Luftgangsters Prisoners of War". The machine guns in the woods would have mown us down to a man. The newspapers would then have explained, that for the safety of the local population the unruly prisoners had to be controlled and having resisted arrest, had to be shot for reasons of security.

Soggy Norton, at six feet three inches, had, up to a point not fared badly on the run, but now had a problem similar to many others in varying degrees of severity. The very short Polish airman to whom Soggy was handcuffed was clubbed so severely over the head by a rifle butt that he was clean knocked unconscious. A heavy kit bag with the shoulder straps around the handcuffs was giving Soggy additional problems, whilst the guards harassed Soggy with stabs and blows and much shouting.

Soggy, with his great frame and strength, was equipped better than most to take care of such a situation as this, and no doubt that huge muscular frame could have lain many of these guards low in a matter of seconds had the weapons been in the other hands. Soggy picked up the kit bag and stuck it under one arm, then hooked up the very short airman under the other and commenced, once again, to run with the column.

Conditions within the column were now becoming quite chaotic. Limbs were tired, everyone perspired heavily from the heat of the day and the pace of the run. Thirst was severe. Injuries were rapidly growing in number and severity, obstacles of kit and fallen men were numerous. More men were tripping over, then being attacked by guards and dogs. Sometimes we would collide with a guard and receive his vituperations.

At this stage it now became very obvious that a clean up operation was under way to release the remaining packs being carried. Airmen still with packs were being severely attacked. Guards in number would get around a man on the ground and hack the straps through with bayonets. This was surely all part of another plan, – outright looting or stealing. The vigorous way in which guards would run from one pack carrier to another and hack him down, became very evident. Some boys had over fifty stab wounds, yet survived.

My pack had served me well by affording me welcome protection from the blows and stabs. I only had six bayonet stabs. I saved the underpants with the blood ringed holes until I got back to England, then somehow they went missing. Lew Korsen had seventeen stab wounds, but it would take a lot more than that to beat a tough man like Lew. Jack (Curly) Lawson had a bayonet thrust which passed through his privates, his testicles were blue, purple and magenta. They were also swollen to massive proportions, but he would not yield. Ross Jones and Jimmy Abernethy were suffering badly but would not give in and like very many more too numerous to print, kept on in spite of their discomfort.

Digger Graham remembered how Tank Shorrock, who was really of double identity as a Prisoner of War, being a Canadian working for No 2 Broadcasting Company actually carried Charlesworth safely through the run after he was injured. The number of cases to be seen, where one of a manacled pair was being clubbed to the ground whilst his partner struggled in his attempts to protect him and get him steady on to his feet, were growing. In many cases both men of a manacled pair were being badly beaten.

Unarmed against such brutal force, there were numerous examples of true grit, resistance, and courage. Although we had a great many wounded men, it could not be claimed that the Germans had entirely their own way. There were examples of resistance in the face of these dangers where men intent on protecting their injured friend, come what may, by placing themselves between the guard and the injured, and looking round with a hand raised high to ward off a further attack. Explicit two-word instructions from the Kriegies were oft heard being passed to the guards.

I think through our exemplary behaviour we came out top in this exercise, and by despising the Germans for their totally inhuman practices one could truly say that we had a right at that moment to feel proud to be British or belong to a column of allied forces.

Changes were taking place in Germany, as we were soon to discover, regarding the extension of the already widespread licence to kill. For we British it is not easy to fully realise the implications of such a licence. Such practices are so alien and unrelated to our national characteristics and traits. The terror which the Nazis could induce and spread could only be realised by those who either experienced it or who witnessed it. It could be mind bending.

The mental anguish attendant with hunger, thirst, cold, deprivation and physical violence is something very few Britons experience or perhaps even think about sufficiently. It was totally inhuman and was expertly prepared and carried out by the gloating Nazis who dispensed it and who seemed to derive a certain satisfaction from someone else's misfortune. We had just had an unquestionable demonstration, and had some more to come. The brutes carried out their beastly practices, also with some twisted kind of collective compulsion. Destruction of all mankind on this entire planet would have been a more generous and satisfactory outcome, than to have mankind subjected to rule by the Nazis. Oh that the world should appreciate the victory.

There were, as always of course, exceptions. Some of the more mature guards, and a few who had guarded us for quite some time, had during the run dropped back somewhat to the rear of the column, where Harry Pettie saw them. Their enthusiasm for the run was not that of the young guards or those with the automatic weapons. Harry quite well remembered one of them who had tears in his eyes. The scene obviously upset him. He was obviously ashamed.

Our behaviour had obviously not gone unnoticed. A Feldwebel of the Marina said to Bob Pegg, in a congratulatory tone, as we stood at the end of the road, "That was a wonderful run you boys just made." and he nodded his head and pursed his lips in obvious admiration for the competent handling of what otherwise could have been a very much more unpleasant event.

The 'Run up the Road', 19th July 1944. An artist's impression of one section of the column by one who was there, Curly Franklyn.

As John B. Lee, of the *Evening News* wrote when he was with British troops in Orbke, Germany,

> If there are any addle-pated civilians in Britain and the USA who think the Allies ought to soft pedal the treatment of Germans they ought to talk to some of the British and American Prisoners of War who underwent typical Nazi brutality. The notorious 'Run up the Road' was one of the most insensate atrocities committed by the Nazis on Prisoners of War in this entire war.
>
> Of about eight hundred British airmen who made this run one hundred and sixty were wounded by bayonets and ninety were injured by bites from dogs. Others had scalp and other wounds from clubbing. Others were entirely exhausted and fell easily to clubbing.

It was over forty years after this event that, for the first time, I met Ed Houston again.

"Never before that day in 1944 did I question our chances of survival," said Ed, "but that was an entirely different ball game as we clouted up that road with bullets whining overhead, crazed Alsatians ripping at us, raining rifle butts and stabbing bayonets."

Like very many more, Ed admitted that for once he had grave doubts for our future. Ed had already had a rough time some time ago in the hands of the Gestapo but he had never doubted that he would survive. Then he recalled how Hugh Clee was so badly injured about the head by rifle-butt blows, whilst he was running close by with little Jock Barrett, that great little Scot footballer.

The scene of the 'Run up the Road' taken by Cec Room in 1985. The spur-road leading to the memorial can be seen. It crosses the ditch into which I fell.

"This is the toughest game I ever played in Ed." said Jock as his twinkle toes deftly stepped over and sidestepped the strewn kit-bags and prostrate bodies still handcuffed together.

Even after arriving at the camp site Ed was of the opinion that the game was not yet over. Like so many others he was of the opinion that the 'Run Up the Road' had not gone the way the Germans had planned.

Why was there no camp as such, when we arrived? No accommodation, necessitating us to sleep in open fields without water supplies or sanitation?

Doug Waters, running with his usual combine, Ron Akerman, Reg Cullen etc, said his suspicions were aroused when a middle-aged Feldwebel of the Luftwaffe guard came running, panting, gasping, and coughing alongside. He had been a POW in England in the Great War and had been well treated.

"I do not agree with what they are trying to do to you," he said to Doug, "to avoid injury you must at all costs keep close together. Do not break ranks and do not try to escape."

It was only then that Doug said he noticed cameras in the woods actually filming these very interesting proceedings.

Some of the boys were shouting relayed messages down the length of the running column, as the Gerries stabbed and clubbed. "Do not break ranks, help the injured, don't let them force you off the road, do nothing which looks like escape."

Doug then saw the reason for these instructions. Machine guns were mounted and manned amongst the trees lining the road along which we were being forced

The stone memorial erected by the inhabitants of Tychow.

to run. "One can imagine the carnage had we panicked." said Doug. It was a bizarre and outrageous scene emphasised by the air of pungency caused by the heady awful scent of the perfume used by that demented German major.

We were a very assorted bunch that day as we supported each other in that very sinister situation. Canadians, Australians, Rhodesians, New Zealanders, Tahitians, Irish, South Africans, Polish, Czechoslovakians, and British, and over forty years later many of us meet quite regularly.

Copying from some notes, made by Jack (Judy) Garland, that ebullient, amiable ambulant from Australia, I find:

"...we eventually arrived at the gates of Gross Tychow, Stalag Luft 1V, an exhausted, scared stiff and subdued bunch of Kriegies. The Germans sat outside and ate some of our food they had picked up from our packs."

Barney Smith and Judy had started the run perhaps a hundred men back from the column head and with a few rugger side steps had progressed to the first twenty to go through the 'gates', little knowing we had to indulge in quite a bit more side stepping. Side stepping and variation of pace was very necessary to successfully negotiate the 'Guard of honour' that our hosts had laid on for our arrival, just to ensure that we all received our full measure of Nazi hospitality.

'The Run up the Road' was over. 'The Run of the Gauntlet' was about to begin. We had now reached the end of about three miles of utter madness. Low flying fun on the squadron seemed a long way off, and a cool pint in the mess seemed even further away, but after thirty ops on troops, tanks and ship

Two more cartoons depicting 'The Run' and 'Running the Gauntlet'.

busting one felt a hell of a long way ahead of this bunch of food looters which now sat smirking at us as we attempted to rest our exhausted bodies.

One could look back down the road and with sadness view the spectacle. Hundreds of personnel packs now to fall as loot to the Oberkommando der Whermacht. Bob Bell and Chas Harrison and a few other boys, who had been right at the head of column had of course managed to arrive with their packs complete. It was however clear, from the further treatment which awaited us that they were shortly to part company with them. Bob and Chas, without hesitation opened up their packs and distributed the contents amongst the boys. Vests, underpants, socks and all kinds of lovely essentials which the folks at home had sent, through the channels of the wonderful Red Cross. Hundreds of these lovely things lay down the road perhaps never to be seen again, which made these few articles worth more than their weight in gold, but confiscation had been avoided.

Chas had a kind of lucky charm. Up to that time, all of the searches and strippings he had experienced, the watch which he received from his mother as a twenty-first birthday present, had remained on his wrist. Thousands of other airmen had lost their watches, rings and other valuables soon after capture. Denys Taaffe had repaired the mainspring for Chas, by shortening it, and made a new face glass from a toothbrush case. Ask Chas what time it is now, more than forty years on, and he will proudly consult that very same watch, and if you press him he may perhaps give you a little bit of the history.

Pickhardt was relentlessly continuing to agitate, fussing about having guards running hither and thither, coming to a halt with much heel clicking, and much repeating of, "Jawohl, Jawohl Herr Hauptmann!" The guards, I honestly believed, had a much greater fear of him, than did we. To them he was a superior officer to be respected and obeyed, to us he was merely a raving idiot to be disrespected and disobeyed.

Although we were all loosely assembled approaching the entrance to the camp, there was nothing within our range of sight to suggest there was a camp in being. There certainly was no entrance to the main gate, but merely two huge gate posts let into the ground where the gates were intended to be.

Pickhardt lined up two rows of guards facing each other, leaving a pathway between them. The guards were armed with rifles and fixed bayonets. Pickhardt gesticulating madly, screaming in a voice which threatened to crack up, left the guards and ourselves in no doubt, what he expected them to do as we were forced to run the gauntlet, over about twenty yards, between the two rows. The surrounds appeared to seethe with guards as they all bustled around giving the impression that they were all busy on some important task. Guards on the outside of the gateway threateningly approached to force the advance party through The Gauntlet, the twenty yard long steel channel. It was a case of being stabbed by the marshalling guards if you refused to go through or take a blind run at the Gauntlet and hope to get through. The first few boys bravely but apprehensively approached those lines of glowering guards, then suddenly made a wild dash through. Some got a few stabs, but no one fell, they all reached the other end, but what was also very noticeable was the fact that the guards in their eagerness to stab and follow through, then turn to catch the next one coming, were in fact interfering with each others movements when rifles would crash together and general chaos reigned for a while. The outcome from this was that the guards spread themselves out considerably more, making the Gauntlet run twice the original length. The guards stabbed incessantly and some injuries were quite serious, the blades grinding on the bones, and one willed the already injured boys through without further injury. My secret fear was sustaining a punctured bowel or kidney.

Up to this point in time many of us owed our lives to physical fitness and a parachute, and even now, in our weakened condition perhaps some remnant of our high physical endurance was seeing us through these past five days of no food, water or sleep. Now through these floggings the fit were yet to assist the injured. Many instances were to be seen where the fit would sandwich between them the injured men and half carry them through The Gauntlet to safety, defying the enemy. He could injure our bodies but not our will. We of course had become accustomed to being shot at in aerial operations. Sometimes we were hit and sometimes not. We had seen our closest friends and crew members, not three feet from us, shot dead or badly injured with shattered legs or similar. So perhaps our mental approach to the present situation was tempered by our past experiences in aerial combat.

Physical fitness, we were to be further reminded within the next following few months, was yet to play another major role in the saga of our survival. The soccer, rugby, running and physical exercises, carried out in the past for enjoyment, was to play a material role towards building the basis of our general resilience.

More of us were forced to Run the Gauntlet. Those side stepping dummies we learned to sell in rugger, to wrong foot the opposition, were now being practised to advantage, as many of us successfully negotiated our paths through the walls of bayonets. Some of us considered we had scored a victory by getting through unscathed, doing some snappy footwork as we pushed some of the muzzles aside to foul the one next to him.

Almost a thousand men take time to handle, so by the time the Krauts changed guards at the Gauntlet and got our boys through, the day was fast wearing on. No concern was shown for the injured by the Germans. There were swellings, bruises, gashes, pulped bleeding flesh, aching limbs, and limping men but no medical treatment. There was not even water to wash off the blood, or water to drink. There was nothing to eat, there was nowhere to rest or sleep, in fact there was just nothing, not even a camp.

We were not to know at that time, that we were to be forced that night to sleep, or rather attempt to sleep, in that very field in which we then stood, on the grass under the heavenly vaults of the star spangled German sky. Gone were our greatcoats, gone were our underclothes, socks, towels, razors, and all the other one hundred and one things normally taken for granted to be the daily bare necessities. What of the two blankets we had set out with? We had discarded the blankets, and our kit, so the Germans reasoned, so why should we now ask for them back again? They argued that the fault was ours.

Guards again began waving rifles and brandishing bayonets. They were forming us up in ranks once more. This appeared to be just as absurd as the order to run had sounded a couple of hours or so ago. Rifles descended on our shoulders with the order to, "Lie down. Lie down". They screamed hysterically as at first we knelt down. What madness was this new tactic? We had ceased to be surprised at anything those Germans thought up.

"Wouldn't surprise me if they now shot the bloody lot of us," said Dave, "and quite frankly I'm almost past bloody caring."

"Faces down. Faces down," the guards bellowed, as they dug us between the shoulder blades with muzzles, butts, and bayonets. "Lie flat. Faces down." the order echoed far, and for hundreds of yards hundreds of sick, thirsty, tired and perspiration soaked shivering Kriegies were prone, faces down, cursing the Germans with all the swear words possible.

"It wouldn't be any good trying to tell the folks back home about this bloody shambles, Dave, they just wouldn't believe it." said Eric.

"No talking, no talking!" bellowed a guard, as he searched for the culprit. The order echoed down the line. "Faces down. No talking or we shoot."

This was surely the end of the line, but we were now convinced that they really meant what they said. There had been enough bullets loosed off for one day, so there we lay, the super race of the fatherland acting with authority and self-satisfaction, but totally void of dignity or venerability, soon to be wallowing in abject wretchedness to which they would now subject us.

A section of guards were now getting some of the boys back on to their feet and forming them all in small parties. With your eyes amongst the grass it was not easy to see what was going on, but I sneaked a little look now and then. A line of trestle tables had appeared, over to which the standing boys were taken. Here they were stripped naked. Their clothes were passed along the tables where every button was inspected, every pocket and seam was meticulously searched. At the slightest excuse one of the huge Feldwebels, who even had the Germans scared, would lash out at our knees, legs, buttocks, and curse us as, "Englische Sweinhund". What a sadistic man that was, and so large that he instilled fear merely when he scowled.

After stripping and searching one was allowed to dress then led over to a separate area where one was ordered to "Lie down. Face down. No talking or we shoot."

Christ it did really become cold. The sun went down below the horizon and the perspiration which was soaked into our clothes set up those uncontrollable shivers when it felt like ice next to your skin.

At long last some buckets of water were allowed to be distributed, but gone were our mugs, towels and everything else. We had to scoop up some water in our hands to drink. It was like nectar.

"I was just thinking about that night we were shot down", said Curly looking up at the star decked skies, "and how those bloody searchlights tormented us... I'd prefer ops to this bloody circus," he said as he held his injured groin, "At least if we were injured on ops we stood a good chance of a meal a warm bed and some expert attention jolly quick."

> You who have seen across the star decked skies
> The long white arms of searchlights slowly sweep,
> Have you imagined what it is to creep,
> High in the darkness? Cold and terror rise.
> Forever looked on by those cruel eyes
> Which search with far flung beams the shadowy deep,
> And near the wings unending vigil keep
> To haunt the lonely airman as he flies?
>
> Have you imagined what it is to know
> That if one finds you, all their fierce desire,
> To see you fall, will dog you as you go,
> High in the sea of lights and bursting fire,
> Like some small bird, lit up, and blinding white,
> Which slowly moves across the flak torn night?
> *Tychow, 1944*

That night under the stars was agony. Those who were injured really were uncomfortable, and some were desperately in need of medical attention. We attempted to preserve some warmth by bunching up together, but there was no real escape from the cold. Later that night a doctor was allowed in amongst us, but there were so very many needing attention that his job was quite impossible. He could not attend to all those who needed him. The injured men were racked with pain. Limbs were stiff with cold, and they were swollen. It seemed that more men than expected, were quite unable to walk, and many were not even capable of getting on their feet.

Whatever the underlying object of 'The Run' may have been, the effective outcome was to denude us totally, every man, of his kit and to ensure that all the contraband and acquired assets were parted from our company before we entered the new camp, wherever it was likely to be.

Whether it was really intended that we should never survive that journey, to arrive at that place, is still I suppose a matter of speculation; one will never know. It was rather odd that no accommodation whatsoever had been prepared for us.

Personally I do not think we would have arrived had we broken ranks or attempted to seek cover, on the Run, when the shooting started.

Pickhardt at least did ensure that on arrival we were again to start from square one all over again. He maintained his argument that we discarded our kit rather than he having confiscated it, and it was only after quite some time later, after a visit of a party of representatives from the Protecting Power that some of our kit was returned.

The morning light revealed an almost unbelievable spectacle. Vic was now overworked. There was so much to do. He cajoled and bustled and pleaded. We desperately needed medical attention, food, water, clothing, blankets, and not least of all protection for the coming night; tents and Marquees.

Pickhardt and his satellites were in no way orientated to listen, but Vic, in no better condition than the rest of us, kept relentlessly on, even threatening that there was now already enough to report to the Protecting Power to cause much discomfort. He won the day. Some medical attention did arrive and so did some tents. We also had two issues, however scanty, of water, and a little very weak watery soup which was made from nothing other than a very few potatoes. We knew only because of some skins floating on the top and the grit in the bottom.

England, home, and sanity, seemed a whole world away. It was of course too easy to become dispirited when suffering from all our hardships, and so how lovely to hear the humour which kept surfacing in the conversations between groups of Kriegies as we sat around. Morale was so much higher than one could have wildly hoped for, and this was the Germans worst enemy. Here was a true example of German piggishness pitted against British gumption and grit and it annoyed the Germans intensely that we should keep coming back at them.

Vic was to serve us well during the next few following months; he deserved some recognition, and many of us, especially those of us who spoke German, were to attempt to assist him as much as possible in his struggle with and against the Germans. He certainly deserved more from life than life was to offer him. He died shortly after returning home to England.

Hopes of having a decent camp with reasonable accommodation were slim. To our amazement the Germans commenced to bring on site dozens of prefabricated wooden 'dog kennels'! Gangs of workmen were brought in to erect these bizarre contraptions measuring approximately 14 feet by 8 feet by 4 feet high which were each to accommodate ten men. We lived and slept in these 'dog kennels' with great difficulty and much discomfort, but needless to say of course, life in these was much better than in the bare field we had at first experienced.

Sleeping on the hard wood floor without blankets, with less than eighteen inches width of floor space each was something we learned to accept. It was the best available. Passing the days was not really easy. Ten men per kennel was gross overcrowding. The Germans still had all our kit, they ate our food, and generally enjoyed reminding us that we were the poor English cousins.

A water pump was installed which assured us of our twice daily thirst quencher but it was rather a protracted operation pumping and delivering the ration. There was in this world somewhere, cups of tea, slices of toast, bacon and eggs, roast beef and Yorkshire pudding, fish and chips, tatie hot pot, and watery potato soup. We received about a cupful of the latter daily, and we were all fast losing weight.

Sometime later, activity was evident in what was to become a compound. Conventional type barrack huts were being built into which we were eventually to move.

Up to that time we had been reasonably fortunate with the weather, but it seemed that a typical summer thunderstorm was about to break. I have never experienced a thunderstorm of such severity and duration. The rain was torrential and continuous. The thunder and lightning was severe and simultaneous, well beyond that normally experienced. The dog kennels shook with the vibration, and the field became totally flooded, large lakes of water forming all around. Lightning became extremely intense as the heart of the storm approached nearer by the minute and lower it seemed by each succeeding flash. One eye-piercing flash brought disaster. Dog kennels were hit and shattered. The lightning caught the nails which held the kennels together, turning them blue with heat and charring the wood around them. The kennels would then collapse into heaps of individual planks of wood, the heads of some of the occupants peeping out from the piles. Many of the boys were struck, some injured, some were killed. Roy Stevens in a nearby kennel was killed outright. My memory on some details is not quite so clear, but Alan Hamer remembers well that four lost their lives during this storm. It was indeed sad to see the way the Germans regarded them. They buried them in sacks.

Ironically, Roy, mentioned above, was the only member of his crew to survive being shot down, and one of the boys, in tribute to Roy wrote the following.

>What fate has man when close at hand
>Was freedom liberty and his land.
>What fate had he who flew so high
>Who lost his plane but not his life,
>And then to die in a prison camp,
>With peace so near.
>
>What fate had this young flier who'd braved the foe,
>Who flew his plane with others row on row.
>O'er German field. He whom destiny singled out
>Of all his crew to live, then turned about,
>And dug his grave on German soil.
>*Tychow, 1944.*

Dave Davidson was also moved to verse, and at the same time referred particularly to a section of the community back home in Britain for whom Dave had a positive dislike; the strikers and shirkers.

> Some men who work for Britain
> They have their graves at home,
> Where birds and bees of Britain
> Around their cross can roam.
>
> But they who fly for Britain
> Following a distant star,
> Alas. Alas for Britain
> They have their graves afar.
>
> To strike and malinger in Britain
> In stately conclave met,
> Alas. Alas for Britain
> They have no graves as yet.

Ken Gosney and others were injured. One of the boys I saw personally had a scoop of flesh burned clean out of his back, as though taken out by an ice cream scoop. He was utterly dazed by the experience. It was July 28th, another never-to-be-forgotten day. The lightning struck some of the wrist watches which had escaped confiscation, and severely burned the wrists on which they were being worn. One of the boys had a flat Longines pocket watch inside his battle dress pocket which was pitted through the three and the nine, yet the watch worked normally. It really was quite amazing that more of the boys were not killed outright.

Danny Willcox-Jones was at the doorway of the 'dog kennel' where Roy was killed, when the fireball struck. So was Ken Gosney, Dennis Shepherd and Tim Fry. Ken kindly called on Roy's family when he returned to England and explained Roy's tragic end. When the fireball struck, Danny was shot clean into the air. The fireball seemed to hit the static tank which stood diagonally about twenty yards from the kennel. Danny's left leg was somehow paralysed for many hours afterwards. Fred Burtonshaw was standing opposite Danny and could scarcely believe the happenings to be credible, as the large glowing, highly charged fireball shot into the kennel. He can remember,

"I was very tempted to kick that 'Big Blue Football' clean out of the door, but I'm glad I resisted the temptation otherwise I wouldn't be writing to you now."

The far corner of the dog kennel, diagonally from the static tank was completely ripped out. Danny remembered they had some Red Cross food tins which were pitted at 180 degrees as though the electrical force had come from the static tank.

One boy was struck, swallowed his tongue, and was refused medical treatment by the Germans, and died.

Some barrack huts were, ere long, completed, and we moved in, whilst the Germans continued to build a further compound.

Of the library boys from Hydekrug, Georgie Wood had been repatriated just prior to our move, but the remainder had lost their precious books; until one day the boilers arrived from Heydekrug. One boiler was found to be filled to overflowing with hundreds of the precious books. Now at least there was a nucleus on which the boys could go to work.

Gone however, for all time was our hope for a return of the theatre. Frankie's hard work on the production on which he was working at Heydekrug when we left, was completely up the Swanee.

Some new arrivals even started to come into camp. Somehow when one witnessed these boys arriving one felt a genuine sorrow for them. They would now have a new battle to fight. From flying high, on top of their profession, expert and dedicated to the destruction of the Hun, they would be reduced to the humility of incarceration and to the indignity of standing naked and being harangued by the hateful Hun, and to become hungry beyond belief. To witness this transformation was very distressing.

How did they view the emaciated frames of some of the older Kriegies? Would they have the thought that only time would see them similarly gaunt and angular? They appeared to be so well fed and healthy. Perhaps only a few days ago they were in the local, happy and laughing, or having a shindig in the mess. They knew the terror of the flak and the fighters. They knew the relief and satisfaction of the undercart touching the runway again – and now for them it was all over. It ought not to be. I was one of the angular ones they were viewing; about two stones under normal weight and about half as much again to lose o'er the next few months.

Being shot down seemed to close a chapter in your life, until you found the beginning of another one, but to these new boys it seemed to be the close of their living. I had escaped and been recaptured. Did they have a clue how heavy the dice were loaded against them? To shake their hands was to make some contact with home and England.

IN TRANSIT

The number Six of Lager Luft, was in Ost Preuzen wild and bare,
In Lager 'K' a thousand men of RAF were captive there,
In wooden huts crammed to the brim, on minimum food existed they.
The cold intense was raw and claimed their whole attention night and day.

'Twas here at Stalag Heydekrug where we had planned and schemed escape,
Where we had various plans and tricks employed, a bid for freedom make.
Where we had hours on end in cold damp sand, deep beneath the turf,
Dug tunnels long and smuggled up the soil, to scatter round as earth.

Where we had seen some pals, who daring more would be, and take in hand
A danger scheme some effort wild that they make a freedom stand,
Where they'd been caught in open land, unarmed, defenceless, without hope.
They'd been shot dead by ruthless Hun, who could have captured him with rope.

The Russian front although slow pace, was heading westwards day by day,
And so our captors move us would, 'ere Russian armour come our way.
So into cattle trucks once more they bundled us some eighty men,
Which bore the notice, "Forty men or horses eight", be packed therein.

Each man upon his back did take his worldly goods, ingenious packs
With shirts sewn up at base and front, the sleeves were used as shoulder straps.
But food and water there was nil and sitting room was not to find,
And sanitation was the last of things to come to German mind.

We jogged and jolted back and forth, and shunted into sidings where
It seemed for hours did we stay, and German Postens could not care
If burst we should, from nature's call. The padlocked doors would open not.
Our hopes would fade 'cos we had thought, the journey may be one short hop.

Short was the hop by standards past, in distance 'twas one-fifty,
It seemed to be a thousand 'ere to Memel quay we'd shifted.
De-trained we then, hungry men, tired, motley, cold were we,
What e'er could destination be? It seemed a journey by the sea.

The metal hull of coal ship foul, we entered through a hatch on the deck,
From one single ladder, frail and worn, to bowels of the ship did trek,
'Twas cold and damp and dark and bare; the only light or air to vent
To us below, we saw least thirty feet above, if back we bent.

The black bilge swilled around as ship did pitch and roll with sickening sway,
As more men forced down hatch to go, stumbled and fell in awkward way.
The protests from below did echo loud, "No room for any more."
Five hundred men were down there now, and still five hundred more to go.

No means of finding place to sit, of sleep or rest was hope too much,
Consideration man to man, was then, with knees drawn up, to touch
The toes of he in front, and back to back in pairs to sit, head down,
And, when a leg stretch one required, to side of he in front be thrown.

Guards took position by the hatch, the miserable sight to guard and watch
But call of nature, hunger, thirst, began to tell, and we would match
Call upon call to guard, that we may up the ladder climb, relief
From pain to find, and fresh air breathe, before returning to the deep.

At one time had I privilege, some time on open deck to spend,
And into conversation came with a lone guard, who fain would lend
His rifle to my friend, who made no move this weapon to accept
Opinion held my friend, that guard had hoped to mutiny we'd leapt.

From there, my friend had reasoned, that o'er Baltic we could sail, in charge,
The Swedish shore to make, where guard would gladly make escape at large.
But had the plan gone wrong, it could have meant the death of all who sailed,
Then suffering all this dreadful hell, would then be all to no avail.

So three days more conditions foul, and four dark nights of abject misery,
In clothes which stunk like putrid slimy waste, a break came to our story.
Unshaven, dirty, smelling, angry men were we, from hunger weak.
No water 'cept from dirty tins passed man to man, had we to seek.

News from the open deck came down, that in to port we'd soon be drawn.
With hopes of land of any kind our psycho buds would lose their frown,
And we would once more improvise and scheme how best to work the best
Of what was worse than we had hoped. We'd even crack a gag and jest.

We stumbled and fell against each other now, as tortured limbs we stretch,
And some were much too sore to even stand, we had these men to fetch,
And hours it seemed as, one by one, we climbed that ladder place to take
On deck. No more than one would ladder hold, two would have it break.

In cattle trucks once more would we entrain, Ye Gods. How far to go?
It's times like these one felt so proud an Englishman to be, and so
Felt sorry, in a kind of way, for those darned Huns, who stooped to deeds,
In England never would have come to mind, however dire the needs.

So being English, we just knew our pride to keep, and honour hold.
More substance was in any man, than any ten from Nazi mould.
Superior then we proved to be, in human values understanding,
When Nazi Hauptman greeted us, minutes after de-train landing.

On quiet country road, each side belined with pine trees, straight and tall,
He mustered scores of Hitler Youths, who armed with rifles, one and all
Commenced to scream in frantic way, gyrating there, with head and arms,
That we, the very murderers be, who children killed and bombed the farms

He ranted and raved so red in face, telling how that we did kill
Their mothers, sisters, brothers, aunts, and now that we should take a pill,
He set them off their bolts to rattle in guns almost as big as they,
And elder guards now bayonets fixed, and dogs were seen in woods at bay.

They then pulled handcuffs by the score, together held by link chains strong,
From sacks they dropped along our ranks, and we together chained along
The column, here and there at will, and put the handcuffs all to use,
They started in a Hunnish way, to call us names and shout abuse.

The situation had assumed a very ugly character,
It seemed as though a single move, may bring total disaster.
But those of us who understood the words of furious anger,
Were able to interpret with "At all costs keep good order."

"We must keep calm, no panic moves, from column do no roving."
For Hauptman now was screaming out, that column should start moving.
Screamed he, "You've got to make them run, and make them go much faster,"
The guards commenced to strike with butts, as ordered by their master.

They slashed at packs upon our backs, with bayonets did they cut them free.
They now commenced to stab at flesh, my bottom soon told this to me.
And some boys took hard blows on head, and shoulders many pounded red,
And Lawson stabbed clean through his privates. Many thought we'd soon be dead.

Some were now quite badly hurt, but friends came to their comrades aid,
If they'd been left to fall to ground, nothing more would need be said,
Then trampled underfoot to death, by heavy running feet in hundreds,
And chaos would have broken out. It would have been quite murderous.

But British be and British act, to all, deserving recognition pass,
Behaviour was exemplary and showed the Germans "who's the ass".
They'd hope for widespread flap and panic, dashing off into the wood,
To shoot us down and leave us lie they then a reason have had would.

In woods we cameras saw set up, which would have filmed the break to wood,
And then have filmed the shooting, when no doubt the propaganda could
Have told the public, how these men attempted mass escape to make,
And to protect the local folks, to shoot them must for safety's sake.

The boys ran on in order good, the guards lashed out with heavy butts,
The injured aimed to centre run, avoiding therefore further cuts,
The stronger men then formed the flanks, where guards renewed attacks with strength.

And as to so incite our fears, some bullets shot along our length,

At first we thought they aimed to kill, but their intentions did we twig,
A thousand men kept finding strength to combat awful German rig.
The Huns were furious we would give them no devious reason, so
That they could shoot down prisoners who, 'Their freedom had been running for.'

A blow across my shoulders, sent me into sloshy gutter tumbling.
A stab in buttocks shook me up as guard yelled, "Kugel", roughly fumbling.
Like hundreds more I lost my pack, with clothes and razor and nick-nacks,
And saw no more of it I fear. The Hun would sort it out in sacks.

Our fears of his intentions bared, were then at camp arrival firmed.
There no accommodation stood, except few huts were built we learned.
And so we sat around on ground, aching with hunger, tired and worn,
But we were then to find out soon, to sleep outside so cold and lorn.

Medical aid was not to hand, and some were sorely so in need,
But later in the day there came a doctor, and some tents indeed,
And dozens of small huts, wooden, fourteen by eight and four feet high,
And crawled we into these with joy, what luxury for somewhere dry.

Then thunder did the heavens rent, the storm by any standards fierce,
Lightning crazy patterns danced, and thunder did the ears pierce.
Rain bounced from 'Kennels' in a spray, and tents were soon in disarray,
The ground would not the water take, and soon the camp looked like a bay.

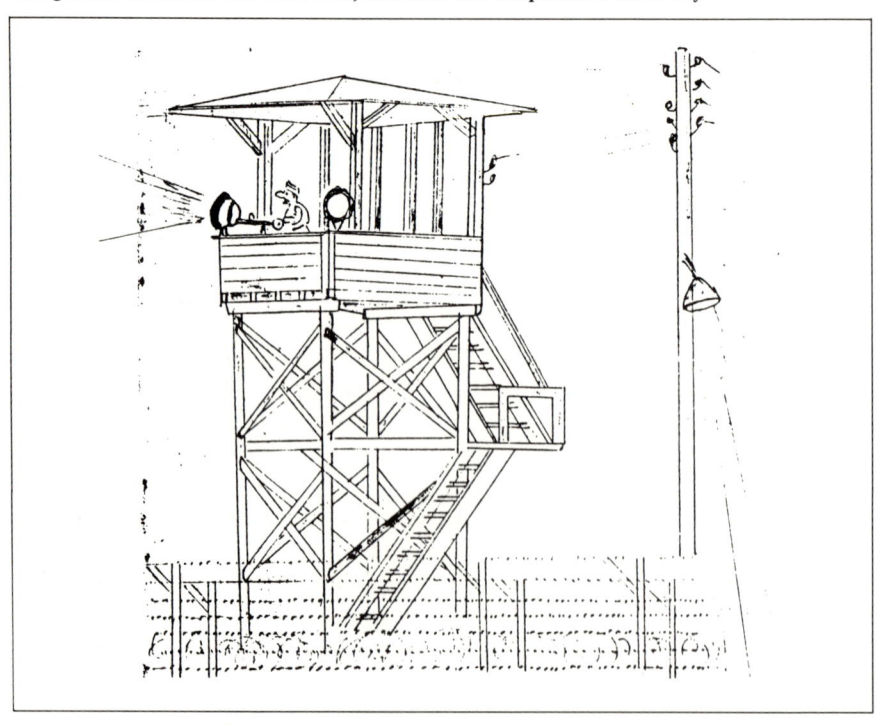

Vantage Out, Gross Tychow (Luft IV), September 1944.

Lightning struck the ground, where steam would rise as water boiled,
And tent broke out in flame and two men died, instantly killed,
And kennel struck with lightning sharp, some shattered were but men took rout,
Another flash, another hit, and flesh was from his back scooped out.

The lightning so severe was, that shattered 'kennels' fell apart,
The nails which in construction used, were blue with heat and then did start
The wood in which they had been driven, to burn, and then apart were riven,
And as a pile of dominoes would tumble down, we were out driven.

One often found a humorous mood in 'dog kennels' of doubtful fame,
'Cos in these cubes we lived for weeks until the larger huts then came.
Then slowly camp life took some shape, we had from scratch to start once more,
As representation to the Hun brought nothing of our kit to'fore.

Kiefheide was the area known, Gross Tychow was the Lager name,
And we had not been there 'ere long, American airmen along came.
More RAF too joined the band and brought good news to spread around,
Then close by, Yankee plane got shot, and parachutes came down to ground.

The camp one day reverbed with cheers, a German would connections new
Make to electric pole on top, and got his wires all askew.
One glorious flash shot wires across, and Jerry shot up, fell back limp,
He then hung swaying in the breeze, all curled up like Morecambe shrimp.

Some Jerry pilots one day would, above our camp, show how it should
Be done by experts in the air, and got controls crossed, what a dud.
And earthwards screamed, not part of plan, and got out smart on parachute.
And then resounding crash we heard, and Kriegies stayed no longer mute.

Their wild-like cheers and shouts were heard far off by Krauts in admin block,
And Komandant thought of all this, we were a sympathetic lot,
So thanked us for our sporting cheers because the pilot had got out.
Misunderstanding twist then brought, more cheers unbounded for the Kraut.

Cec Room, our stalwart Kriegie Call member, with great enthusiasm, held us spellbound as he addressed us at Kriegie Call some forty years later.

This was following his nostalgic and historic solo return to the scene of 'The Run up the Road'. He left the boat, The Stefan Batori, at Danzig, to face the challenge of exercising the ingenuity, tenacity and resourcefulness he had exhibited in that very area, some forty years earlier. It was not easy covering the round overland trip to Tychow of 450 Kilometers, it required some measure of wangling and some degree of bartering, the area now being under Russian domination.

Cec eventually contacted an old inhabitant of the area who recalled 'The Run' and other atrocities, directing Cec to the 'Memorial' which stands in a clearing in the trees, about halfway up 'The Road', and bears the following inscription:

>   WDZIECZNOSC NARODU BEDZIE WAM ZAPLATA.
>   J.R. Becher

>   POMODOWANYM JENCOM OBUZU W. MODROLEZI
>   LOTNIKOM ALIANCHIM. MIEZNCY GMINV TYCHOWO.

The interpretation, I am told, is:

> The gratitude of the Nation will be your reward.
> *J.R. Becher*
>
> To the murdered prisoners of the Modrolas concentration camps and the Allied airmen. From the inhabitants of the community of Tychow.

It seemed there was no doubt that a very great many of the reported 10,000 Russian prisoners who were held there, were either murdered or allowed to die, by their German captors. From what information which could be gleaned it appears that when the Russian forces over-ran the area, they were reported to have shot Pickhardt without question.

Although Cec was operating under supervision, and of course certain restriction, he was successful in obtaining some very valuable photographs of the memorial, and had it not been for his dogged persistence we would have had neither knowledge nor photograph of this venerate reliquary.

We, as members of Kriegie Call feel honoured that the memory of the atrocity of the 'Run up the Road', has in some visible and tangible way, been established on site.

The Germans were shaken by the news of the ill fated attempt on the life of Hitler, not that they would discuss the matter, but their general attitude was tinged with a certain air of clumsy indifference as they avoided being drawn into conversation.

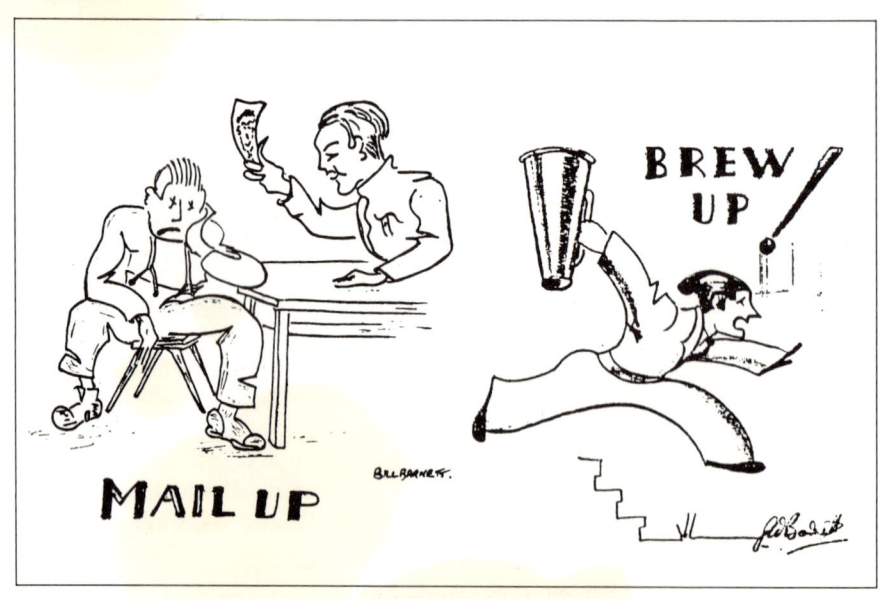

Cartoons by Bill Barnett and Jock Barrett.

"Wie geht es, heute, mit dem Fuhrer, den?" (Well how's the Fuhrer today?)

"Warum verweisen sie darauf?" (Why do you ask?)

"Hoffentlich dass er sich verbessert hat." (Hoping that he's getting better).

"Ja?" (Yes?)

The food situation at Gross Tychow was bad and slow to improve. Some Red Cross parcels did arrive but the Germans played their detached type of game and would not even allow us a stock record to help us plan distribution.

Representatives from the Protecting Power eventually arrived surrounded by masses of German guards, officers and interpreters, but no Pickhardt. Vic gave them some details of 'The Run' and also of the very bad conditions that existed in the camp. The Deputation said they would extend their stay in order to interview Pickhardt, who was supposedly on leave, but permission was not to be granted. Following this visit however some kit was returned to the camp and distributed as well as possible. It was fantastic to regain some items which were to help pass the time and give us something to do besides just conserving energy and living with the pangs of hunger. A pack of cards, for example, worked miracles. Someone made some balls from the leather legs of flying boots, and from somewhere a set of stumps grew and some implement resembling a cricket bat came on the scene.

Camp life slowly shook off some of the shortages and restrictions whilst the winter advanced and more Kriegies arrived to fill the rooms even fuller. Quite a number of Americans were coming in to be mixed in with us, regretfully not always to the furtherance of good tempers and domestic harmony. Much more overcrowding was the forecast. To meet this problem, the initial plan was to have two men sleep on the floor in each room, there being no room for any more beds. Beds were the usual three-tier wooden types carrying loose slatted boards for a palliasse base.

It became quite important to retain the British character of the rooms and keep at bay the tendency for too much American influence to be brought to bear. The Americans were not generally consistent in their behaviour and wherever the proportions became unsuitably balanced the standard of behaviour and general discipline deteriorated. It was obvious, that of necessity we would have to keep our influence dominant. Good administration and morale depended on it.

As many more Americans arrived it became necessary to house them on their own, and so, after much argument and negotiation with the Germans, they finally agreed to this move, much to the benefit of us all.

Some American Red Cross parcels arrived which the Americans claimed were solely for their own use. Our stocks were very low, so Vic approached the American camp-leader to rule that whatever Red Cross supplies arrived, whether American, Canadian or British, they should be considered to be for the use of us all. Before a decision was made, I believe the whole American compound had to be balloted, but it was only carried by a very small majority, and only after the camp-leader had forcibly pointed out that they had been quite willing to share our meagre stocks when they were billeted in our compound very recently, and that they could not just change the rules to suit the state of their stomachs. Some months later, during the three months forced-march which we were to endure in snow, rain and shine, sleeping rough in fields barns and woods, a column of Americans approached our column, of which I was leader at the time, and paid us a great compliment by asking if we would agree to allow them to join us. They said that the British standard of discipline appealed to them, that we behaved like gentlemen and that they felt that they had a better chance of survival with us rather than with their own countrymen. They respected our exemplary method of distribution of all available food... Now what a change of attitude was this?

Additional electrical power lines were needed, and one day a German, an electrician we presumed, shinned up one of the poles and attached himself by his safety belt, before commencing to juggle with the wires. He must have got his negative and positive knotted. There was one almighty flash and the poor blighter fell back limp, swinging lifelessly from his harness. There was a resounding cheer all over the camp from every Kriegie aware of the accident, but oddly no reprisals were taken. Whether the dangerous 'gun practice' which was shortly to follow, was precipitated by this incident, was debatable but quite possible. This so-called 'gun practice' was quite alarming. The German guards in the watchtowers would train their machine-guns into the compound and fire bursts amongst us causing the earth to spatter up over us. We would throw ourselves prone on the ground whilst the firing took place hoping not to be hit. We were of the opinion that the exercises were intended to undermine our morale and cause psychological disturbance. Aim would soon be diverted to a bank of earth within the compound and termed by the Germans to be 'gun practice'. No doubt it was. It was, I think, a form of twisted Hunnish entertainment. It appeared to be a national trait to have a good laugh at the discomfort of others.

As winter drew nearer the problem of keeping warm occupied hands and minds. Too little fuel was supplied by the Germans, and so we heaped up the snow high all around the huts to keep in what warmth we had and exclude the draughts. The Germans suspected this was some deceptive move to conceal tunnelling activities, and forced us to move all the snow away. There was no increase in the fuel delivery however so we were compelled to burn anything we could lay hands on. We even resorted to stuffing the cheap, coarse furniture into the stove at the risk of being punished. At Tychow there was no undressing to go to bed. It was quite the reverse; we dressed up in anything we could muster to help combat the cold.

Earlier we had lost the blowers made from Klim (milk spelt backwards) tins, which came via the Red Cross, containing powdered milk. These home made blowers, acted on the blacksmith's hearth principle, the air being forced through by a hand driven revolving fan. It was an extremely efficient contraption, extracting unbelievable amounts of heat from the merest amount of fuel, so one can imagine that anything combustible was avidly collected.

Many claims to the design and invention of this Kriegie contraption have been made. Those which I have seen in print I know to be quite false, because I know that the contraption was giving many Kriegies very good service before some of the claimants were shot down.

Allied air-raids were becoming quite frequent, so we devised a system of our own fire watch, two men at a time per hut.

Bridge tournaments were really well contested with fervent fanaticism. For those of us in our room who were obsessed with the game, there was much enjoyment. Neville Feraneyhough really did not mind us playing, he had done quite a bit himself but was now deeply steeped in his studies. Eric Else who however was a non-sympathiser, but a great character, put down his feelings on the matter, in writing, for me one day in my log.

BRIDGE

(A bitter observation by a non-sympathiser)

"Two Clubs". My God when will this bedlam cease?
"Three Spades". Oh give me peace, oh give me peace.
But where is peace to save me from the bend,
When rubber follows rubber without end?
When Culbertson and Blackwood rule the scene,
Thrusting aside from thought all that has been
Or might be; no, it matters not the hour
When sits the fiend with features grim and dour,
And mutters now and then a smothered, "Damn",
When smug and smiling Foeman tries a slam.
My mind is numbed, a mist enshrouds my brain,
Who are these fellows Culbertson and Crane?
What is a "Goulash", "Yarborough", and "Finesse"?
Small slam, Grand slam, Leg on Game, no less?
I cannot say, but this I firmly trow,
Such things are not for me, and well I know.
Proceed then Masters and o'er the table stump,
Play on. Play on, until the last "No Trump".

Eric G. Else. Tychow, Oct. '44

Food, just at this time was extremely scarce. The German rations were not sufficient to maintain life, and we were of the opinion that the exercise was quite intentional, to keep us under the thumb. Red Cross supplies were not great but kept us from starvation.

What better means of riveting the attention of a human being could there be, or what better means of undermining his resistance could one devise, than enforced hunger? What better training in discipline and self control could one demonstrate than asking a man who had not just missed a few meals, but had not had a meal as such, for perhaps a couple of years, to apportion to his friends some little quantity of food which had come their way? The rules said that should he be found to cheat, he forfeit his portion, and that when having carried out the apportionment, all others had the right to choose which portion they desired, the last one being his. How scrupulously fair one learned to be and with no choice of menu, and frequently no food at all, how unfinicky and unfussy one became regarding food. One did not question what it was, whether it tasted good or not, or even whether it was cooked. None of these things were of any consequence. Even now over forty years on, how sorry I feel for the selfish child who grumbles to the parent that the fare for the meal is not suitable because it was on the household menu the day before yesterday, or the adult diner in the restaurant who inspects the menu list of a dozen main dishes and remarks that "there's nothing very appetising on offer". They have never been hungry. It is all, to me, lovely food.

Whether it was intended as a morale booster for the Germans or a demoraliser for Kriegies, one cannot say but three FW109s came over the camp one day on a show-off beat up, giving an impressive display, until one of them got his controls badly crossed and piled straight into the ground. It is no guess-work as to who came out top on this psychological exercise.

On a particular search one day, we were herded, as usual, into the compound area, clear of the huts.

Machine guns from the perimeter towers opened up in a frightening metallic chatter and not knowing the objective we suspected the worst and threw ourselves prone to the ground. Shots were fired over our heads and some into the ground around us. Some bullets in fact smashed into a hut splintering the wood and causing a nerve-shattering racket.

We suspected some Hunnish plan to cause panic amongst us and further put our nerves on edge. It seemed to be the weekly gun testing exercise from the posten boxes gone badly wrong. They then directed the fire into the earth mound on one side of the compound.

The Goons exhibited their rather bizarre sense of humour in a variety of ways. Their greatest enjoyment, generally, as a nation, one could claim, was derived from the misfortunes of others. They would even laugh at one of their own number who may be caught out in some embarrassment, and experienced great delight if some poor Jew or forced worker or a POW were to suffer. Thank God they never set foot in Great Britain as a ruling power.

Many Kriegies really thought during this particular incident, that it surely was our end. After all, when the bullets start flying and whining in various directions you don't remain standing to survey the scene, or to see who or what is being hit, you are flat with only a worm's eye view and you hear the muffled thuds as they travel through the ground.

It was not until I formed our Kriegie Call Reunion Group in 1980 that some written evidence came to hand via Des Dunphy, that, "...preparations and training were in progress (at Tychow) for organised shootings in the camp compound. ...Hauptman Pickhardt was strongly backed by the Nazi Party."

These statements were contained in a letter, written by Helmut Whale of Bad Neustadt, in conjunction with Baron Wolf von Gottenberg, who both claimed to have been interpreters at Gross Tychow. The timing was correct because of their mention of Vic Clarke as Lager Leader (see letter, page 196/7).

Reflecting as I did on the Desert Campaign, with all its memories, the quote of Rommel kept returning to me, "Krieg ohne Hass" (war without hate), but how could one reconcile that with the behaviour we were now experiencing at the hands of these ankle-length coated strutting brutes and the leather-clad Gestapo with their homburgs and fine boots with swine like eyes and ghostly features. Their clumsy brutal hands would grasp fine leather gloves as they would bark out their raucous staccato orders. Their manner alone would suggest that their mandate be death with no questions asked.

What chance had we of penetrating that steely barbaric wall of evil power. No recognition could be hoped for, our qualities of decency, honour, integrity, esteem and respect. Such qualities would threaten to undermine the basis of their evil cult, and so must be totally suppressed.

Conditions at Tychow were undoubtedly the worst we had so far encountered, the German attitude without doubt being very much more aggressive. Camp workers however were not to be dismayed and toiled hard in an attempt to make life just that bit more bearable. There were those who would 'launder' others' washing; there was George Dummett who kept an up to date list of the occupants of every building in the camp and used it effectively for the lightening distribution of all incoming mail. Even little Sammy Bunyan was a form of entertainment in his book-making (betting) activities. Then the lectures, the Debating Societies, the County Clubs, the Bridge Tournaments, the Sports Committee, the Medics, the Entertainers, the General Admin team, the Librarian, the Coal party, the Kitchen party, the XYZ Committee (i.e. security, escape, illicit dealings in essential items and the many other virile organisations which bound us together and helped many to retain their waning sanity). Sadly however we did have a few for whom the strain was to prove too much, and self destruction was attempted.

Working hard and with great ingenuity, our radio engineering experts, for whom I had the greatest admiration, had again built a receiver, one which fitted into a cigar box, and we began once again to receive the BBC news. Frank Hill recalls the moments when Roy Mirfin, under great secrecy, would assemble the various detachable parts of the radio, (usually distributed for security reasons), and commence receiving. Even months later on the three months march, Roy, on gaining the relative security of a farmer's barn, after a day's march, tired and hungry, would diligently assemble the receiver in the dim evening light, then disappear under a pile of straw, and emerge with the morale boosting BBC news we all awaited.

Herschfelderstrasse. 13.,
Bad-Neustadt/Saale. (13.a).,
Germany/America Zone.

November 26th. 1946.

Dear Mr. Clarke,

According to circumstances I would like to contact you again. It is now a considerable time we have seen us last and obviously my letters of the last year never reached you. It is now by some important reason I write to you again; the case Pickhardt. [Vic meantime had died]

I have met my friend Baron von Gottenberg (formerly in the mail censoring department) again and today I am with him for some days. We have discussed the case Pickhardt and we find it our duty to bring this case before the authorities providing you or T/Sgt. Paules have not yet done it on your part. We trapped Pickhardt and found that he made for the Russian Zone. This is the situation. Furthermore I remember our last meeting in the camp before we were transferred to the Russian Frontier. You and T/Sgt. Paules told us to contact you as soon as possible after the war for any support or help if necessary. In view of the fact we have decided to follow the advice of our friends and relatives abroad we want to emigrate when an opportunity is given. A statement of yours would certainly give us preference in obtaining the permission for leaving the country. Would you therefore be kind enough to give us a statement as soon as possible, which shows the situation in the camp and our activities. I am certain you will remember if you read as follows: "Baron von Gottenberg and Mr. Helmut Whale have been interpreters from 1941 to 1945 in POW camps in the

Two cartoons by Spike Howard, NZAF.

OF PLOUGHS, PLANES & PALLIASSES 197

German 'Luftwaffe', holding Airforce personnel of the Allied Forces. During that time they have been very helpful in every respect in alleviating the strain of POW life, thus gaining our confidence. In summer 1944 I have been British camp-leader at Stalag Luft 4, Gross Tychow, Pomerania. By the brutal mistreating on the part of the guards under their Cpt. Pickhardt by about 30 POWs were bayonetted. *Preparations and trainings were in progress for organized shooting in the camp.* When the a/m interpreters were transferred to this camp, I – the British camp-leader and T/sgt. Paules have asked them both to help us in our more than desperate situation knowing that these two were the only ones who would have some understanding in our situation and who would be prepared to take the considerable risk of taking up activities against the a/m Cpt. who was strongly backed up by the Nazi Party. Thereafter we have asked these interpreters to do their best to prevent this Captain in carrying on in his activities pointing out that they would certainly save the life or at least the health of the hundreds of POW's and to do away with the enormous strain on the whole camp of approx. 10,000 inmates.

We have offered them any possible help if necessary after the war, which was refused by them in claiming that they would do everything possible, but would hate any idea of 'payment'. Both interpreters were completely successful in their efforts. I can only state that we, the camp-leaders, feel grateful that these interpreters had the courage in resisting a powerful party officer in that camp."

This was the situation, dear Mr. Clarke, as you will well remember, and if you would acknowledge these facts both of us would really feel more grateful, because it possibly helps us to build up a new life somewhere

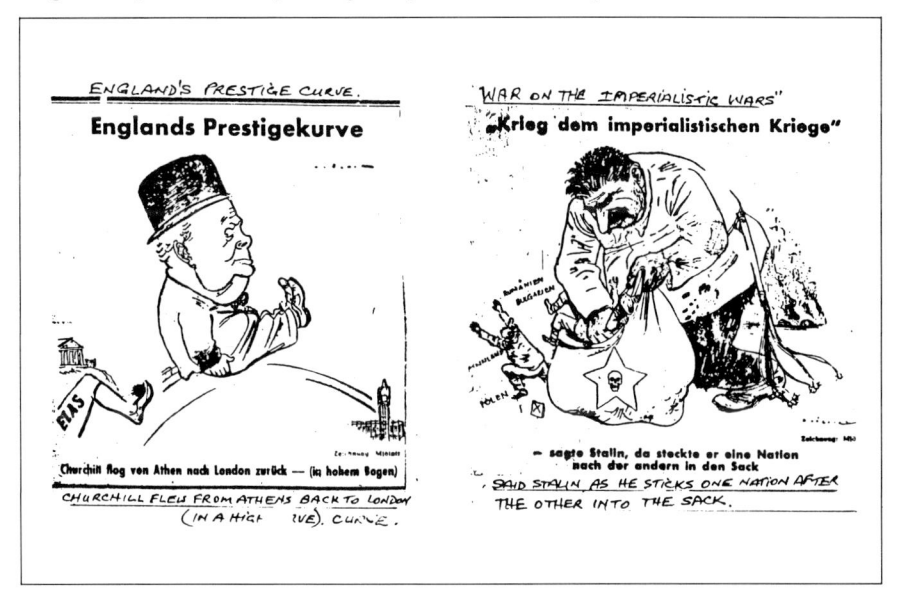

Two cartoons taken from German newspapers, 1943.

abroad. Will you please therefore send your letter containing this statement in double to:

Baron von Guttenberg,
Herschfelderstrasse 13,
Bad - Neustadt/Saale. (13.a)
Germany/American Zone.

I would like to hear from you about your well being and would appreciate if this correspondence could be continued giving all of us a new start for understanding each other.

Kind regards from me and Baron von Guttenberg,

Yours - Helmut R Whale

When Des passed this letter to me I was extremely sad to learn that Vic was extremely ill when returning from Prisoner of War life and in fact died within a few months of his return.

* * *

Radio reception was now daily. It was a very wonderful asset, and the news 'readers' once again started to circulate the huts to communicate the up-to-date news. This time however they did not read it, because for security reasons it was not written down for them. It was a good memory exercise.

A further new compound had been erected, just in time to receive hordes of weary dishevelled soldiers, obviously British mostly, with some Russians

Fitness was necessary for successful escaping...

and other nationals, all arriving on foot from the east. They were footsore and limping, dirty, ill-clad, obviously very hungry and appeared to be exhausted.

By their very appearance one knew instantly that they had shared miseries from which they would love to escape. Did their arrival at Tychow signal for them welcome rest and decreased rations? Was it the end of one suffering and the intensifying of the other? It seemed that perhaps their stay was just long enough to allow their blisters to heal. There were thousands more to come, and soon we ourselves were to be herded out onto the road and to the fields and woods, in snow, frost, rain and sun, to experience frostbite, hunger, thirst, blisters, swollen limbs, spastic muscles, colitis, dysentery, pneumonia, freezing cold and many other afflictions we would never have contemplated. We were to make room for others, more unfortunate than we, being quickly force marched against their will, away from the advancing Russian armies. These forces had now reached the Oder to the south of our camp, had taken Breslau and were moving north.

Flap and panic took charge. We were to leave the following day. Kitchen wagons would go with the column, drawn by oxen or horses. We were also told the march would be by easy stages in a south-westerly direction where an empty factory was reported to be suitable for housing us. This information of course was quite untrue, as we were to be marched west as quickly as possible with the object of crossing the Oder before the Russians were able to cut us off.

Hurriedly we once again made our makeshift packs from shirts and whatever other suitable articles we could find. The brew pot was never still and we drank tea continuously whilst we prepared to leave. (Thank God and the Red Cross for the tea, beverages, food and clothing). We worked late into the night. What Red-Cross parcels we had in store, to ensure a small issue over a period of time, would now have to be brought out and distributed. Carrying it would be the problem.

· CHAPTER 11 ·

THE FINAL MARCH

Packs were filled with clothing and the recently issued Red Cross tins of food. Torn up letters and other things to be discarded were heaped up outside the barrack doors. The camp presented a very untidy spectacle as we formed up the following morning, February 6th, to march away in a north-westerly direction. It was extremely uncomfortable attempting to walk as the snow stuck to the soles of our boots. We slipped and stumbled. The packs were heavy; we were not accustomed to this and it soon became obvious, after the first ten miles, that many of the boys were going to be in deep trouble. It was soon to be proved that those who had attempted to keep fit were to stand the test much better.

Many of them had already resorted to what I considered to be absolute folly; throwing away the heaviest items which happened to be tins of food. My instinct was to pick them up, but there were dozens. The action was precipitous and thoughtless but what could one do about it? They would regret it, and very soon.

We would occasionally stop for a ten minute break, after which some of the boys could hardly pick up their packs to continue. I was glad I had kept as fit as possible through exercise. The marching was not troubling me quite as severely as it was many of the others and I had confidence in myself of being able to last as long as anyone.

We were then on really rough ground, away from the road. It was a deep rutted track like those I had been familiar with on the farm. Snow covered the depressions and the boys did not appear to be able to 'read' the surface. Many of them were falling heavily having walked a distance far in excess of what they ought to have attempted. The column halted. There appeared to be some confusion amongst those guards attempting to read a map up front. It was becoming dark, the boys were very tired and it was not the time to tell us that we would have to retrace our steps. Eventually we came to a small farming village through which we had passed earlier and it was here, in the barns, that we were to spend our first night on what was to become a feat of endurance, an exercise of the survival of the fittest, lasting for three months over a distance of 600 miles. Ignorance once again was bliss. The village was Naffin – we had walked a distance of about 18 kilometres. Part of the column was housed in barns at Boissin. We were issued with a loaf of black bread to share between every three men.

The following day was somewhat of a shambles. Through rain and sleet the Germans drove us over mud-plastered fields and lanes, for a further 27 kms, housing part of the column at Zeitlow and the remainder in Reselkow.

Some 'pig potatoes' (potatoes boiled in their skins, mud grit and all, with no salt) awaited us, four per man. We were now extremely uncomfortable, even our blankets had become soaked in the sleet. Trousers, socks and boots were quite soaked with no means whatsoever of drying them out. Miserable night.

The third day was yet another pressure day, the going becoming tougher as the day progressed. Blisters and aching limbs took their toll during the 28 kms through Stolzenberg and Roman, where the column was split and housed.

We had now covered over 70 kms in three days on four potatoes and one third of a loaf of bread, so it was now that some of the boys would have enjoyed one of those tins of food they had discarded. Who needs a slimming diet?

Some watery potato soup and pig potatoes came up the following day, whilst most Kriegies attended to foot care, bandaging up blisters with anything they possessed that was suitable. The medic boys were in very great demand, but one had to remember that they too had to march, and like cookhouse volunteers and other helpers, had to keep going whilst the column rested for the day.

When the column was split up between two or three villages, Vic could not possibly attempt to cover all sites and so the situation spawned a number of recognised leaders, who either by vote or just natural selection and tendency, were regarded as being deputies, especially if they were German speaking. Over the following three months we were to find, when our column became somewhat fragmented, that it was possible, given the correct approach to the farmer (if one could winkle him out) to have our diet of spuds supplemented by carrots, turnips, peas or beans – and frequently barley from his granary and on many occasions I took part in these successful negotiations. Sometimes we were known to come up trumps with a sheep, or on occasions two, plus other incidental finds. My farming experience certainly helped me at times. I well remember one farmer, on whom I had applied some mild pressure and English gentlemanly charm, saying, "The way you handle these sheep suggests you know what you're looking for. Choose one yourself". So I did, a lovely, broad, flat-backed one, not much amongst so many men, but at least it added a flavour to the stew. Later I was to become more successful when bargaining for more than one sheep. On occasions I would make no progress when meeting up with a 'dyed in the wool Nazi' farmer. To torment him we would surreptitiously ensure that he saw our cigarettes and chocolate being used with great enjoyment, and being traded to other Germans who were willing to part with some food.

A truly, dedicated and worthy stalwart to be seen here, there and everywhere, was Jack Laing. His characteristic walk, which suggested that his stride be at least a foot longer than anyone else's, carried him up and down the column and around the barns, at all times helping and enquiring. Jack was endowed with energy and enthusiasm which he shared with all, but regrettably about eight weeks of such strain put him into hospital, as did it Vic Clark too, and we missed seeing them about from then on.

On the fifth day we were issued with a quarter of a loaf of bread and then urged on, with much fluffing on the vibrissa, by Three Times Whistling, to complete a further twenty kilometres. We passed through the little peasant village of Polzin, where near the village pump and duck-pond the inhabitants had set out buckets of water and ersatz coffee. We were amazed at such kind considerations but the guards prodded us on, shouting, "Move! Move!" Was such generosity sparked off by the local hordes of Polish forced workers who came milling round the column bringing us cups of soup? One guard was seen to knock the soup out of the hands of those who brought it saying, "Sie kommen gleich in Quartieren." (they will soon be in their quarters).

One old lady quite stooped, hobbled alongside the column, obviously disturbed by the sight of our plight, saying, "Och. Kinder. Kinder. Warum Kampfen wir?" (Oh children, children, why do we fight?) As we bedded down in barns that evening we longed for that soup which lay spilled in the roadway. We had nothing. Twenty painful kilometres behind us, and still no food.

The ice-covered roads glistened in the morning sun as we attempted to put a further twenty kilometres behind us on our way through Greifenberg to Kukahn. Many of the boys were now in a very rough state and it would seem, were soon to be in real trouble, but the pressure was on as we approached Goerke having covered the next twenty kilometres beyond Kukahn. On arrival, at least we did get clean water and a cup of barley. The wind was an icy blast, our feet were cold and very wet and the barn we eventually occupied was bare and draughty. It seemed now that endurance was stretched beyond limits.

Jack Paul celebrated his 24th birthday there at Goerke, blisters, chilblains, dysentery and all. It was the 12th February 1945, the seventh day of our trial of endurance. We had now done over 135 kilometres in extremely cold, wet weather on less than a loaf of bread and a few boiled potatoes, along with weak potato soup and a cup of barley. Little wonder we had all lost a lot more weight. The conditions were also producing some serious coughs and colds, the coughing being quite alarming. Broken blisters could not be properly cared for and many were becoming infected. This was a situation which was to become extremely serious, claiming the life of Ken Stanley and threatening the lives of many more. Not only had our bodies to stand the natural shocks which flesh is heir to, but had to endure the ills quite unaided by modern medicine. Such was not available to the very much overworked Dr Forest-Hay who, after all, was just another Prisoner of War. How long could we endure?

Knowing how slowly the Germans reacted to any of our needs or emergencies, it was time we called a halt to this punishing marathon. The reader can attempt to picture the discomfort of having to walk every day, averaging twenty kilometres per day in all weathers. Even if you had good food, good beds, suitable clothing, warmth and medical care, you would say it was too much, especially over country lanes and rough tracks. Without these important things life at that time was torturous, and it was really most important that we rested up. The Germans

OF PLOUGHS, PLANES & PALLIASSES

The three months forced march in cartoon form...

would in no way listen to our pleas and insisted that we complete over 140 more kilometres during the next seven days. This was a most ominous prospect. It was clear that there would be many serious casualties ahead, and how we would cope with the numbers? The dysentery situation was also deteriorating. Many were already too weak to be expected to go further, and were burning wood to make charcoal and eating it in large quantities to help combat the complaint. Thankfully it did seem to ease the burning rawness.

Representations were made to the Germans, but the answer was given by a finger pointed to the sky, denoting a higher authority, with the remark, "Befehl is Befehl." (Orders are orders) as the Feldwebel patted his revolver and then pointed his index finger to his temple. That was final.

We occupied many barns at Goerke and explored their surrounds. A sheep was forthcoming, as I completed some negotiations with the farmer, which Godwin had commenced but which were beginning to turn sour for some reason not obvious. Some of the boys found a large circular tub in one barn, filled it with water and crowded their bodies into it with great satisfaction.

Willie milked a cow in another barn and became extremely ill, whilst Keith Pettigrow devoured large quantities of the milk without ill effect and thoroughly enjoyed it. In one of the other barns the farmer cut up very rough indeed when he discovered that every cow he owned had been thoroughly milked dry. To keep the peace the boys had to leave the barn and find an alternative one. Real hunger knows no limits.

February 14th was truly a miserable day indeed. It poured continuously with rain and we were in no mood for going marching. We were so desperately hungry and rejoiced when we received half a dozen biscuits, 2oz of margarine and 3oz of corned beef – not very much, but an awful lot more than nothing. We had already known too many nothings over the past 135 kms.

The guards firmly told us that it was more than ever important that we all stay closely together as we were to pass through an area of great military importance, and anyone who straggled or got out of line would without doubt be shot. With that thought in mind our concern was even more keenly concentrated on those boys who were suffering badly from blisters, aching muscles and exhaustion.

We were now, after a relatively short march during which our blankets had become very wet, near to Swinemunde, where some seven months earlier we had disembarked from the 'Hellship' *Insterburg*. The object of this short march was to be nearer the Oder which we were to cross the following day. We would then be able to make the Swinemunde ferry and clear the area in one day of marching. Little were we to know that even so, it required us to make a day's march of 38 to 40 kilometres over islands and bridges. Torture indeed.

We were ousted very roughly from our barns at 0600 hrs and the Germans left us in no doubt that they clearly meant business. It was Cec's 25th birthday, one he would surely never forget. We passed through Tessin, Hagen, Wollin and on, goaded by the guards over the whole forty kilometres with further threats to shoot anyone who lagged behind. On the way we saw many dead horses – evidently the journey they were attempting had proved too much for them. Their flesh, though meagre, had been hacked from their bones by many marchers as they passed. Such an act, at one time, would have been to me quite reprehensible, but I found no compunction in hacking off a handful of meat from the nose of one of the unfortunate animals, as did many others in our column. Real hunger, as we then knew it, knew no conscience. It was a question of survive or perish.

It was evening as we approached Pritter, where the guards herded us into some large fields bordering onto some pine woods. The evening was intensely cold under one of those lovely clear crystal-domed winter skies, which always portend frost and body-numbing temperatures. We longed to have the shelter of some barns, but it was 1900 hrs and from where we stood no habitation was in sight. It would be lovely just to gain the shelter of those woods just beyond where the guards were lined up. It was then we were told that we would have to spend the night just where we stood. This news, to say the very least, was shattering, after such a totally exhausting day of forty kilometres and no food. Many of the boys were in such an advanced state of physical fatigue that they just folded up on the wet ground where they were standing. We would most certainly have to do something to prevent them freezing before the night was through.

I cannot remember seeing, in the whole of my life, a gathering of British subjects presenting such a totally dejected and alarming sight. It is difficult to grasp the drastic implications of this situation without having being one of those involved. There were well over a thousand Kriegies of varying nationalities gathered together on this site. There were many Polish and Russians who were, it appeared, glad to be near the British. It meant, perhaps, that they would be better placed for receiving some small quantity of food rather than none at all. But what hope was there for any of us in a snow-covered field?

The guards relaxed their vigilance somewhat, whereupon we made for the woods, broke off and gathered boughs and branches of pine needles with which to make beds of some kind. Twigs were gathered under the star-lit sky, and soon dozens of small fires were built, the boys crowding around in an attempt to thaw out frozen limbs. You would warm your back, then turn around to warm your frozen front and your back would immediately lose all the heat it had gained. How could we hope to survive the night?

Many were collecting the charred wood from the fires, cooling it off and eating it in an attempt to soothe their tortured bowels.

Then miraculously, there appeared a field soup kitchen, a hope of some food. Even some Red Cross parcels appeared, sufficient for one parcel per five men. It was like lightning the way every one arranged themselves into groups of five to effect a satisfactory distribution.

A huge queue soon formed on the field kitchen, but how long would it be before one reached the kitchen, or would there be anything left if you were near the end of the queue? It turned out to be about ¾ of a cup of barley soup, which grew thinner and weaker as the queue diminished. It was now midnight and unbearably cold. Johnnie Theckston and others tried to find comfort in crutches of trees, but the intense cold drove them out. It was totally unbearable.

"Lucky you didn't end up in the stew pot Thecko!" shouted some joker, "Somebody might have taken you for a rooster up that tree!"

"With the state of my socks and undies, I wouldn't give much for the flavour!" quoth John.

Hundreds of us dared not to sleep on the sodden ground, and it was much too hard where it had frozen. Fires were built all night through and it helped us to stay awake walking around from one knot of men sitting around their fire to another. It would have been disastrous to remove your boots.

I was somewhat fortunate. I had purloined, en route, a large multi-layered brown paper sack, which I had tightly rolled into a bundle to prevent it becoming wet. I wished we had a thousand of them. I made a base of pine needles, unrolled my sack and pulled it up over my head. I was soon as snug as the proverbial bug. It was sheer luxury and I felt a twinge of guilt as though I was cheating. With a certain measure of discomfort perhaps the sack would hold two, so I put the offer to a sufferer, of sharing. We were firmly wedged once we were installed, but he warmth was worth every bit of the inconvenience. The bonus was that, at least, sleep came.

We awoke to see everything and everybody covered white with frost. How some of the boys had survived the night I shall never know. I was therefore much better equipped than most of the column to face the following hazardous day, which was the 16th February, my 26th birthday. This was another day of total abstinence from food; we did receive some water, later in the day for drinking, and looked forward to the soup kitchen, which never came.

At 0700 hrs we were marched off in parties. We passed through Zirchow, most of the boys having great difficulty, after such a punishing night, in keeping going. We passed many civilians on the way to Swinemunde ferry, who obviously did dislike us intensely. They sneered at us, made extremely rude remarks, and threatened to strike us. Some walking stick strikes could not be avoided, which very much displeased the recipients.

Having the ferry now behind us, we had gained the western bank, pressing on in great discomfort as it was then pouring with rain. In the last two days we had covered just under seventy kilometres, most men not having slept and no one having had even what one would describe as a poor 'starter' to a meal. But it was at times, when hunger was one of our most serious problems, that another of our Kriegie Greats would surface, with his expertise, to augment the Wally Oakley stews. Mention has been made earlier of the potent distilled grog produced by that wonderful character, Ferdie Farrands.

Geoff Neeves reminds us of the positive contribution which Ferdie made to the wellbeing of his fellow Kriegies whilst on the March. At the end of a day's footslog Ferdie would be in his element exercising his fluent Deutsch which he could employ both at the 'Hoch' and 'Platt' level. With the Goons he would use his 'Hoch Deutsch' with an extremely haughty manner so effectively that many of the guards all but clicked heels and threw up a 'Heil'. With the Farmers Frau he would go all idiomatic, flutter his eyelids and virtually charm off her knickers. In consequence we would be favoured with the full use of the farm's spud boilers and often an illicit extra bag or two of spuds for the boys. He would enlist several of the boys to do the work, and as Geoff remembers, Basil Craske, Don Goddard and himself were acting as spud loaders and distributors one evening whilst Ferdie was chief boiler operator. It was on of those occasions when Ferdie exhibited his true value*.

German boilers came in a weird and wonderful variety. Some were simple 'coppers' under which one built a fire, and merely heaped in the potatoes and poured in some water. Some of them however, were complete mysteries which, when coaxed, operated on a pressure-cooker principle. When confronted with one of these, Ferdie would go into ecstasies tracing the pipework, valves, inlets, outlets etc, and his face would light up with satisfaction. He met with success every time, recalled Geoff, except once.

"When we opened the discharge manhole we were somewhat apprehensive because of the extreme difficulty Ferdie had experienced in controlling the steam-pressure valve. It was defective. Sure enough there were no cooked potatoes as was usual ... we peered and poked in through the steam ... and there we found one massive heap of hot white flour ... I was aghast" said Geoff.

Ferdie, however, just smiled, ordered that the flour like product be shovelled into buckets, flickered the eyelashes, picked up a couple of buckets and said,

"Follow me gentlemen."

Ferdie walked into the nearest barn to pronounce to the starving and expectant troops, in a very proud manner, that tonight he had prepared a very rare and special dish – mashed potatoes. He was, of course, favoured with the ovation which he richly deserved.

The column split in order to obtain barn accommodation for the night at Gorki, Grenzow and Kathryn. Cec cornered a Russian farm worker and wrangled some slabbed cattle-cake from him. I knew somehow he would manage to have cake for his birthday. Everybody appreciated those barns, although there was no food, and slept well, despite the craving stomachs.

Again on the following day, conditions were grim as we passed through Usedom and Finnow. One stretch of the route being 8 km of cobbled road.

---

*Prior to the war Ferdie was a BSc. (London) in electrical engineering, but he was also a pilot in the RAFVR, on the point of operational qualification. He chose to fly his bomber rather than continue in his television research.

Our feet already felt like pulp before we hit the cobbles, and what heaven to reach the end of them. By 1700 hrs on that day we had completed over 30 kms before reaching some barns at Murchin. ME109s and FW190s were buzzing about from a nearby Luftwaffe airfield, but did not appear to be on any detail other than circuits and bumps. Judy Garland traded his beloved watch for a chunk of bread and I recall his raging thirst forced him to leave the column to approach an old couple standing at a cottage door. He asked them for water. The old lady obliged immediately, and as she handed it to Judy a guard came along and with one mighty swipe knocked the water and the container high in the air. Judy, with total abjection and swollen wooden tongue, joined the column. The same guard came up to him saying,

"Cold water would not do your stomach any good, here have some of this." He then handed to Judy his water bottle full of warm ersatz coffee. As Judy remarked,

"How in the hell do you begin to understand the German mind?"

Now on to Anklam and Nardin, a further 20 kms. where the barns were good. Hot water was poured into large tubs in the farmyard, we had pea and onion soup and some hot boiled pig potatoes. At last after three days, something to eat.

Now, Monday really did bring something. We actually got some food before starting out on the day's march. Hot water and hot pea soup before marching off at 0730 hrs. We owed a lot to the Kriegie volunteers who stoked up the fires, got the boilers going and prepared the soup. Wally Oakley was indeed an outstanding organiser when it came to preparing soup. We could, of course, with some imagination, term some of his concoctions real stews when we were able to obtain a bit of meat for him to include. These were usually prepared in the farmers outhouse boiler where the pig-swill was treated.

After a further 28 kms, another small cup of soup awaited us from the field kitchen and a further 4 kms on we found barns at Seltz, but we had to grope around by moonlight in order to get settled in for the night.

The guards were now finding their food difficult to come by, and one of them actually stooped to picking potatoes from a clamp which some of our boys had found. As Barney Smith and Judy where busy digging, one of the other guards spotted what was happening and without warning put a bullet in amongst the diggers, which rather put a different complexion on taking liberties. Even the scavenging Germans obeyed the bullet.

We were still no wiser at to where we were heading, other than that it was away from the advancing Russians. As we had covered 344 kms since leaving Tychow, surely we must be outstripping them.

Many of our guards had disappeared overnight, the younger ones having been replaced by guards much older.

We were now following very rough muddy roads in well-forested areas. Sickness, mostly dysentery, was taking a heavy toll, many of the boys being unable to continue. It became evident that in order to prevent total chaos we would have to remain stationary for a few days of recovery. We stayed at Schossow for a couple of days. Pneumonia had proved too much for Nick Green, and although once a very well-built athletic type, he died.

It was now that Ken Stanley also found matters too demanding, and succumbed. The chips were now really down between ourselves and the Germans, and some confrontation was inevitable if conditions did not improve. Even Vic Clark was looking quite ill and surely could not go on much longer.

We needed someone of higher authority to visit the column and see at first-hand just how serious the situation was, so that recommendations for action could be implemented to bring about some improvement.

Barracks 5, 6 and 7 comprised our column, and we arrived in the village of Schwandt early afternoon after only about 18 kms. We had lost Barracks 8, 9 and 10 but found they had barns some distance away. Jack Laing was looking after 8, 9 and 10, Vic was poorly, which was my cue to take a positive approach to our perplexing predicament.

Food was our most pressing requirement and I therefore had a few words with Graham Godwin and other volunteer workers and sought an audience with the farmer. I introduced myself formally in my best Hoch Deutsche receiving an agreeable reaction with the information that his name was Johan Sinnig. I explained our dilemma to Herr Sinnig and requested to know what quantity of food he had on stock such as potatoes, carrots, swedes, barley, beans, peas, lentils and any other grain, as we needed to assess potential supplies for a few days against our needs. Herr Sinnig was reasonably sympathetic to our situation, but obviously quite concerned that about 500 men in his farmyard were about to eat him out of house and home, but he was prepared to help. I asked him where his stocks of grain were kept and could I please see them. I think at this point, with respect, God bless his German soul, Herr Sinnig wished he had not joined the club, but I had detected that he had some British sympathies. He nervously led me to his granary.

I was, without doubt, impressed. I had never seen such lovely order in a farm granary before, it was so clean. Each sack of grain had the neck neatly rolled back almost level with the contents, so that each sack would allow a sample to be dribbled through the fingers for inspection. This I did and congratulated Herr Sinnig on his standard of cleanliness organization and quality produce. He looked nervously at the guard and then back at me. I told Godwin to get the guard out of earshot on some pretext, which he dutifully accomplished.

I told Herr Sinnig that it was inevitable that British forces would be in his village within a few weeks. He agreed. I then told him I would give him my "Versicherung und Versprechen", (promise and assurance) that if he would supply all the food we needed, "unsere verlangenen Magen zu versorgen", (our craving stomachs to satisfy) I would recommend to our

Hauptquartier, when I arrived in England, that he be compensated and receive favourable treatment. He was very pleased with the arrangement saying he would accompany me to the granary daily for my requirements. He furtively looked around to see if any guards were in sight then shook hands with this 'friendly enemy' who was to take his provisions. I reminded him that if he now parted with this grain to anyone else after coming to an agreement, that he would be in deep trouble.

Wally and his kitchen staff now really had something on which to work – and this they certainly did. They were at those darned old boilers from early morning till night. I would meet Herr Sinnig with my order. Two 55kg sacks of peas and beans, eight 55kg sacks of potatoes, two 55kg sacks of carrots, two 55kg sacks of swedes, two 55kg sacks of onions and salt. We also had an arrangement for some meat.

Keith Pettigrew in his diary wrote, "Strange to feel your stomach full. Wally keeping the soups coming. Farmer playing ball with Percy Carruthers as go-between and getting results. Even got salt and meat."

During our stay with Herr Sinnig I obtained three sheep from him. Not perhaps a sufficient ration for so many hungry men, but one hell of a lot compared with nothing. This was, relative to the past, a banquet.

Apparently however, barracks 8, 9, and 10 were not having it as good as us regarding food, and some of them found their way over to us in search of something to eat. Their farmer was not quite so cooperative as ours. We had, however, to be somewhat cautious; we could not risk an invasion, so gave them each a generous helping of stew and suggested that they rejoin their own column. A hard but necessary decision.

Vic and a great number of boys who were ill had been transferred to a barn in Briggow which was being used as a hospital. Vic had pneumonia, diarrhoea, and frostbite. He really was in bad shape. At last an Inspector General of Luftwaffe POW camps paid a visit and confirmed that those too ill at Briggow were not to be moved. Those in our column who were very ill, but whom we could not get into hospital, were put into a 'sick bay' arranged in a nearby barn. If we moved they would have to be left behind, it would be wrong to gamble with their lives and the Germans realised that the finger would be pointed at them, and perhaps not too far in the future.

We stayed nine days with Herr Sinnig and certainly felt the benefit of the food we had received. The real morale-booster was when we received a whole Red Cross parcel per man. News kept reaching us that some of the boys in the hospital had died from dysentery and pneumonia – young athletic men who a short time ago had been in fairly good physical condition.

The intense cold continued, and it snowed heavily on Sunday 4th March when we said goodbye to Herr Sinnig. I kept my promise on my return to England and put matters right at interrogation, that he be suitably recognised for his help. I have no doubt, he saved many airmen's lives.

Dead horses were again to be seen on the roadsides, their flesh having been hacked off to the bones. We covered nearly 80 kms in the next three days then rested at Monchbusch on the 7th March where Keith celebrated his 23rd birthday. He wrote in his diary, "Good barn. Our column more organised. Good barns, good stews, and spuds. Roy Mirfin and 'The Gen Box' in our loft.

It was about this time, early March, that I had a serious talk with the German officer in charge of us. I was now somehow committed to accept the welfare of the men of former barracks 5, 6 and 7 as my responsibility. My ability to converse quite freely in German was a most salutary investment and had the magic of slicing clean through the captor/captive barrier, which was now somewhat mutated from that which existed behind the wire. Perhaps I found my 'niche' in our current situation.

I explained to the officer that through lack of Mitwirkung (cooperation) we were causing much Zeitverschwendung, (wasting of time), by having no regular advance representative arriving in the villages where we intended to stay. From then on it was not an uncommon sight to see me pedalling along ahead of the column on an old bicycle, sitting on the crossbar, with a German guard seated on the saddle with his rifle over his shoulder. Christ, it was hard work sometimes, those three stones in weight I had lost would have helped tremendously.

I would discuss food supply with the farmers and hot water arrangements. Could the boiler be filled now with water and fired up, to have the water standing out in buckets or troughs when the boys arrived? They could then wash whilst the stew was being boiled. The arrangement was extremely successful and cut down waiting time a very great deal. I then had to cycle back to the column and complete the walk along with boys.

We pressed on to Lankin where we knocked up a super stew. "Best one yet" wrote Keith, who was a connoisseur of 'Kriegie Glop'.

Barracks 8, 9 and 10 were somewhat distanced from us now. Some days they marched when we rested, and vice versa. Generally we seemed to be in better shape than they. Keith wrote on the 19th March. "Got bread, brew and spuds. Built fires; got other spuds from clamps. Barracks 8, 9 and 10 caught up and are across the way, having it rough. They came over to us."

Harry Bastian, from the 8, 9, 10 column wrote in his diary on the 20th March, "Very hungry. Barracks 5, 6 and 7 turfed us out of their column. We lost out." I did not feel very good about this. It is hard to see your own suffer, but I was becoming somewhat jaded, it was hard work and five hundred in one bunch was just enough. In fact I would have welcomed packing in for a while but never got round to doing anything about it. The trouble is I think in such cases is that you really believe you are indispensable. We continued on through Kremlin, Wantlitz, Eldena, Bresegard and crossed the Elbe on Thursday 22nd March, averaging over 20 kms per day. We received half a Red Cross parcel at Damnatz and a further very welcome half at Metzingen. Many allied aircraft were now overhead close enough for us to see their bombs actually falling, and morale was now weighing in on the credit side.

Wally kept up his soups and stews from the ingredients we were able to organise. We passed through Bevenson and Emmendorf. I did one of my cycling trips and called upon a farm and asked to speak to Herr Bauer (the farmer gentleman). I was told by a very nervous young lady who returned with a pleasing smile that Herr Bauer wished to see me in the house. The guard sat down on the wheelbarrow, pushed his head dress to the back of his head, and motioning me away into the house. I was very apprehensive. Perhaps I had dropped on a right Nazi Kraut. I removed my head dress, bid him 'Good Afternoon', introduced myself, then paused for a moment. He did not even look up as I spoke. He was sitting in a low chair at forty-five degree angle to the fireplace, his elbows on his knees, and his chin in his hands.

I addressed his right ear, saying I had five hundred very hungry men looking for shelter and food, who would be arriving in about two hours. I told him that I was asking for the use of his barns and wood-burning boilers, and of course about 150 to 200kg of grain and a minimum of 800kg of potatoes and vegetables. I thanked him for inviting me into his home, and awaited his reaction. He said something to his wife in a very low voice which I did not understand. Both his wife and daughter bustled to arrange the table and asked me to take a seat saying,

"You can have a good meal well before your men arrive."

Had I found second Johan Sinnig?

I explained that I must return to the men without delay and that it would be unfair to eat food not available to them, but said how grateful I felt for their kindness.

Herr Bauer then spoke to me for the first time, complimenting me, I think, by referring to me as 'an English gentleman', and continued,

"Then your men shall have plenty of food when they arrive." Here surely was a true pro-British German, one of the very few I met. Notes in Keith's diary covering this period read. "We arrived at a nice prosperous barn and bags of rackets went. It was the best day we had for trading yet. Hammer and Pat got on the kitchen party and did well. I felt sick from overeating." For the following morning he wrote. "We got spuds, brew, stew with barley and real pork and carrots. It was the tastiest morsel for a long time. We racketed quite a bit and left comparatively well stocked."

Herr Bauer invited me to stay longer. I thanked him and said I wished we could, but that the guards had orders to move us on. The next place was owned by a 'Terror Flieger Hater', and we had a difficult time. I wrote to Herr Bauer on my return to England and thanked him on behalf of the five hundred Kriegies. He had apparently feared the Russian advance and left the farm to flee further west. His daughter had received my letter and it was she who replied. On through Malzinge to Ebsdorf. We were obviously converging with many other parties on the march and now even water was becoming hard to come by. Keith Pettigrew in his notes, mentions this and remarks how welcome even a little water was which Wally Barber had managed to locate. It seemed to be the end of the line for a great many of the boys when at last we were lined up on the railway station at Ebsdorf and bundled, once again onto the train – as many as eighty men to a cattle truck. Life was a variation of tortures.

After a journey of about two and a quarter hours we arrived at Stalag X1.b Fallingbostel. Harry Bliss, locked in one of the trucks, died unfortunately before we could get the Gerries to unlock the doors. Jim Ruddick was with Harry and remembers that Harry was the only surviving member of his crew, from the crash on being shot down, and it was extremely sad that he should now die in these squalid conditions. Jim recalled having to pull the bier up the many hills to the cemetery. In Jim's weakened physical state the task was indeed arduous. There were seven coffins on this huge contraption and not a lot of reverence was allowed to be shown. Both Jim and Alan Forster remembered how the lids kept springing open from the thin matchwood structures which contained Polish and other nationalities. Harry was a good type and a great friend and Jim wished all the time that things could have been better than this for him.

That cattle truck ride was only seventy kilometres but it was truly hell. We were all so tired and the very sick were totally worn out. As on previous trips, with eighty to a truck, there was no room to sit down. The train remained in a siding all night, but this time the number of men who were capable of standing up all night was very few indeed. This resulted in bodies being heaped on each other, exhausted. There was no order to the heaps, the boys just had to fall where they stood, consequently there were packs all mixed up in the heaps, feet in faces, bottoms on chests and it seemed, legs and arms everywhere. Oh to be in that promised land – England – a land fit for heroes.

It was after midday that we were at last exposed to fresh air and light. The trucks were filthy. There had not been enough room to move to a corner to urinate, and those pinned down with other bodies, and who suffered from dysentery and diarrhoea had no chance. The degree of distress was disturbing, especially with those who had to vomit and cause such an unpleasant inconvenience to their own very good friends. This was a mental torture.

My first and lasting impression of Fallingbostel, after marching the two miles from the train and undergoing a most detailed search, was, as we were released into the camp, coming face to face with a fifteen coffin burial party; one of a great many more which were to follow. The death rate was no doubt quite high, especially amongst the Russians, who were in a separate compound. They presented a most appalling spectacle. Some were lucky to have some worn out boots but most of them had their feet wrapped in rags and sacking. The inadequate amount of food, rough boiled potatoes, was merely tipped on the ground. These men were so dreadfully hungry that they just fell upon the heap of potatoes to shovel them into their mouths. Many could not get to the potatoes for bodies, consequently much of the ration was spoilt, being trodden into the ground. The scene was indescribable. They were so unbelievably thin that when the dead were collected it was difficult to believe that there really was a body under the sheet.

They were really treated worse than animals. One wondered how the Germans could be so beastly to other humans. I have oft said that I feed my dogs more bulk food daily than we received in a week, but more than the Russians received in a month. Death was inevitable. The food was not sufficient to maintain life. The Russians of course did not have the benefit of Red Cross parcels. It would be quite true to say that had we been deprived of them many of us would certainly not have survived either. As it was, all of us had lost at least twenty-five percent of our body weight.

In this camp, in spite of the squalor, some organisation did exist. The French had their own department. It was said they numbered 20,000 and had been there a long time. They were not to be trusted, as one would expect to be able to trust allies. They had a huge stock of Red Cross parcels and guarded them zealously. They were non-cooperative and very selfish. In Fallingbostel, besides French, Russian and British, were Serbs, Indians, Yugoslavs, Colonials, Americans and some minorities mostly living in over-crowded huts which were badly lice ridden.

We were herded on to what we called 'the football pitch'. Aircraft were milling around overhead. Air raids seemed to be almost continuous and deep rumbling of guns and bombs could be heard in the distance. Two huge marquees were brought along and erected on site. As large as these were, with every square foot occupied, there was still an overflow of men. Some of us found our way into some bare wooden huts, with nothing in them whatsoever. They were terribly draughty and so cold that sleep was hard to come by. We soon discovered that these huts were really well occupied. They seethed with lice; it was so very uncomfortable. We would spend hours inspecting every seam in our clothing. We would sit naked doing de-lousing drill, freezing but enjoying some moments of escape. We would go along the seams with a flame to burn the little beasts and roast their eggs to bursting. Judy however had a different view.

"You're not bursting the eggs with the heat of those flames," he said, "you're only helping the little bastards to hatch out."

I think he was quite right, the seriousness of the situation never abated.

One long term prisoner here was a wonderful example to all, and who really earned his salt, was R.S.M. Johnnie Lord. His organisational abilities were superb and discipline flourished in his wake. Morale was elevated, reason and mental equilibrium maintained. His personal turnout was equal to any parade ground standard.

It was rumoured that priority prisoners were to be moved. That, we learned, meant RAF aircrew, but the news did not disturb me, in fact I rather welcomed the thought. The news, however, did seriously disturb many of our boys, who were not in a suitable physical condition to go on the roads again. There was a massive sort out of the fit and the unfit, the fit numbers being greatly reduced below our arrival numbers. Jack Laing was now in poor shape and for his own sake was advised to accept hospital admission. Jack had experienced a hard long slog, working hard, endangering his own health as had Vic Clarke. Others too had been giving more of their time and energies than could have reasonably been expected of them, such as the Doctors, the medics and the stew-boiling brethren. I too felt that I had had enough, and said so.

I of course owed a tribute to a likable Scot, without whose help I would not have been able to do what I did. He was wizard on food management. From Red Cross parcels he would make up the cocoa, chocolate, raisins and milk powder into what appeared to be a huge chocolate bar, and called it fudge. However scarce our food supplies, there always seemed to be a slice of fudge, albeit very thin sometimes. If I was busy and missed out on soup distribution, which was quite often as I never seemed to have the time to join the queue, he would ensure my share was there on my return.

He would take charge of my kit when we arrived at a barn. I would then concentrate on whatever was required whilst he sorted out some sleeping pitch. Howard played an important and unselfish part in keeping me on the go, and if it was a case of preparing food on individual fires, he always had a tin full for me. Perhaps Jack and Vic did not have the same degree of support, I do not know.

Who should we meet here again at Fallingbostel, but Ken Cotterell who had escaped from the column some way back. He had become entangled with some nasty SS characters and some French, who were not very sure where their loyalties lay, and dumped him eventually onto an American column. Here, Ken remembered, the American boys had rather lost their grasp in the face of hunger and were actually fighting over some potatoes. I recall the words of Ken as he expressed his delight that his escape skirmish was over.

"This is yet again one time that I am genuinely glad to be British and to be with British." He very obviously meant what he said; he was never one to waste words.

We were to stay at Fallingbostel only ten very long days and glad to take to the roads, fields and barns once more. There was some reorganisation to be done before leaving. Our numbers had now been considerably reduced through sickness and so it would now be quite acceptable to merge the boys of barracks 8, 9 and 10 with ours of 5, 6 and 7. I was voted to be Column Leader, and although I was not looking forward to the task with any great enthusiasm, I nevertheless felt obliged to accept as the boys all knew me, and in any case I had become accustomed to the procedures and the demands.

What a welcome change, we could be friends with our friends from barracks 8, 9 and 10. Bastian and crowd were now 'us' and we wouldn't need to shoo them off to their own column when they came scrounging for food. Harry was a great Aussie character as many others. He kept a good diary all through the march as did Cec, Keith, Geoff, Judy, Bill and others. I have copies of them all and know the difficulties they had compiling them. Sometimes notes were folded together on all sorts of scrap paper, the inevitable 'bog' type being included.

Reading Harry's notes which he wrote just prior to Fallingsbostel, I am conscious of appreciating his frankness. "Buggered. Everybody weak. Too little food. Six small spuds. Cup of watery soup. Lovely day. Pinched some pig food. Saw two ME262s" One had to admire his coverage. In his entry for the 7th April, the day before leaving Fallingbostel, he paid me a compliment which I don't suppose he ever intended me to read.

"Had three issues of a quarter of a Red Cross parcel since we arrived here. Had fruit, biscuits and nutty which really tasted heavenly to our empty tums. Spuds have been cut to three per man - it seems we're off again tomorrow – Jack Laing confined to bed - Percy Carruthers has taken charge of our column. He's a good type. 'A' and 'C' Lager moved out yesterday."

We stood around for literally hours whilst the Goons exhibited their particular brand of flapping. There was no need to oust us out of our wraps at 0600 hrs, five hours before moving off, especially that it was pouring with rain. The guards were now Wehrmacht (army) but oddly enough seemed to lack the pomp of previous ones.

We barned up at Bleckmar after 14 kms. Bill Rae had already slipped the column and beat us home by a few weeks. The following day Jack and Cec dropped out but a truck picked them up and brought them back to the column much to their dismay. Tempests were strafing any vehicle which moved. Typhoons and Spitfires were continually seeming to stand on one wing as they picked out their targets. A FW190 went belting down the runway of an airfield just over the hedge, lifted its landing gear just in time for a Spit to fill him with cannon shells. The German pilot ejected and landed safely, landing quite nearby. Jim Haskett said he looked alright.

A further 26 kms. to Trauen and yet 26 kms. more to Wettenbostel en-route to which we found propaganda newspapers from the RAF, ration cards and leaflets. There were hundreds of aircraft to be seen and heard and just as many lice in our clothing from that Fallingbostel infestation.

Some forty years later Harry Bastian was reminiscing on these days, on propaganda papers, leaflets and ration cards as the column approached one of the towns.

"You came along the column," said Harry, "full of British 'bull' shouting, 'Gerry town coming up fellows. Shoulders back, heads up, spring in your step and above all, remember you're British.' We used to call you some bloody names at times Perc, but looking back, the treatment did us all good at the time. I can forgive you now. Cheers."

"Do you remember those bloody chilblains which we used to cure by piddling on them?" asked Harry. Then he quipped, "But I could never quite manage a very good aim on to those on my ears."

Betzendorf was our next halt but we were apparently catching up on other parties so had to stay put even though no barns were available. We slept where we were, so just as we had done before, we collected up pine boughs on which to bed down.

Years later, in one of my Chairman's Chatter circulars sent out to the boys of Kriegie Call, I could not resist referring to our sleeping moments under the stars by quoting from King Lear.

> Poor naked wretches where so 'ere you are
> That bide the pelting of the pitiless storm
> How shall your houseless heads and unfed sides
> Your loop'd and window'd raggedness defend you
> From seasons such as these?"

Jock Rae quickly pointed out the appropriate loop'd reference to the radio direction-finding aerial and the window'd reference to the anti radar device thrown out from aircraft and which as long silver strips was to be seen in the area of Germany through which we were then marching. It was festooned from the pine trees presenting a fairy tale aspect of thousands of ready made Christmas trees.

We made for Barnstedt only 16 kms from Ebsdorf where we had boarded those stinking cattle trucks for Fallingbostel. Although food was not really plentiful we were certainly doing better than we would have done had we stayed at X1.b, and certainly better in general than we had hitherto done. A local farmer had just killed a horse and it seemed anyone was free to cut himself a steak – an offer a lot of us gladly accepted. We were also coming across flour, rogen meal, peas, onions, vegetable clamps and barley. Some of this was transportable and so could be used later. We were now seeing shot-up trains and trucks and burned out cars which our strafing aircraft were destroying at will. Oh to be at the controls again helping with the destruction!

More boys were now leaving the column for the woods. Jack and Cec slipped away again. It was now the 15th of April and they were back in England on the 24th. Bob Galloway and Jim Smith left. Harry Bastian, Sam Hall and Vic Hanks went together and later ran into Geoff Neeves and Don Goddard.

Some of the boys did not time their moment of 'slope-off' as well as they might have done, leaving amidst dog barking and the odd bullet being loosed off, but the Gerries did not follow up the chase.

Dixie Deans, the senior Camp Leader, had been with his 'A' Lager since leaving Heydekrug some ten months earlier. They missed the *Insterburg* trip and the 'Run up the Road', having gone by cattle truck to Torun. Now they were near to us again and Dixie paid us a visit, whilst on parole, on an old bicycle which the Germans had loaned him. I was able to assure Dixie that we were on top of the situation and suitably organized. He rode off to locate another column.

Strafing aircraft put on some rather spectacular displays on occasions and we would cheer like hell as they came wheeling around to line up their sights on trucks and other vehicles. The pilot would press the tit and the shells would plough into the vehicles causing them to seemingly jump from the ground, shudder, stop and burst into flames. On other occasions we would not be too well placed relative to the target and would have to fling ourselves quickly into the ditch for our own safety. Regrettably, one of our other columns had been mistaken for enemy troops and badly shot up. Thirty of the boys were killed outright, three dying later from their wounds and forty-three were injured but survived. This happened at Gresse, and was very sad: after so much rough treatment at the hands of the Germans, to lose their lives to allied aircraft was particularly poignant.

Dysentery was still wreaking havoc in the column. Jim Haskett recalled one most unfortunate event which occurred at one of our stop-overs. Many of the boys were spending long periods sitting on the pole which was erected over the very long latrine trench. It was fully occupied by groaning suffering Kriegies, and the long larch pole was taking the strain of the weight well, bowed beyond the limits of acceptable curvature, when a very desperate six-footer came tearing out of the barn, dropping his trousers en-route. Amidst the cries of, "Oh No!" and "Oh Christ!" he quickly shuffled a place for his bottom. There was one almighty crack, and the whole row of tortured bodies shot into the trench of malodorous fetid ejectamenta. What unbelievable chaos. Some bystanders were overcome by fits of hysterical laughter, others just gaped in utter disbelief, whilst some distanced their bodies from the scene before the odour caught up with them. How those boys did stink. How to get them clean? How to bed them down? We would have to do something with their clothes, we could not throw them away, there were no replacements. One had his flying boots filled to the brim. These boys would have to be segregated if only to maintain their friendship. To describe a certain situation one often used the expression "to be in the shit" but this present circumstance was ridiculous.

> For I have known the freedom of the air,
> Commanded every move with confidence and skill,
> But crawled in mud like some coarse starving slug,
> When life seemed short if one were to despair.

The guards awoke us at 0200 hrs to move off to Bleckede in order to cross the Elbe by ferry before the fighter boys got airborne in their search for targets for the day. We waited for an hour and a half in the cold night air before the ferry took us over. We were fortunate to come across a Red Cross stock which allowed one parcel per man – what a welcome find. Spitfires took a look at us as daylight broke and recognised us. We waved furiously and cheered like madmen. Some just stood and gazed, chins wobbling with emotion.

The Goons killed an ox, they too were becoming desperate. In a very short time it was skinned and huge steaks were being carved. I have no idea to whom the poor animal belonged; it was a case of every man for himself. The Germans then allowed us to take a share. We cooked on open fires when the wood parties returned with some fuel but we found the meat to be too rich for our poor stomachs and we became extremely sick.

Shot-up Hun transports were now to be seen all around whilst more and more Typhoons attended to anything on wheels. We covered about 19 kms along the Berlin – Hamburg road to Dammeritz where we found barns in which to pass the night. Two trucks passed by and immediately our fighters literally blew them to pieces. There was a flak post nearby which kept poking a few shots at our aircraft as they wheeled over. A Tiffie pilot located it, swung his aircraft round in a very cocky and confident manner, standing it on one wing, levelled it out and blew the whole thing in the air, guns and men together.

We awoke to heavy rain and consequently delayed our departure until mid-day. We passed through three small villages and arrived at Cammin in the evening. Three smallish barns, well furnished with straw, made a very comfortable and warm resting place. A further barn with a muck floor was used, it stunk a bit but was at least somewhere to sleep.

Meantime, elsewhere the 11th Armoured Division had pressed forward and had met up with Geoff Neeves, Don Goddard and others who had slipped the column less than a week ago. Whilst Geoff and Don were riding on one of the armoured cars they spotted Cec and Jack who were craving liberation.

In our comfortable barns we were enjoying our best rest for some time. It was just after midnight when a low flying aircraft shook us back to consciousness. It turned away and could then be heard to approach once more. As Jim Haskett put it. "There came the roar of the Merlins. A Mossie? Tracer and cannon angled down through the roof. The floor covered with Kriegie bodies – someone had to be hurt. Andy and Jim were out in seconds ploughing through mud and slush. The thatch was blazing like tinder and to our horror the twin-engined shadow was coming in again, low with guns blazing. We pushed off through the rain to the shelter of some trees, others made off to higher ground.

Fred Draycott recalled, "Two barns blazed immediately. Flaming thatch was falling onto Kriegies attempting to get outside. One cannot forget the screams of the boys being set alight and those who were wounded by gunfire. Wally Lowery, Loftie Minnitt and Jock Brownlie were against the wall just where some shells came through. Jock was filled with splinters. Wally Lowery, almost casually, said "Loftie, 'av bin 'it." as he attempted to inspect his shattered ankles. That was the end of marching for Wally who was shipped off to a nearby hospital. Jim Ruddick in the small corner loft saw the tracer coming down immediately in front of him. Harry Pettie and Wendell, with some of the others were throwing their kit out of the barn loft openings, then jumping. Both they and their kit, and others, were landing on those men escaping at ground level. Harry went back in for his boots but did not have time to look far, he ended up with two left footed ones. Alan Schofield was hit in a leg and hand. Ken Gosney and Danny Willcox-Jones were hit. Bob Hart remembered a voice calling loudly after the first attack. "Lie still. Lie still!" came the strong Kiwi accent of Morris Smith.

Jock Durnan was killed. Reg Brown was killed. Sammy Ramsden died later, as did Reg from their wounds. Danny Heath remembered that one of them was lying next to him. Danny dragged him out but the flames at ground level were blazing so intensely, and so quickly, that he just had to drop him. Keith's diary recorded, 'at least fifteen injured'.

Fred Draycott remembered that when we arrived at these barns, a mobile German HQ also arrived but took up a camouflaged position amongst some nearby trees. One wonders whether this was the target the aircraft was seeking.

The guards were fussing around, some of them quite obviously shaken by the affair. 'Three Times Whistling' the German Feldwebel, to give him his due mention, was eager to assist the wounded. I was attending to Jock Durnan and he was there with me helping with the lifting.

I was not making very good progress attempting to get the boys away from the scene onto some higher ground behind, when Des Dunphy came along to lend his ever-capable assistance. We congregated a large number up the hill in a nearby field, up behind the far hedge, until some kind of order could be achieved. Many of the men were too exhausted to stay awake and although it was raining they were bedding down and falling asleep right there.

From other directions men eventually made their way back towards the barns, when some guards came along to complain, saying they were not prepared to return to the barns in case of a renewed attack. I told them that I considered that the warmth from the dying flames was worth any risk there may be so they allowed all to return who wished. Some of the men found shelter in the undamaged barn.

The following morning the glowing embers of the barns served to boil water for drinks, to cook anything one may have for breakfast and to dry out our sodden clothing.

The old man and lady who owned the barns came along, and quite contrary to what we expected, they were amazed at our plight and condition. Perhaps they were also astounded to see us eating the charcoaled beams of their barns, which a few hours earlier had been supporting their roofs. Many of the boys were eagerly chipping off the charcoal and though it was not very palatable, the question of taste was not for consideration when the urgency to rid oneself of the entiritis and dysentery was so keen.

The injured were taken to a field hospital and I then had to concern myself with burial arrangements for Jock who had paid the supreme price.

I was allowed to visit the vicar of the little local church down the road. He was a man of God, and religions, at a time like this did not really matter. I found him to be a true and faithful servant of his religion. He was most anxious to be of assistance and made arrangements for the funeral. He preached a proper service and burial service, albeit in the German tongue, but as he spoke I was by his side throughout, interpreting his words to the burial party of Kriegies who were in attendance. Hymn singing was however not practicable, but it was nice to think that our dead, on enemy soil, had been revered in a manner as befitting as was humanly possible in the circumstances. With true reverence and his inherent skill in the art of woodcarving, Chas Griffin made a small cross from a piece of wood he had acquired and fixed it there 'to mark his place'.

The incident, regrettably, was only one of many such unfortunate occurrences, which must inevitably take place in a battle area. We really were extremely fortunate not to have been directly involved in more. We learned of another incident involving Typhoons at Vellahn on the 20/21st.

We moved to search for other barns. We only went five kilometres to Dodow where we found comforts beyond our belief. There was a Red Cross wagon with a parcel for each of us. There was a field of leeks where Keith was pulling in a good harvest. We washed too, in a lovely clear little stream. I stripped off naked, exhibiting my angular collection of bones, for the purpose of a de-lousing exercise and found a sheep tick with its head buried into my abdomen. I recognised it as such immediately. I wondered if the local farmer had any sheep dip to shake it out, because I knew I must not mishandle the little brute otherwise its body would come adrift and leave the head to fester in my flesh. I tortured it with a sharp hawthorn spine and it surrendered. A curious guard came along, took a peep and asked,

"Whatever is that thing?"

"Which thing?" said I.

He guffawed.

"The literal translation," I said, "would be Schaf-tick."

"Ach so. Ach so. Das Ticken, das Ticken. Baa, baa, baa." and he shuffled off. Here we really got some good organization going. Although many of the boys had lost all their kit and some of their clothing in the barn fire, they shared in their combines and got by. We ate the best meals here that we had seen for a long while – and many of us had our first bath for eleven weeks. We actually boiled clothes for the first time in three months, on fires we built on bricks and stones.

We had a good flow of rations from the farmer, until some clown stole some of his pearl barley. He was furious at such dishonesty and promptly insisted that he reduce our allocation.

I had a word with the culprits telling them that it was just not the way to go about obtaining food when we had an understanding with the farmer, and that their action made things much more difficult for me. The farmer insisted that I reprimand them, but could not understand why I was not doing it the German way by having them stand bolt upright to attention and bawling and screaming at them with my eyes bulging, spit flying and my nose six inches from theirs.

"Oh piss off Perc and tell him he's bloody lucky we're not confiscating the lot, the bloody Kraut."

Do you have to fall out with your friends to keep you from falling out with the enemy?

"Now fellows you either toe the line or I don't consider you one of my column. I'm not having it. These bods are still top dog until we get their guns, until then remember they're swinging on your balls."

We had no further trouble and I apologised to the farmer, and retained his cooperation.

It was Anzac Day. Up the Aussies and the Kiwis, in the nicest possible way of course – they were a great bunch of guys and I enjoyed knowing them.

Things were turning for the better, decidedly so. We would attempt to stay here. The Tiffies and the Spit boys I think had got to know us and would come belting over fifty feet up. If a truck took their eye they would give it a squirt and it would be no more. We could clearly see the pilots as they flashed up. We cheered them and waved encouragement.

The Goons issued milk specially for those with dysentery, and we got spuds, carrots, barley, swedes, leeks, chunks of good bullock beef, 4oz each of horsemeat and lots of fresh brews. Dare I say it, some of us were noticeably regaining some lost weight. It was a lovely day, we were even having haircuts, in a fashion, and Keith noted in his diary that he even heard someone singing for the first time. "A bit corny," wrote Keith, "but there it was, 'Would you like to swing on a star?'"

The old Volksturn guards (home-guard) who were now in charge of us were very relaxed – a very different cry from the "Run up the Road" the previous July.

It seemed now that perhaps we only moved to where we could find food and orders appeared to be somewhat confused. It had been, for quite some time now, easy to drop out of the column and make your own way west. As for myself leaving the column, I suppose I had some feeling of loyalty to the boys which prevented me going – after all, I was more use where I was.

On Friday the 27th of April the guards hounded us out at 0630 hrs then madly panicked us down the road for about 1½ kms, stopped, and waited for two hours, then returned us from whence we came.

For almost two weeks now, as Judy used to do, one could stand outside the barn after dark and watch the fascinating flashes of the artillery fire. We set off through lovely wooded country to Bodow off the Schwerin autobahn. It rained a bit then turned to snow, but who cared now whatever the weather? We were eating again. Fires were going all around. Duffs and scones from flour and rogen meal were in a great supply and I was even being offered some on my way about.

I had a communication from the main control and told the boys of the content. Keith wrote in his diary for that day, "Had a nice quiet day. Pat is improved. Percy told us to be ready to leave at a moment's notice. We are to head west to avoid 'JOE' with the hope of meeting up with British troops rather than the Ruskies catch us up. The Goons are apparently afraid. A FW190 landed in a field nearby."

For May 1st the diary continued. "Rose at 1am and started marching at 3am. Weather-wise it was a miserable day. From the date one would call it 'May Day'. Well it rained, hailed, and snowed and the sun shone. It could only happen in Deutschland. Reached destination at 2pm." End of quote.

'Dixie' Deans called to see me. He was driving around POW columns in a German staff car with a driver at the wheel and a Goon on the running board spotting for Spits and Tiffies etc. Something surely must be close to brew point. Dixie told me not to move from where we were in the village of Luttow as our troops would be through the following day. This countermanded our further 'stand by to move at short notice' instructions from the Goons and so I went round the barns and announced to the boys that we were to resist any attempt to move us from where we were. Stay put until our troops arrive within the following 24 hours. Liberation and freedom. Great cheers went up and totally drowned anything further that I may have intended to say. Some danced around like crazed natives in a war-dance. I stood there enjoying the spectacle. Harry was within yards, shouting at the top of his voice.

"Shut up you unruly shower, and listen to Perc!"

"Thanks Harry anyway. Don't spoil their fun." and I went my way to the next barn. More wild cheers rent the air, hand shakes, back slapping and questions of where to get some food and grog to throw a barn party.

A great wave of enthusiasm swept the boys along in their search for food and they ate and talked late into the night in their barns and in groups around their little cooking fires. They were extremely happy and certainly well-behaved as the then typically young exuberant British airman. It was a wonderful opportunity for hooliganism, but not one case was reported.

There were more essential, fundamental and prerequisite matters demanding attention. They were caught in the prop-wash and peripheral speed of the vital and quickly unfolding events. I was proud of their behaviour. One could have excused an outbreak of uncontrolled mayhem, but we witnessed emotionally self-disciplined scenes of utter joy. Deep emotions were widely displayed by all these young men who together had looked death squarely in the face on many dramatic and incredibly precarious occasions, when they had stuck together, supporting each other in moments when everything appeared to be against them. There were melodramatic instances where men were unable to put their feelings into words and openly wept at this long awaited delightful news. It had not occurred to us previously what form liberation would take – but now it was taking shape right here in this small agricultural village of LUTTOW. Behind us were years of barbed-wire incarceration and the last three months of strength sapping, lice-ridden, hungry marching, in rain, hail and snow, having slept in woods, fields and barns in wet and filthy clothing and covering a torturous footsore 600 miles which had claimed many of our respected friends and crippled many others, forcing us all beyond the point of human endurance.

I had some news on the bush telegraph of a gaggle of trucks up at Boisenberg. If I got some drivers I could have a fleet of trucks standing by on the tick-over when our troops arrived, to on-load our men and get heading west. We ought to be safe then out of the way of the fussing Tiffies, and have a trouble-free ride.

It was 5am when I hollered, "Wakey Wakey!" in the doorway of the bigger barn and I called for the first dozen drivers to volunteer to get up to Boisenberg to collect the trucks. Keith was first down out of the hay loft. We picked up the trucks and some spare cans of fuel, returned to the barns and parked up. At least it was a start, we could pick up other vehicles as the opportunity arose, or as we made the opportunities. The boys were cooking all manner of foods on their little fires and every one was caught up in an impatient atmosphere of expectancy.

It was May the second, 0920 hrs when the small village of Luttow echoed to the cheers of crowds of happy, bony, ill clad, lice ridden Allied Prisoners of War. Scout cars of the 6th Airborne Division drove into the village street.

I cannot explain the feeling as I rested one hand on the wing of the first car and shook hands with the Commander with the other. As Geoff Blackett's notes read, "Percy Carruthers announced that we can expect to be picked up within twenty four hours. Hope he's right. Brewing at 0930 hrs when the boys came through. Everyone was so excited. Real white bread. We shall never forget those red berets of the 6th Airborne Div." The deafening cheers rose high in the air. Quote from log:

> We went mad. Fellows were crying and laughing and hugging and congratulating each other, conscious of the struggle they had shared over a long period of time, just to survive. The heavy stuff came through at 10.30am. We got cigarettes, biscuits, choc, compo, matches, beautiful white bread which was so white we could hardly believe it was true, and many other impossible little treats. Some of the boys could not act normally, they were so overcome with excitement. This was the most momentous moment of my life. I realised the true meaning of the word cornucopia.

I too felt a great satisfaction, tired as I had been of late, it was as though a whole new world was opening up before my very eyes. It was an event to dwarf the feeling on that day I entered RAF. It even exceeded the satisfaction of my first solo flight. It certainly surmounted the experience of my first enemy sortie, perhaps because it was a culmination of all those events, with the exciting realisation that the Nazi horde had been crushed and we were free from their beastly oppression.

Now was our official moment of transferring the boot to the other foot. With my shoulders square and my neck pressed back on to my tunic collar, I called to the German officer who, in charge of the guards, did not really appear to know what he should do. It was now my turn to do a spot of organising.

"Hauptmann, komm mal her!" (Captain, come here.)

The British troops had now motored on and were not a bit interested in the guards.

"Shoot the bloody lot if you feel like it." said a smiling British Captain riding atop a lone armoured car, or if you want to hang on a bit the infantry bods will sort you out ... we're off scouting.

I felt like saying to the German Hauptmann the words which many a British airman had heard on his capture.

"For yoo der Vor ist ofer."

"Sie mussen die Manner andordnen, die Waffen her zu stellen. Denn sick daruber versameln." (Tell the men to pile their arms over here, then have them fall-in over there), I commanded.

"Von her aus, gebe ich alle Befehl" (From here on I'll give all the orders), I continued.

I felt no emotion in these proceedings, they were mostly poor old lads who had been brought in at the last moment, and were long past the recognised age of combat. If we had any scores to settle we would have to go on searching, as some did, feeling so strongly about it. Obviously the Germans knew what they had deserved to expect if the previous guards were still with us at liberation, and so they spirited them away during the hours of darkness for their own safety, bringing in these old boys as substitutes.

The Germans were no longer guards and they filed over to the concrete base where Des and Wally and I stood. They quite expertly piled their rifles, after removing the bolts, stepped backwards and made their way over to the clearing I had indicated. A few even threw me up a salute before turning off, goodness knows why.

Des, Wally and I stood there on the concrete base in the farmyard where before us stretched the dozens of little piles of rifles as though they were little stooks of corn towards the end of harvest.

This was our harvest. Here were the fruits of our labours, our hardships, our sufferings, and our hunger. Beyond the piled arms there were the knots of British airmen, ex Prisoners of War, clad in the worn, untidy, filthy clothing which they had been obliged to wear continuously for the past three months, often lice-ridden. They were laughing and joking and mixing about looking for other acquaintances and friends from the thousand strong column. Tears of joy were quite unashamedly being shed by some, others sat down and buried their faces in their hands. This was the day they had lived for through their torture, degradation and hunger, but sometimes doubted whether they would ever live to see it. These were the boys whom Des and Wally and I understood as we viewed them over the piles of arms which were once wielded against them in anger. But where were those who had done the wielding? We recognised the gaunt features, the dysentery wracked lean, angular hungry frames which now milled about in a state of complete happiness. One could also recognise many of them who were some short time ago so fatigued that they could not stand. Their clothes had been soaked in urine and caked with excreta. I remember their hollow eyes as they stared at you in their misery, but did not appear to see you. One remembered that many of them would not have survived had it not been for the help of their firm and true friends who at great expense to themselves laboured to bring them some small degree of comfort.

To appreciate the depth of feeling of these boys you would have to have been one of them. In order to understand the special bond experienced by these Kriegies of Insterburg, The Run up the Road, and the Death March, one would have to have known the anguish and desolation they knew in their illness and when danger leered at them at every turn with rifles threatening injury. One would have to have experienced the tormenting grief that followed the thought that it would all be there again tomorrow – or there again that there may not be a tomorrow.

* * *

With these pictures in mind one may begin to understand the electric atmosphere which permeates the environs of the aerodrome motel at Sywell, when as many as possible of the two-hundred of those boys on the mailing list gather together for the annual weekend reunion of Kriegie Call. They do not have to speak, it is all said in the handclasp of the Kriegie Call Logo. The aura is unmistakable, and they remember those who did not survive to liberation.

These are the boys who learned to recognise a new dimension in appreciation of food and freedom, of human rights and values, of simple structures such as a bed, a clean set of clothes, food to eat today, and still have some for tomorrow, actually on a plate, and to be not looking down the wrong end of a gun barrel when it pleased the holder.

* * *

As we surveyed the scene, Wally, without giving any indication of his feelings or emotions, which I well knew he was very capable of exercising, quietly said,

"Well Perc, it's all over at long last."

Philosophical old Wall, judicial, staunch, inveterate. A true anchor man. Doug Moore told me sometime later, that he met an army sergeant in Brussels who told him that Pickhard $\frac{7}{8}$ $\frac{7}{8}$ had stayed behind at Tychow when we left. The

Russians dropped in to release their men, who told them of the antics of Pickhardt, and it was said that without question or trial the Russians stood him up and shot him on the spot.

"What the hell are we going to do with all the Krauts we've got lined up over there fellows?" I asked Des and Wally.

"You heard what the British Captain said Perc." came the reply.

"If we'd had the original guards here I wouldn't have had time to put a stupid question like that, you two would have supplied the solution before we knew we had a problem." Their silence confirmed their thoughts.

The Burgomeister's residence is always a good place to start in Germany if you are in any doubt, and so having located it I marched the prisoners round there. I was very conscious of the smart leather belt and holster which I now wore, complete with Luger and ammunition, but regarded it as a souvenir rather than a persuasive side arm. There was a huge walk-in cellar, at ground level, below the Burgo house, so I reconnoitred quickly, noticed it had quite a low ceiling, about six feet from the spotlessly clean floor of concrete, decided without hesitation again, that they were all going to go in there, men and officers alike, discomfort or not, I wouldn't keep them in there any longer than they kept us in Cattle Trucks. I promised them.

The officers objected, saying they ought to be housed as officers and in different accommodation than their troops. I spoke very quietly.

"Sie sind alle meine Kriegsgefangenen, so bitte sei Meine Gast. Bitte einzutreten, jeder Mann." ("You are now all my prisoners of war, so please be my guest. Get in there every one of you.")

I brushed about a dozen of the men aside, preventing them blocking the entrance, they could go in later.

"Bitte Herr Hauptmann, Sie durfen erstens wohnhaft nehmen." ("With my compliments Captain, you may be the first to take up residence.") and I placed him between myself and the entrance. He faced me closely all the time and I walked slowly towards the entrance. He went in backwards, protesting all the time, but I wasn't going to allow him to disturb my cool.

"So mein Herren, alles ein, und lass kein ubrig." ("So gentlemen, everybody inside, without exception.") I still had about twenty to go, and I could see the face of the protesting Captain peeping over the shoulders of the others, well to the back and I must admit to quietly enjoying a moment of mild requital.

Just at that moment, along came a bustling little Scot, complete with a Sten gun at a very cocky angle. He was about five feet three inches tall, or short whatever your mood, and appeared to be almost as wide.

"What's the set up here?" he enquired, waving that menacing looking weapon around. I explained the recent reversal of the captor and captive relationship and said that I still had a couple of dozen bods to pack in to the cellar which was bulging at the sides already.

"Dinna worry yer heed aboot it sir," said the little dour one, "Gae yoursel haem yer folks'll be await'n."

Any packing problem which I thought may have existed evaporated immediately. I have never seen so many bodies go into such a confined space in such a short period of time.

"Wie kriegt Mann Wasser herein?" shouted Hauptman. ("How does one get water in here?")

"Sie brauchen kein Wasser, denn es kein Toilette darin gibt." I replied by way of advice. (You don't need any water because there's no toilet in there.)

I had seen a lot of German guards handling a lot of British prisoners over the past two and a half years, with much brutality, much shouting and not a little measure of indignity, but never with the firm professionalism of that young Scot. It was that quiet unassuming air of authority which one could sense, but then the Krauts had lost their guns. There was no need for screaming undignified behaviour, where veins bulged from red necks and eyes protruded like golf balls. There was no doubt about it, the Brits had something which was somehow indescribable, indefinable but easily and immediately recognisable. We had it all the time, all of us, and the Germans knew it, and no doubt respected it. Never in a hundred years however, would they be able to acquire it.

The boys went on the rampage for food. They brought back eggs, which we had not seen for years. There were chickens, home baked bread, ducklings, plates, pans, wine, schnapps, bicycles, and cakes which the Hausfrau had just taken out of the hot oven for the family meal. We did not commandeer one house. We would spend the remainder of the day here in our barns, cooking, eating and sleeping and set out for Luneberg at 0800 hrs the following morning. We had plenty to eat a good warm barn and freedom – happiness. The last three months had been the greatest test of physical endurance any one of us was ever likely to experience. As Des Dunphy, an ardent student of Deutsche, wrote to me some years later,

> Ein ruheloser Marsch war unsere Leben,
> Und wie des Windes sausen, heimatlos,
> Durchsturmten wir die Kriegsbewegten Erde.

Or as Coleridge said in his translation,

> Our life was but a battle and a march,
> And like the chill wind's blast never resting, homeless
> We stormed across the war convulsed heath.

No doubt he had Luneberg in mind, this time.

Freddie Simpson, who was one of Lofty's faithful boy scouts on that lunatic parade at Barth some two years earlier, related a story to Gordon Clubb and others. Apparently, before being shot down, he had arrived home one very dark and stormy night, on a very short and unexpected leave, unknown to Freddie at the time it was a secret overseas posting leave, and his wife refused to open the door, suspecting an impostor.

"OK by me," shouted Freddie through the letterbox, "it'll be a long time before I'm back here again," and he pushed off back to the squadron. He was then pushed off to the Middle East and the Deutschers pushed him behind barbed wire for three years.

"You know fellows," said Freddie with a grin, "She is just not going to believe my story!"

Up to Fallingbostel we had covered between 600 and 700 kilometres, and since then about a further 200. Whilst on our feet since commencing this march, winding back and forth and taking detours, I estimate we did at least 1000 kms (App. 600 miles) and according to notes kept by various boys we did it on 4½ loaves of bread, 37 cups of soup, 44 spud ration issues, 4 Red Cross parcels plus what we stole and bartered, give a mouthful or two either way, and after three months of snow, rain, frost and sun, some 40 to 50 pounds lighter in body weight, we survived to freedom.

The trucks started to roll, or frog leap, or buck jump, or stall, depending on who was doing the driving, but honestly they did roll – eventually. I would rather have written to the effect that 'the motorised column drew smoothly away, as planned, at 0800 hrs' However, I must tell the truth, because before commencing to write this epic I did promise not to novelise, fictionalise or romanticise, otherwise the title to this might have been, *Bulldust be my Guide*. Hence the trucks frog leapt or whatever, midst calls and shouts from the unfortunate passengers in the back as they rocketed back and forth, worse than in any cattle truck, acting as back seat drivers in a positively advisory capacity, to wit, "Sort the bastards out, up front!"

McGuiness and Geoff Blackett, along with their followers, commandeered a coach. Basil Craske would by nature act as a skipper and took the wheel. Judy and gang got a car, full of typewriters, cigarettes and other items. They were picking their way gingerly across the pontoon bridge over the Elbe at Artlenburg, bucking and swaying, when the thing ran out of fuel. The Military Police were keeping the traffic flow as smooth as possible. There were a lot of vehicles to cross over.

"Get that bloody thing off the bridge quick." hollered a very large MP. Judy and gang, ever cooperative, started with all their strength to push for the opposite bank. The bull-like voice once more filled the air.

"Not that way for Christ's sake – over the bloody side."

Regrettably their nice little car, cigarettes and all was tipped into the swirling Elbe, lost forever. The boys then took their lives in their hands, running like pursued men over the heaving, snaking, bucking bridge, with vehicles lumbering over threatening to pitch them headlong to a watery grave.

Traffic chaos was building to an alarming degree. Long queues of vehicles headed both east and west down to a crawl and frequently at a standstill for ages. Thousands of men were on foot. Allied Prisoners of War heading west and defeated German troops heading east.

I ousted twenty German soldiers from a truck, filled it up with Kriegies and set off. We ran out of fuel. I stopped a BMW combination. Doug Grundy insisted on driving. With myself on the pillion and a gang heaped up on the side-car Doug attempted a bend much too quickly, ran out of road and plumetted us all into a very deep ditch. We all got away with bruises except Doug who did his ankle. Doug writhed in agony and then turned ashen as he lay groaning. Dave had no sympathy. "Serve you bloody right Grundy." I then stopped a car full of German officers. "Rote Kreuz. Rote Kreuz", they pleaded (Red Cross), and prepared to move off. I stuck the point of my Luger in the left ear of the over arrogant driver.

"Alles sofort aus steigen", I bellowed. They reluctantly climbed out, and I lined them up in a neat little row by the hedge telling them in no uncertain manner that if they moved I'd put one through their fancy boots.

Following de-lousing, documentation and re-kitting we pulled into Soltau and then Celle. Dakotas were coming in. We counted off in groups of 35. A young pilot came over asking for the next party. I stepped forward and we turned for the aircraft.

"I'm on my own today," he said, "how about doing the flying whilst I take care of the navigation?" he queried. I was delighted and thoroughly enjoyed flying myself away from captivity, something I had attempted to do some eighteen months ago when I escaped, and failed.

I could never forget my emotions when we crossed the channel and I searched the horizon for land ahead. The coastal cloud bank came into view and then, soon, the coast line, the white cliffs of dear old England.

My eyes filled up, I hoped my pilot friend did not have anything to say, I could not possibly answer him, my throat was so full. I tried to swallow, it was so painful, the lump was too large and it was so hard. I felt I would choke. I gripped the stick and breathed through an open mouth. We were silent. I'm sure he knew my difficulty. Perhaps he'd seen it all before.

I reflected on my England as I knew it when I left for Egypt some four years earlier. I remembered the bombing attacks I had done on troops and tanks and vehicles and ships to halt the Nazi hordes. I remembered the beastliness of the Nazis and I felt a satisfaction of having helped to crush them and preserve this

England I could now see coming up on the horizon. The engines of the old Dak sang sweetly in my ears as I checked temps, pressures, fuel, revs, mixture and pitch before commencing a very shallow descent to the soil we had all longed to tread for so long.

FACING WEST

Heydekrug rigors now in distance wane,
The Lithuanian cattle trucks long behind,
The horrid Insterberg of Baltic fame,
Now seemed, a nightmare leaving mind.

The bombs of Allied aircraft furnace forged,
On Swinemunde yards, as we at last
From hold of hell of 'Insterberg' disgorged,
Lay 'neath the railway trucks which rocked with blast.

This now a world apart appeared to be,
And even Hauptman Pickhardt's screaming voice,
Had somehow faded faint beyond the lea.
A life more quiet now would be our choice.

The flogging, stabbing, shooting, biting run,
From Belgard station through the pine trees tall,
Kiefheida Kreis to traverse had been done,
Flesh wounds and bruising healed, good news on call.

From Heydekrug we'd come the front to 'void,
But front had followed westward steady on,
And so with further thoughts of move we toyed,
Until one night instruction came, "Move on,"

Move must we, as first light brushes sky,
Chaotic scenes of sewing in the dark,
As make-shift packs some shirts we modify,
And talk of yet another 'running lark'.

'Twas in the cold first light of February morn,
That Kraut would, sheep-like herd us out of fold,
Down pine wood retraced we steps with scorn,
In column kilometre long we rolled.

On icy road we stumbled, slipped and fell,
Saw sentry boxes empty for first time,
And on to one another firmly held.
To keep our feet from slipping on the rime.

The Krauts would not a clue to us reveal,
What mode of travel we now take on would,
Nor destination would he volunteer,
Or where we'd sleep, or eat, beyond the wood.

We turn'd from road to cart track rough and torn,
With snow and mud our boots are caked, and weigh,
A ton apiece, as strength becomes outworn,
But on we pressed. "No rest," the Hun would say.

Some boys however apprehensive were,
And having yet the 'dog run' still in mind,
Thought now the Hun, perhaps without demur,
By common grave would shoot. No more to find.

Two hundred sick we left behind. With glee
They Russian infantry would meet, with hope
That they'd be fed, and kindly treated be,
Some medic care and wash with real soap.

Ten miles ahead past French Stalag 3.D.,
Wet to the knees came we, with hunger sore,
In barns a welcome rest and sleep took we,
But food or drink was not to come to fore.

To Reselkow came we on second day,
A further twenty Kilos down rough tracks,
In sleet and rain our clothes sag, and we sway,
As packs grow water logged upon our backs.

One slice of bread and cheese do we become,
A thousand hungry airmen now are we,
And in the barns again we find some room,
And break some ice our choking thirst to free.

Our blankets wet, our clothes with rain a-sog,
A very miserable night spent we in hay,
Prickling our skin just like a hedgy-hog,
Tormented, hungry, shivering there we lay.

One German guard with pail of luke warm soup,
Our barn passed by, the guard dogs now to feed.
With care placed he the pail for doggie troupe,
Whilst he forth went to bring them out on lead.

Returning, – dogs leapt forth with ravenous bounds,
Expecting supper now to wolf straight down,
But somehow pail had now avoided hounds,
This chance allowed to pass, we'd have been clowns.

The pattern had become to form, for we
Convinced now were that never would we stop,
This life of vagabond, and captive be,
Our lot to bear, until the final flop.

But following morn we reasoned with the Kraut,
That hungry men, all wet and tired and worn,
Could this day not proceed to venture out,
And so we stayed, and spuds to us were borne.

Some twenty miles were target for today,
But sure some boys were much too ill to try,
So to a local farmer did we pray,
His horses, carts proved transport, harsh but dry.

En-route saw we now refugees by crowds.
Bicycles, carts, wheel chairs, prams they pushed
With worldly goods were laden. There were hoardes
Of sad-faced children, to their parents rushed.

Miles yesterday were eight and twenty long,
And food today we somehow must obtain,
It is my birthday and I must give song,
Some cattle cake we found. No candles gained.

Now Swinemunde came to sight once more,
And by the road a dead horse lay half carved,
Our hunger was much worse than e'er before,
We ate that meat in chunks before we starved.

We now would take some risks, food to acquire,
A straying hen or duck would meet its lot,
In darkness milk a cow, and crawl through mire,
To steal some spuds. Alas some boys were shot.

In common now these last few weeks had seen,
The flesh roll off our frames with dreadful speed,
Most men lost fifty pounds, were lean
And gaunt, with bulbous knees through lack of food.

The German tongue with reasonable ease I spoke,
Had "Column Leader" for our men become,
With farmers would I oft have lucky stroke,
With spuds, and peas, and beans, and other grain.

Our highlight was one sheep to throw in pot,
And, under coats, some boys sneaked an odd fowl,
Unseen, to dangle in the bubbling lot.
So ate we better from 'Klim' bowl.

To sleep at Pritter nowhere could be found,
Full were the cowsheds, pig styes and the barns
So trudged we o'er the slushed and snowy ground,
To woods, which lay on hill beyond the farms.

From branches pine, a thousand weary men,
Made beds, and covers, where to sleep the night,
Degrees of frost, no mercy, gave us ken,
When morning broke it was a sombre sight.

With swollen blistered feet and frozen hide,
Frost-bite and dysentery took their deadly toll,
A dozen men had now already died,
And now it seemed for more, no hope to hold.

Upstanding, fine and intellectual boys,
In early twenties most of good physique,
Reduced to state of cast and worn out toys,
It saddened us, but Hun it did not pique.

Now lice and even ticks infested us,
No change of clothing, wash of hair or bath,
Despondent in wet dirty clothes we'd cuss
Our luck. We were the ghastly aftermath.

Events deplorable as these, could not,
Have come to mind of western civil man,
But we who closely lived to Nazi plot,
Appreciate good food, and freedom, can.

Apart from all his foul and horrid deeds,
For western allies showed Hun some regard,
Far in excess than to the Russian needs,
To them he was most foul. Most horrid. Bitter. Hard.

Their lot was worse than ours without a doubt,
Expendable their lives in numbers great,
From us they'd even beg in front of Kraut,
And with some hope would even hours wait.

Recall I once a crowd of Russians, who
So desperate had become they clambered mad,
Although we were half starved, we threw a few
Odd valued items to them. 'Twas most sad.

They desperately grabbed and grovelled, snatched and clawed,
Poor things with hollow eyes and sad expressions wan,
They even ate the soap we threw and gnawed,
At soil in hands, as through their fingers ran.

A mobile kitchen for us down the hill.
We speed, and search for 'Klim' down hill to pelt.
Some watery soup for those who yet lay still,
Ice from the eyebrows, moustache, then to melt.

At Nerdin farmer kind to us would be,
A large trough of pea soup he did produce,
Then water, hot, in quantity, did he
Pour into trough, when soup had all been used.

To drink some first was very obvious move,
Then wash whate'er we could, should we be bold,
Oft did I marvel, in the frost it proved,
To be not fatal, catching death of cold.

More rain and snow, now early March had come,
Four weeks we'd been in hunger, forced to March
Two eighty miles, we'd plodded bravely on.
With filth our clothing now was stiff as starch.

Had we then thought we'd still two months to beat,
And more than yet four hundred miles to plod,
Ere we could get some decent food to eat,
We may have all thought we'd be under sod.

Shrunken stomachs, shrunken frames re-act,
Some boys now vomit when they're given food,
And some dejected, much too weak in fact
To stand. Whatever done does prove no good.

The end of March some warmer weather brought,
A welcome change from sleeping out in the cold,
But feet were badly blistered as we wrought,
Some daily twenty miles, – a story told.

At Ebsdorf back to cattle trucks came we,
Eighty men per truck which forty filled,
'Twas hell. – Hot, stuffy, what a shame
For those sick boys, the journey almost killed.

The padlocked doors no ventilation gave,
The sick boys pleaded, "Let me sit or lie,"
But this we dared not do, their lives to save,
From trampling feet, with jolting train, they'd die.

To Fallingbostel came we now at last,
Two miles to walk to Stalag. X1.B.,
Where Indians, Serbs, and French and Yugoslavs,
And 'Airborne' by the hundreds formed melee.

Oh Lord. This overcrowded milling band,
Ten thousand schemed and planned to rest and sleep,
Where medic aid was in such great demand.
Mass funeral passed us by with feelings deep.

The chaos of it all we ten days had,
Then once more on the march we were to flog,
Perhaps a blessing in disguise. How sad
Jack Laing was serious ill and could not plod.

This Fallingbostel Chaos would we swop
For hoofing o'er the heath and country tracks,
Then food was scarce where e'er we were to stop
But on the farms at least we got some snacks.

Assumed I then Jack's column part of mine,
And off to westwards shuffled we once more,
Hoping the best for Jack, who left behind,
With struggle hard and tough, health to restore.

To Bleckmar, fifteen miles through heath and wood,
'Tis eighth of April now, some flowers peep out,
We sleep in open, bedding where we could,
My six-foot paper bag can't do without.

One evening resting up in farmer's barns,
Mosquito pilot must a brief have had,
That enemy was in sheds and village farms,
And shot us up, results of which were bad.

As boys from lower barn ran out to clear,
The top floor boys crashed down upon their heads,
Unconscious, burned and injured lay too near,
The blazing hay, which just had been their beds.

One boy was wholely blown apart, and some
Were sorely injured, did they quickly die.
The Scot, Jock Durnan was the first to come
To sight, as I him saw in roadway lie.

The hay and straw ablaze in seconds, meant
That boys were trapped as flames engulfed the scene,
And lots jumped down some thirty feet, and rent
Their blazing clothes off, mid shout and scream.

Scho through leg and hand had got the blast,
And many various wounds were common place,
And some lay dead, disaster here at last,
To fields and hedges did remainder race.

Across the road and up the hill I walked,
To where our men in hundreds were with guards,
Suggested I that plans for casualties be talked,
And sleep arrangements should for men regard.

The guards I found more timid than our boys,
They'd stay the night out there beneath the hedge
But not to village go, as some decoys,
Might fall to gun, for them would be no fledge.

The village Vicar showed his brotherhood,
And funeral for our friends he gracious led,
And I at service with the Vicar stood,
Interpreting the words he kindly said.

Then some days on, bless all who helped to free,
Some parcels through Red Cross from Lubeck came,
And one between two airmen shared could be,
Morale then soared and helped the sick and lame.

The RAF now often low flew past,
And recognised that we some prisoners be,
'Cos Dixie had some news to Allies pass,
And pinpoint without doubt they had on we.

But Typhoons on day strafing moving trucks,
Banked low round wood along a nearby track,
And bullets stray did catch us in the rucks.
Some boys were killed. A problem hard to crack.

The Elbe we'd crossed where snaking pontoon swayed,
Where Jerry trucks and cars seemed everywhere,
Where Spits and Tiffies round the heavens played,
Some one-o-nines and one-nine-ohs were there.

'Twas daily march, first north, then west, then south,
The Germans now less irksome did become,
And information would pass on by word of mouth.
They even seemed to want to help us some.

Some days we almost eastwards walked, as though
From Allied front escape would they have us,
But morale in the boys did daily grow,
The journey home now seemed a certain must.

May now broke on us with a kindly smile,
More food had we one day than in two weeks
Before. Now oft we'd go an extra mile
Or so, a better barn and food to seek.

Since Fallingbostel did we yet four weeks
March here and there, which seemed with little aim,
As Jerry now full realised the creaks
In Nazi force, foretold the obvious end.

On cycle rode up Dixie one fine morn,
And told me here in village hold the throng,
That Allies would be with us in the dawn,
To Luneberg to make our way 'ere long.

We'd had three months in snow and rain and fine,
Spent marching miles six hundred and a score,
Friends had been shot, some died, some dropped from line,
Escaped. For those lives spared we thanked the Lord.

Second of May, a glorious sight to see,
Sixth Airborne Div. into the village rode,
The boys went wild with shouts and whoops of glee,
To be the first to meet them, many strove.

The guards I had them bring their arms 'heraus',
And pile them neatly in the yard, – what luck,
Then marched them to the Burgomeister's house,
In cellar squashed, as we in cattle trucks.

A Scottie soldier then took charge of site
And crammed more in than even I could bear,
With muzzle forced he them in real tight,
As Krauts complained aloud, "Sei nicht so schwer".

With belt I now strapped firmly on some guns,
And stopped a German convoy formed of trucks,
And threw out all the angry spluttering Huns,
Then filed them to a clearing, just like ducks.

We clambered all aboard and off we set,
Full pelt along the road which headed west,
Then spluttering halt, climb out. We had to get
Some fuel. So other transport would we quest.

A Bay-Em-Vow, with side-car rounded bend, (BMW)
And two shots fired I up, the air to rend,
The Huns stopped quick, I asked them if they'd lend
Their lovely outfit to a needy friend.

"I'll drive a bit," said Doug, so willing I
As pillion rode, a Colt in either hand,
Whilst Phil and Jack and Ron the 'car' piled high,
And off we went, a very happy band.

I really ought to not have trusted Doug,
He drove as madman, head down, seat in air,
And rounded bend flat out, I was a mug
By ending up in soggy ditch full square.

"You've bent the bloody thing beyond redeem,"
But Doug was not for hearing what I'd say,
His ankle urged him on to moan and scream
With pain. So on the turf we had him lay.

A German car I stopped, full up of Heer,
And bid them all climb out, but Hauptman said,
"Red Cross." – I stuck a pistol in his ear,
He changed his mind, to save his square shaped head.

Where e'er we drove the scene was chaos pure,
Thousands of Germans heading East, intent
The cosmopolitan mass ignore for sure,
But Kriegies saw on foot the rest they went.

The cheering boys had transports of all kind,
And stopped to frisk the Krauts when e'er it pleased,
And held white bread which almost sent you blind,
A dazzling brilliance seemed it to our eyes.

Some boys would travel home in leisure style,
And German car, with fuel, would take on charge,
Old Taaffe and gang would head for Brussels, while
Some others talked of taking trips on Barge.

So Luneberg at last, then Celle next,
Where we new clothing, bath and food enjoyed,
And Kriegie friends called in all heading west,
Together we'd on next Dakota ride.

A stench more foul than any I had known,
Of death it reeked, a sinister tale did hold,
As o'er the air towards our nostrils blown,
'Twas Belsen,- hunger, death and misery untold.

With pilot walked we o'er to aircraft neat,
"I'm on my own today," said he to me,
"So you can take the 'second dickie' seat,"
"And navigator I will gladly be."

As 'Dak' I flew feelings cannot be said,
And when the shores of England hove in sight,
I gripped the stick, and swallowed lumps like lead,
I knew then what we'd done had just been right.

The menace of the Nazis as depicted in a wartime cartoon, kept from our shores thanks to the English Channel and the RAF.

OF PLOUGHS, PLANES & PALLIASSES 239

> Church Fenton RAF I duly came,
> Mosquito sleek my pleasure was to fly,
> And thoughts of 'barn' would blaze into my brain,
> Both ends of this machine I'd had a try.
>
> To fly I'd choose 'gainst fighter, shot and shell,
> Than slowly waste away in hunger hell,
> Because had Hitler's Nazi's won the war,
> We'd known no family unit evermore.

Having mentioned the worth of the English Channel in the history of the British Isles, I cannot help bringing to mind the words of Wordsworth as he stood near Dover facing east.

> Inland, within a hollow vale, I stood
> And saw, while sea was calm and air was clear,
> The coast of France, the coast of France how near,
> Drawn almost into frightful neighbourhood.
> I shrunk, for verily the barrier flood
> Was like a lake, or river bright and fair,
> A span of waters; yet what power is there;
> What mightiness for evil and for good;
> Virtuous and wise: winds blow and waters roll,
> Strength to the brave, and power and deity,
> Yet in themselves are nothing. One decree
> Spake laws to them, and said that by the Soul,
> Only nations shall be great and free.

THE KREGIE CALL PLAQUE

The Kregie Call Logo was expertly copied and etched onto a slab of South African granite (17 inches × 11 1/2 inches) and figured in gold leaf by Curly Franklyn (ex-Kregie). It was then mounted onto a beautifully carved oak surround, figured and fashioned by Master Woodcarver Chas Griffin (also an ex-Kregie). The complete assembly weighs 20lbs. The logo, designed by the Author, depicts the basis of our background, a twin-engined aircraft and Kregie Call circle which embraces our square of friendship with our true handclasp. The surrounding winged barbed-wire denotes flight from the distatsteful German captivity. The oak mounting records certain dated events from our captivity.

· CHAPTER 12 ·

AT HOME

We landed at Wing in Oxfordshire, and how could one ever forget the scene as some of the Kriegies, British, Commonwealth, Czech and others fell on their knees, on alighting, and kissed the English soil.

The W.A.A.F. admin girls were wonderful as they greeted us home to the RAF and England. The organisation was fantastic. The Women's Voluntary Service were outstanding too. Everyone there could not do enough for us, it was almost embarrassing. Lovely baths, new uniforms, haircuts, medical checks, lovely beds with actual sheets on them, beautiful food and as much as our shrunken stomachs could hold. Wing was certainly a busy place.

During the month of April the staff there handled 14,794 returned prisoners of war. In May 1,269 aircraft landed there to drop a further 38,000 happy Kriegies. In one day alone, the 15th May, there were 132 Lancaster aircraft attempting to land to disgorge their scruffy louse-ridden cargoes.

Next day, off to Cosford. Full medical, interrogation, more uniform, a few pounds in the pocket and away home to my Cumbrian hills, the little village on the hillside, the little farm at the top of the bank and the folks with a lot of tears and a lot of smiles.

"You are so thin," was my first greeting. Nothing had changed in my absence. The same old black leaded fireplace, shining like a jewel, the ten foot settle under the window and the dear old wall-clock on which I learned to read the time.

A posting took me to Church Fenton RAF, where the busy looking Mosquitos stood around the perimeter as though they eagerly awaited you climbing aboard and commanding them to take to the air. The last time I had seen a Mossy was when at the barns at Cammin, when we were on the receiving end of the firepower. It was here I flew my first Mossy, and how I wished I had known the aircraft some years previously.

Bill Reay and I travelled home at weekends in my old Austin Ruby saloon. I walked down to a familiar shopping area on the crossroads. There were the same old names above the doors and shop windows, but I felt somehow a little strange. There appeared to be a display of a frightening variety of goods on the shelves. Eggs, vegetables, cheeses, fruit, even bananas and many other lovely items I had not seen for years. I marvelled at the apparent richness of it all.

I then came face to face with an old school friend, and there was immediate recognition by both of us.

"Hello Perc, long time no see," said John. "What do you think of all these restrictions, rationing and all that? We ought to be getting rid of it now don't you think?"

I was searching for an answer.

"It's high time we had some better weather too." complained John.

I wanted to say that everything was lovely and had never been better; that I felt like shouting it all from the house tops; that what he termed 'restrictions' were to me 'a land of milk and honey', providing four meals a day, and that as far as I was concerned the sun shone from morning till night. But obviously he would not understand what I was talking about. He looked so terribly healthy. I saw him then, not as a friend but as a dissatisfied grumbling critic of all that, to me, was good. We were on entirely different planes, our senses of values were worlds apart.

I learned that day, he had been in a 'reserved occupation' during hostilities and had made himself a nice little fortune on the black market. I regarded him as being the ice-cream salesman visiting the hazardous ball game selling his wares at enormous profit, not even knowing the score of the game or who the players were. He only wished to sell his wares. Perhaps he was right, some might say, but I, as one of the players, would have made a lousy ice-cream salesman.

At least I felt a certain satisfaction from what I had done and my conscience was clear. Perhaps John might claim his conscience too was clear. Perhaps he did not have one.

I felt I wanted to be alone and spit. I would go to my Cumbrian hills. I would absorb the panoramas, unmoved in place and beauty, I had known.

I remembered the furrows I had ploughed on the farm those years ago, and my pride in their arrow like perfection. I remembered too the furrows I had ploughed with steel of a different form through the columns of advancing Nazi hordes in Africa, and I found peace of mind that both these furrows had been for England and humanity.

I retraced my steps to the valley and stood by a familiar hedgerow feeling the peace of the countryside. Some small happy giggling children ran by. A young mother pushing her pram, flicked a momentary side glance in my direction, and was gone.

I contrasted the fate of thousands of small children at the hands of the brutal Nazis against that of the happy bunch of voices which receded round the edge of the wood. A blackbird, startled, flew low along the tree lined road and piped it's shrill warning. I remembered Wordsworth.

> One impulse from a vernal wood
> May teach you more of men,
> Of moral evil and of good,
> Than all the sages can.

Had I not now, in some measure, become a sage, of sorts? Could not my experiences to some extent claim to have mellowed me beyond my twenty-seven years? Nostalgia deepened, I looked high into the sky and recalled.

> I wandered lonely as a cloud
> That floats on high o'er vales and hills...
>
> ...Which is the bliss of solitude."

Then quite alone, exhilarated and thankful for my return, I did wander lonely as a cloud o'er those vales and hills, at the earliest opportunity, in a way Wordsworth was denied.

From the cockpit of my aircraft I viewed the golden shafts of sunlight as they played on the hills and valleys, and as they reflected from the mirror-like surfaces of the jewelled lakes, turning them from silver to vast sheets of gold, and remembered 'his' words again.

> There was a time when meadow grove and stream
> The earth and every common sight, to me did seem,
> Apparelled in celestial light
> The glory and the freshness of a dream.

Speechless and enchanted, I struggled again with that same lump which came to my tortured throat on crossing the channel in that old Dak... I was truly now,

> In the land of my own,
> In an England of hedgerow and field,
> Where the wounds in my mind would be slowly healed,
> And the graves in my heart would be overgrown,
> And I flew into sun.

THE HANDCLASP OF FRIENDSHIP

And so the years have rolled away,
Now deep nostalgia comes our way,
We think back to that former day,
When we were young, so far away.

We'd little food and little hope,
Made silver moulds from Gerry soap,
We made our lamps so we could cope,
From Taffel Margarine and rope.

Our pleasure was a Baltic cruise,
Chains on ankles to amuse,
A first class coal hold was the ruse,
But still the bods survived abuse.

We ran and sweated up that road,
With Goons and dogs that stripped our load,
With blows and jabs they did us goad,
But still we're here in better mood.

Aussies, Kiwis, and Cannuks too,
British brothers, and even now
We stick like thieves and never rue,
That Handclasp of Friendship we'll pursue.

We think of those who've passed away,
We think of them on better day,
We saw White Cliffs again in May,
Our bond will hold us, ne'er to sway.
Jim Haskett. (Down Under).

THE KREGIE CALL ROUNDEL
I wrote to Jim Haskett's only known address (in Norfolk) in 1981, and within two weeks I was reading his reply from Melbourne, Australia, telling me that he had lived there for 27 years. He was so delighted to renew old friendships, and promised to make me 'something' which I would 'treasure for the remaining years of my life!' After 200 hours of expert craftsmanship, the laminated wooden roundel was shipped to the UK. It bears a copper plate on the reverse side saying: 'To commemorate a reunion of RAF POW survivors organised by P.W. Carruthers, DFM, also to remember our comrades we left behind for ever.'

APPENDIX
ABBREVIATIONS AND EXPLANATIONS

ACH/GD	Aircrafthand – General Duties
Ack-Ack.	Anti-aircraft Gunnery.
A.C.M.	Air Chief Marshall
A.L.G.	Advanced Landing Ground
Angels Ten.	Altitude. Ten thousand feet.
A.O.C.	Air Officer Commanding
Artz	Doctor or Surgeon
Asymetric Flight	Flight with one of the engines either shut down or shot out.
A.V.M.	Air Vice Marshall
Balt	Baltimore Aircraft
Beaus	Beaufighter Aircraft
Beezer	B.S.A. Motorcycle.
Bivvy	Small one-man miniature-size tent. Bivouac.
The Blue	Out in the Desert Wastes.
Bowser	Large cylindrical fuel container on wheels
Brass	Headquarters staff
Canary	Radio receiver built out of odds and ends
Chance Light	Portable electric beam-light, downwind of landing run beamed upwind.
C.O.	Commanding Officer
Colt	Side Arms
Critical Speed	The lowest possible flying speed in asymmetric flight where the directional control of the aircraft can be maintained.
C.S.C.	Course and speed calculator
D.A.F.	Desert Air Force
Dak	Dakota aircraft
Dog Leg	Variation of courses steered
Dhobied	Laundered
Erks	Airmen (various trades)
E.F.T.S.	Elementary Flying School
E.T.A.	Expected Time of Arrival
Flak	Ack-Ack or Flugabwehrkannone. Air Defence.
F/O	Junior Commissioned rank (Flying Officer)
G	Measure of gravity exerted on body, eg. Two G, Three G, etc.
Gardening	Laying mines in water from aircraft
Gen Box	Radio receiver
Gefreiter	Luftwaffe rank. App. Corporal
Gharry	Truck, Lorry.
Gills	A circular arrangement of small metal shutters to admit cooling air-flow to the engine
Glop	Sloppy watery German food. Mostly water and potato peelings and grit.

Goolie Chit	An official identification note, printed in Arabic or other relevant language, promising a reward for the safe delivery of the airman to his unit (complete with Testes).
Heer	German Army
i/c	In charge
I/O	Intelligence Officer
Ities	Italians
Katabatic	The off-shore breeze which occurs after sun-down. Anabatic is the reverse after sun-up.
Kite	Aircraft
Kitties	Kittyhawk aircraft (Fighter/Bombers)
Klim	Tinned milk powder (Milk spelt backwards)
Krank	Sick
Kriegie	POW Abbreviation of Kriegsgefangener
Kugel	Bullet
Lager	Camp – compound.
L.A.C.	Leading aircraftman
Link	Aircraft simulator
Lazarette	Hospital
L.G.	Landing Ground
M.O.D.	Ministry of Defence
Mercators	The cylindrical method of projecting the surface of the earth in sheet form (A map)
Met	Meteorological
Mickey Mouse	A jettison arrangement for releasing the total bomb-load simultaneously.
Millibars	A measure of barometric pressure set on a calibrated scale on the altimeter to indicate the height above a given point.
M.P.	Military Police
M.T.	Motorised Transport
M.U.	Maintenance Unit
Mutti	German for Mum
My Jack	On my Jack (Alone)
Nav	Navigation
One-One-O	Messerschmidt 110 (twin engined fighter)
One-O-Nine	Messerschmidt 109 (single engined fighter)
O.A.T	Outside air temperature
Ops.	Operational sorties or operations room
Oberkammando	Headquarters command
Orged	Organised
Plappermaul	Chatter box (German)
P.F.F.	Path Finder Force
Planted	Mines dropped (planted) in water whilst out 'gardening' or 'sowing vegetables'.
P/O	The lowest commissioned rank. Pilot Officer.
Postens	German armed guards
Pontoon	Temporary bridge over water, supported on floats.
P.T.	Physical training.
Q.D.M.	From the Q code. Magnetic course to steer.
Racketting	Trading or swopping illegally.
Shalufa	The name of a certain Delta airbase.

R.S.U.	Recovery and salvage unit
S.A.A.F.	South African Air Force
Shufti Kite	Reconnaisance Aircraft
Samlung	Collection point
Stacheldraht	Barbed wire
Three Ten	310 mph
Tin Fish	Torpedoes
Tit	Gun or bomb button. Cockpit switch etc.
Three Greens	The green cockpit indicator panel lights denoting the undercarriage (or undercart) down and locked.
Three Times Whistling	The nickname we had for a certain German Feldwebel (Sergeant) who once said, "Ven der Kommandant into das Lager coming is, vill I be Three Times Whistling.".
Unterseeboten	Submarines
U/S	Unserviceable
Veefers	Free desert issue cigarettes, of doubtful content. Often suspected to be of camel origin. Official name: 'V for Victory'.
Very Lights	Coloured flares shot into the air from a Very Pistol for illumination or distress warning.
Wires	The Drift Wires fitted to a Course Setting Bomb Sight which when correctly orientated, and with your eye on the sight aperture the target would appear to run along and between the parallel wires.
Wallah	Native boy or servant.
WOP/AG	Wireless Operator/Air Gunner
Waffen	Weapons
Wimpies	Vickers twin engined Wellington bombers.